# GREEN LIES

## HOW GREENWASHING CAN DESTROY A COMPANY
### (AND HOW TO GO GREEN WITHOUT THE WASH)

By

## PASCUAL BERRONE

ISBN-13: 978-1523373567

ISBN-10: 1523373563

The author of this book has been beneficiary of the "I edition of the BBVA Foundation Grants for Researchers and Cultural Creators". BBVA Foundation accepts no responsibility for the opinions, comments and material contained in this project and/or the results of the same, which are solely the responsibility of the author.

Fundación **BBVA**

# Dedication

*To my wife Andrea and my daughters Milena and Valentina, who permanently inspire me to work for a better world.*

*To my parents, Jorge and Graciela, who taught me a sense of responsibility and the value of kindness to those who surround us.*

# Table of Contents

# Preface

The world cries for repair! According to the World Health Organization seven million premature deaths annually can be linked to air pollution. Scientific research compiled by National Geographic reports that sea levels worldwide have been rising at a rate of 0.14 inches (3.5 millimeters) per year since the early 1900s as a result of global warming caused by a damaged atmosphere and depleted ozone layer. Aquatic life is no longer viable in many lakes, rivers, and other water bodies around the globe due to water pollution caused by industrial waste products, while the United Nations states that almost one billion people lack access to clean water. Wildlife populations and natural ecosystems are confronted with a bewildering array of pollutants that are released into the environment, either by intent or accident, placing around 19,000 species under threat of extinction, according to International Union for Conservation of Nature.

Clearly, showing concern for the natural environment is a trend that has been growing during the last four decades. We, as a society, have become more aware of the impact that we have on our surroundings. In this process, prominent public figures from different fields have actively helped to raise awareness. Movie stars and celebrities like Julia Roberts, and Leonardo DiCaprio have been long-time supporters of solar energy. Former Vice President of the United States and Nobel Peace laureate, Al Gore, is well known for his participation in the movie "An Inconvenient Truth" and credited for reenergizing the environmental movement. Scientist David Suzuki has increased international public awareness of climate change with a catchy short online experiment known as the Test Tube Theory (http://testtube.nfb.

ca/) that expresses the scale of overconsumption. New organizational forms like Greenpeace and other NGOs have engaged thousands of individuals who fight social ills as a collective responsibility. Even religious representatives are including the environment in their discourse. Take for instance Catholic Pope Francis's recent encyclical on the environment, where he directed sharp criticism at global leaders for their failure to combat climate change, considered today a landmark intervention in the global climate change debate.

Of course, the corporate world is not silent about the negative consequences of their actions on the environment. Business leaders such as Unilever's Paul Polman, Body Shop's Anita Roddick, and Patagonia's Yvon Chouinard are preaching—and at least trying to practice—an approach on business that assumes an active role in improving social welfare, beyond maximizing the wealth of shareholders.

Corporate environmentalism is not surprising. First, firms have helped to create much of the environmental footprint. It is hard to forget the noxious impact of oil spills such as the Exxon Valdez (1989) and more recently the BP oil spill in the Gulf of Mexico (2010), which took the lives of 11 workers, cost up to 1 billion dollars in clean up, and caused a devastating ecological impact on the region's flora and fauna. Second, the idea that a growing green economy is emerging while creating new business opportunities has become a dominant paradigm. Indeed, the proponents of the "business case" for sustainability suggest that environmental concerns can be seen as opportunities for innovation, spurring more efficient products and processes, granting access to new markets, improving outdated business models, and, at the same time, reducing costs, risks and liabilities. Thus, many companies have engaged in environmental activities not only because "it is the right thing to do" but simply because it is good for business. Who would be opposed to implementing practices that not only save the planet, but that are financially rewarding at the same time? This is how sustainability became one of the most popular buzzword in the corporate world to begin with.

However, practice has taught us that profiting from environmental initiatives is a long and winding road. Most companies have a difficult time when it comes to bridging the gap between green concerns and green consumerism, to manufacture green products without sacrificing quality, and to understand what it means to be a green business in the first place. For the most part, becoming a green company takes a sizable amount of resources, time, and risks. These difficulties have not stopped many opportunistic companies from attempting to reap the benefits and derive value from greening the company on the outside without making the necessary investments on the inside.

Perhaps the most evident and recent case is Volkswagen AG that, in September 2015, was caught using a software program rigged to cheat emissions testing in 11 million diesel-powered cars owned by consumers around the world. The truth was that VW engines emitted nitrogen oxide pollutants up to 40 times above what is allowed in the US. At this very point in time, the consequences are still unfolding and the total impact of the scam is yet to be seen. In economic terms, during the first week of the scandal, Volkswagen's share prices plummeted more than 35 percent, the company's market cap contracted by more than $25 billion and CEO Martin Winterkorn stepped down under pressure. From a reputational stand point the hit was also hard. The Dow Jones Sustainability Indices removed Volkswagen from the investor-focused corporate social responsibility rankings. In the meantime, law firms are beginning to file class action lawsuits, which could ultimately force the automaker to buy back the cars altogether, in addition to monetary compensation. Perhaps more importantly (and largely absent from the discussions in the news) is the impact on human health. The pollutants involved (nitrogen oxides) can contribute to respiratory ailments and premature deaths that have been linked to breathing contaminated air.

While the VW scandal may be seen as an extreme case, the reality is that many organizations publicize their environmentally friendly actions to convince their stakeholders they are taking steps in the right direction. However, these actions may be merely superficial and cosmetic, completely decoupled from the organizations' noxious environmental impact. That is, there is a gap between what they say they do and what they actually do: they tell "green" lies.

This practice has been generally termed as Greenwashing—a form of spin in which corporate actions are used deceptively to promote the perception that a company's policies or products are environmentally friendly. But, considering the above example the key question that emerges is: *Are these efforts paying off?*

This book is an intentional effort to answer this question. After laying the groundwork in chapter one regarding the urgency and reality of environmental issues in our modern world, chapters two and three go on to offer a historical perspective on global environmental challenges in order to understand how the concept of sustainability has become a central notion in our everyday lives. This includes understanding the role different societal actors have played in the process, particularly with regards to corporate involvement. Chapters four through six of the book adopt a more scientific approach, delving into the type of actions and strategies firms implement that can be classified as greenwashing, what key drivers lead to favor this kind of corporate behavior, and most importantly the consequences greenwashing actions can have on firms' legitimacy, reputation and economic performance. In the concluding chapters of the book, we present a blueprint for transforming a brown firm into a sustainable company with a solid business model and we discuss the implications of this process.

In addition to the qualitative analyses performed for this book, we also conducted a series of interviews with CEOs, sustainability managers, corporate social responsibility (CSR) and environmental consultants, as can be seen in the quoted excerpts found throughout the chapters. The goal was to make both a practical and scientifically based book in order to better understand the implications and consequences of this corporate misconduct we all know as greenwashing which in the end has an impact on us all.

What we do today, will affect our tomorrow.

# Acknowledgments

I would like to express my most sincere gratitude to the many people who saw me through this book. First of all, I am grateful to the BBVA Foundation, that provided financial support to this project and that has shown, one more time, it is an institution seriously committed to pushing the frontier of academic knowledge. A special big thanks goes to Alejandra Castañeda Ferrer, who acted as more than a research analyst/consultant. She was instrumental in articulating this book, gathering data and stories, and much more importantly, being able to capture my complex way of thinking and translate it into an understandable text. This book would never have found its way without her.

I would like to thank all those who provided support, talked things over, read, wrote, and offered comments. In particular, I would like to thank Emmanuel Lagarrigue (Chief Strategy Officer, Schneider-Electric), Antoni Ballabriga Terreguitart (Global Director of Responsible Business, BBVA), Ángela Sáenz de Valluerca (Sustainability Director, EDP Renovaveis), Xavier Houot (Senior Vice President – Group Environment, Safety, Real Estate, Schneider-Electric), Luis Piacenza (Managing Director Global Sustainability Services, Crowe Horwath International), Antonio Fuertes Zurita (Reputation and Sustainability Senior Manager, Gas Natural Fenosa), Philippine de T'Serclaes (Chief Advisor, Schneider-Electric), Pablo Bascones Ilundain (Director, PwC), Gael Gonzalez (Sustainability expert, luxury sector), Ernesto Lluch Moreno (Senior Manager in Environmental Innovation, G-advisory), Carlos Salvador (Sustainability Expert, Oil and Gas sector), and Valentín

Casado (CEO, ELMET) who generously allocated time to me to interview them and allowed me to quote their remarks in this book.

I am also grateful to a long list of coauthors with whom I have had the honor and the pleasure of working over the last 15 years on the passionate topic of sustainability. I have learned a lot from them.

I also thank Anaik Alcasas who provided professional editorial input on this book. I also acknowledge my home institution, IESE Business School, in particular the department of Strategic Management and the Research Division, for providing the necessary space and time to pursue projects of this caliber. I am also indebted to the Schneider-Electric Chair of Sustainability and Business Strategy, for which I am the holder, and that provided material support. Above all I want to thank my wife, Andrea and my two daughters, Milena and Valentina, who are a continuous source of inspiration and support. I love them with all my heart.

# 1 Green is the New Black

> **"** A point has been reached in history when we must shape our actions throughout the world with a more prudent care for their environmental consequences. Through ignorance or indifference we can do massive and irreversible harm to the earthly environment on which our life and well-being depend. **"**
>
> *(UN 1972)*

There is no denying the impact human beings have on the planet. Our demands are constantly increasing, straining the fragile balance between our short-term needs, and our long-term survival. During the last century alone, the world extracted 34 times more natural resources than in previous times and the use of fossil fuels went up by a factor of 12. In other words, the use of resources at the current rate is not an option, as some predict that by the year 2050 we would in fact need two planets to sustain us (EC 2014).

As a result, the preoccupation with sustainability has reached new heightened levels in institutions, organizations and society alike. Since the mid-twentieth century, the environment has become a number one priority as the challenges we face continue to evolve and public awareness continues to increase. Who hasn't heard about hybrid cars or smart cities? Who isn't concerned with climate change and water depletion?

We are constantly bombarded with green products and green companies on one front, while issues such as climate change, low carbon economies, and strained resources are at the top of the international agenda (Figure 1.1). One of the major highlights of 2015 was the Paris Climate Conference (or COP21) which brought together more than 190 countries, while one of the most notorious corporate scandals of the same year featured Volkswagen tweaking cars to cheat $CO_2$ emission tests. There is no denying that sustainability, eco-friendly and "green" have indeed become the buzzwords of our generation.

Our approach to protecting the environment has evolved from worrying about a few endangered species, to pushing for a change in the way we do business, the way we operate, and the way we live. Sustainability has become more than just a word. It is a target we are all trying to hit.

Figure 1. 1  Global Megatrends

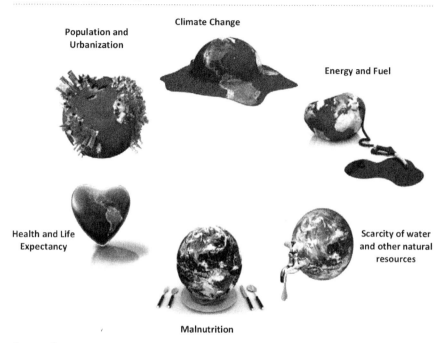

*Source:* Own

However, this wasn't always the case. Amidst the industrial growth experienced during the last century, the environment was the least of our worries. We were so busy with improving our living standards by modernizing businesses through assembly lines, shortening travel times with cars and planes, and overall, increasing consumption, that we never gave a second thought to what we were doing to our planet. So how have we gone from raising our living standards to focusing on sustaining our way of life? How did the environment become the center of debate in the first place?

## 1.1 The Call for Change

Towards the end of the 1960s, the questions raised through the voice of the popular hippie movement gradually went global as concerns about the future of our planet occupied the international arena for the first time. The Conference on the Human Environment held by the United Nations (UN) in 1972, constituted an important turning point. The sustainable use of the planet and its resources was addressed and defined as the most pressing challenge of the future and gained unprecedented international support. The negative impacts caused by continued economic growth and industrialization were starting to emerge and raise red flags.

Although many believed this to be a fad, a fashion that would soon become outdated, the truth is that the actions taken since to re-right past wrongdoing have been numerous. The biggest feat of the UN conference was its final declaration which included the 19 principles on which to base subsequent measures with the intention *"to inspire and guide the peoples of the world in the preservation and enhancement of the human environment"*(UN 1972). This was shortly followed by the UN Environment Programme (UNEP), and the report *"Our Common Future"* by Dr. Brundtland (covered further in 2.3.2 and beyond) which introduced a ground-breaking concept: **sustainable development**, defined as "development that meets the needs of the present without compromising the ability of future generations to meet their own needs"(WCED 1987). Far from being a catch phrase, the influence of the term in national and international policy making has only increased over time, and with it, the globalization of environmentalism. And for the first time, the notion that sustainability obliges firms to make intertemporal trade-offs to safeguard intergenerational equity was introduced.

The term was internationally endorsed a few years later during the Earth Summit celebrated in Rio de Janeiro in 1992. Defined as the convergence between the three pillars of economic development, social equity and environmental protection, the foundation for the global institutionalization of sustainable development was created. Over the years, the UN has followed through with its commitment, hosting landmark conferences that have brought together world leaders to promote initiatives, frameworks, programs and principles to guide implementation.

At a continental level, the leading role adopted by the European Union (EU) must also be noted, having stepped up to the challenge by assuming its responsibility almost immediately. As a result, since the 1970s over 200 pieces of legislation have been established that are intrinsically linked to the protection and preservation of our environment, shaping Europe's environmental policy while endorsing and supporting international measures (EC 2014).

Both the UN and EU have become international key players, having occupied major roles in the drive for a sustainable future. They constitute an invaluable source of leadership, driving the integration of sustainability as the only way to go. Nevertheless, they cannot do this on their own. From the very beginning, the common denominator of all initiatives has been the importance placed on the actions of national governments and corporations as major vehicles for change. Efforts have been directed towards standardizing policies and business practices, increasing intervention through legislation and control systems, and urging both governments and corporations to accept responsibility for global environmental degradation.

## 1.2 A Change in Direction

Since the 1970s international aspirations and expectations have heavily influenced policy orientation, forcing progressive change to mirror the evolution and redefinition of environmental challenges (Table 1.1).

In the early years, policymaking was conditioned by traditional environmental themes such as protecting species or reducing contamination. This approach shifted in the early 90s as focus moved from remediating specific sources to preventing further environmental degradation on a global scale. From then on, policy orientation pointed towards integrating environmental concerns within all sectors, encouraging further collaboration and engagement with other stakeholders, and most especially with the business community. Their role in the matter had to be effectively redefined if sustainable development was to succeed in the long run.

| Characterization of the type of challenge: | Specific | Diffuse | Systematic |
|---|---|---|---|
| Key Features | Linear cause-effect; large (point) sources; often local | Cumulative causes; multiple sources; often regional | Systematic causes; interlinked sources; often global |
| In the spotlight in | 1970s/1980s (and continuing today) | 1980s/1990s (and continuing today) | 1990s/2000s (and continuing today) |
| Includes issues such as | Forest damage due to acid rain; urban wastewater | Transport emissions; eutrophication | Climate change; biodiversity loss |
| Dominant policy response | Targeted policies and single-issue instruments | Policy integration and raising public awareness | Coherent policy packages and other systematic approaches |

*Source:* European Environment: State and Outlook 2015 Synthesis Report. Copyright by European Environmental Agency.

The reorientation towards corporations was fully embraced giving way to a new era of CSR. The best known example is the Global Compact Program, a UN initiative launched in the year 2000 which established a platform to diffuse and help firms develop and implement sustainability oriented strategies and policies. It was the first business-directed program launched by an international organization, constituting an important landmark which would trigger many more thereafter.

Much has changed since. Driven by new levels of social awareness, political agendas have converged as national governments have gradually adopted similar governance principles and structures aligned with international and continental strategies. Meanwhile, accepting the impact of business activities on the surrounding environment, firms have redefined corporate strategies to accommodate sustainable practices and guarantee regulatory compliance. Both efforts and resources have been redirected towards achieving new levels of transparency to demonstrate the degree of this commitment.

All in all, sustainable development has been universally accepted as the solution for safeguarding our future, having become the ultimate goal and guiding principle of institutions, governments, businesses, NGOs and civil society. Nevertheless, in spite of this apparent transition we must ask ourselves whether these outward commitments are truly being held up, or on the contrary; have they been taken with the sole purpose of *seeming* legitimate. The question still remains, have the last fifty years really made a difference?

## 1.3 Where We Stand Today

To this day, the EU is one of many institutions that has repeatedly brought attention to the major challenges linked to unsustainable systems of production and patterns of consumption. In this regard, the overall progress in environmental quality has been documented over the years throughout various reports, all of which have concluded that by and large, "environmental policy has delivered substantial improvements [...] however, major environmental challenges remain" (EEA 2015).

The analysis included in the most recently published report (Table 1.2), supports this belief as the state of key environmental trends and their corresponding projections indicate the considerable deficiencies that are present across all major areas. Even where short-term trends seem positive, predicted future outcomes are still insufficient. For example, although greenhouse gas emissions have decreased by 19% since 1990, the estimated rate of future reductions will leave Europe far from reaching their 2050 target of reducing emissions by 80%-95%. Moreover, the estimated annual cost of damage to health and the environment caused by air pollutants from European industrial facilities exceed EUR 100 billion. In other areas, the urgency of remedial action is more than obvious as prime sources of negative impact are not being successfully managed. For instance, the levels of fossil fuel consumption are still dramatically high, accounting for at least 75% of the EU energy supply, a trend that is not foreseen to improve in the years to come (EEA 2015).

Table 1. 2  An Indicative Summary of Environmental Trends

| | 5-10 year trends | 20+ years outlook | |
|---|---|---|---|
| **PROTECTING, CONSERVING & ENHANCING NATURAL CAPITAL** | | | |
| Terrestrial and freshwater biodiversity | ▓ | ▓ | ☐ |
| Land use and soil functions | ▓ | ▓ | No Target |
| Ecological status of freshwater bodies | | | ☐ |
| Water quality and nutrient loading | | | ☐ |
| Air pollution and its ecosystem impacts | | | ☐ |
| Marine and coastal biodiversity | ▓ | | ☐ |
| Climate change impacts on ecosystems | ▓ | ▓ | No Target |
| **RESOURCE EFFICIENCY & THE LOW CARBON ECONOMY** | | | |
| Material resource efficiency & material use | | | No Target |
| Waste management | | | ☐ |
| Greenhouse gas emissions & climate change mitigation | | ▓ | ☐ |
| Energy consumption and fossil fuel use | | ▓ | |
| Transport demand & related environmental impacts | | ▓ | ☐ |
| Industrial pollution to air, soil & water | | | ☐ |
| Water use & water quantity stress | | | ☐ |
| **SAFEGUARDING FROM ENVIRONMENTAL RISKS TO HEALTH** | | | |
| Water pollution & related environmental health risks | | | ☐ |
| Air pollution & related environmental health risks | | | ☐ |
| Urban systems & gray infrastructure | | | No target |
| Climate change & related environmental health risks | ▓ | ▓ | No target |
| Chemicals & related environmental health risks | ▓ | | ☐☐ |

| INDICATIVE ASSESSMENT OF TRENDS & OUTLOOK | | INDICATIVE ASSESMENT OF PROGRESS TO POLICY TARGET |
| --- | --- | --- |
| Deteriorating trends dominate | ☐ | Largely not on track to achieving key policy targets |
| Trends show mixed picture | ☐ | Partially on track to achieving key policy targets |
| Improving trends dominate | | Largely on track to achieving key policy targets |

*Source:* European Environment: State and Outlook 2015 Synthesis Report. Copyright by European Environmental Agency.

The overall conclusion seems to be that the benefits reaped by environmental policies have been cut short by the success of globalization. Global economic growth has been achieved at great cost with increasing resource use and levels of pollution—the same outcomes we've been trying to avoid for decades. The blame cannot entirely be placed upon governments and corporations, but there is reason to believe policies are not being fully implemented by nation-states, and the environment has not been successfully integrated into corporate policies. These factors contribute significantly to environmental pressures and impacts.

The steps taken towards creating a low carbon society, a green circular economy and resilient ecosystems are far from being enough, as the dependency on many natural resources remains untenable as does the ecological footprint which exceeds the planet's capacity (EEA 2015). Despite having recognized the importance of the environment for future economic growth and general well-being, on a smaller group-by-group scale the urgency is not sinking in.

## 1.4 Questioning True Intentions

Governments are constantly faced with high levels of skepticism and mistrust, because while some progressive steps have indeed been taken, the disappointing outcomes have definitely fallen short of expectations. To explain these shortcomings, many have argued that nation-states are merely acting with superficial intentions of compliance, mimicking what happened in the past with human rights treaties (Hafber-Burton and Tsutsui 2005). Environmental laws and policies are indeed being adopted, but little is done to implement and monitor the changes and impacts that should be taking place.

Corporations have also fallen short of society's expectations. Even though more and more companies seem to genuinely embrace sustainability, the degree of corporate implementation is forever doubtful. In fact, many corporate responses have been considered little more than window dressing, with companies being accused of adopting much-dreaded *greenwashing* strategies to divert public attention. After all, if being green can pay off, surely *seeming* green can have similar effects, right?

From a corporate point of view, the push for greener firms is clearly there. Consumer awareness has risen drastically in recent years, a trend mirrored in the estimated expansion of the green market that is predicted to increase from $230 billion in 2009 to approximately $845 billion in 2015 (Tolliver-Nigro 2009). This in turn has influenced the direction of marketing strategies. As a result, during the last twenty years green advertising has increased almost tenfold as companies have responded by repeatedly bombarding consumers with "green eco-friendly" products in an effort to satisfy new demands (TerraChoice 2009). Websites now have entire sections dedicated to disclosing environmental and social policies and performances which reinforce the green image most companies seek to establish (Alves 2009). My early work on greenwashing has also shown that the number of green trademarks (those containing the words "green," "renewable" or "clean") has increased more than ten times in the past decade.

At the same time, corporate disclosure has gained tremendous attention as external actors—not only consumers—seek unprecedented levels of transparency. Over the last few decades, new means of sharing corporate environmental and social impact have emerged as a growing number of stakeholders expect information and reassurance that traditional indicators can no longer provide. Governments, investors and consumers have increasingly advocated that a firm's sustainability should be evaluated according to a "triple bottom line" of environmental, social and financial performance (Elkington 1998; Marquis and Toffel 2011).

Consequently, the scope and nature of corporate reporting has gradually broadened to include social and environmental issues. Company reports have in fact become a fundamental tool in the transition towards sustainability, providing the performance information needed by both stakeholders and the corporations themselves to track and monitor their progress. Reporting was first driven by voluntary initiatives but due to the increasing urgency of compliance, policymakers have gradually introduced regulatory requirements in an effort to standardize the practice. As a result, the amount of mandatory initiatives established with regards to sustainability reporting has increased significantly over a period of seven years (Figure 1.2) which can also explain why its use has skyrocketed within most advanced economies in such a short period of time (Figure 1.3).

Figure 1. 2 Trends in Mandatory and Voluntary Sustainability Reporting

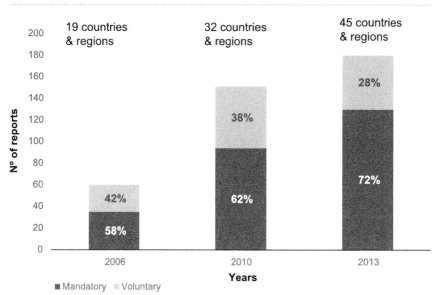

*Source:* Own based on "Carrots and Sticks: Sustainability reporting policies worldwide." United Nations Environment Programme (UNEP). 2013 Edition.

Corporate reporting (CR) is just one example of the many actions firms are taking to respond to increasing external pressures. Corporations have demonstrated a broader change in attitude with a variety of practices and policies in recent years. However, to determine whether these actions are merely superficial, we must dig deeper.

Figure 1. 3 Comparison of Corporate Reporting between 2008 and 2011

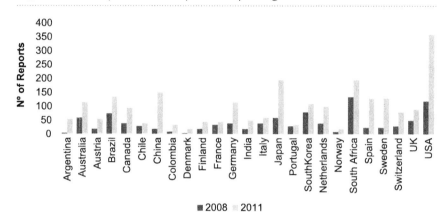

■ 2008  ▪ 2011

*Source:* Own based on "Carrots and Sticks: Sustainability reporting policies worldwide." United Nations Environment Programme (UNEP). 2013 Edition.

## 1.5 Greenwashing: The Uncomfortable Truth Behind Corporate Greening

The efforts corporations are putting into showing their newly found commitment is a fact, *show* being the key word here. Taking the stats in these two figures, the truth is that while reports have been widely used to assess a company's overall performance, voluntary disclosure cannot firmly indicate the extent of a firm's commitment.

Reports continue to vary significantly in their content and comprehensiveness and ultimately will always depend upon the company itself and its willingness to share information (UNEP, GRI et al. 2013). Companies can exaggerate social and environmental credentials and highlight positive actions, while omitting negative impacts. These misgivings are present in various environmental reporting studies because while organizations may very well be paying attention to environmental issues, the general public still believes that the reports fail to accurately reflect an organization's behavior (Marquis and Toffel 2011). Some may argue these claims to be unfounded, but the truth of the matter is that in many cases the gap between what is being said and done actually does exist.

> 66 As long as external communication is humble and fact-based, one can empathize with a company's efforts, and it need not necessarily be accused of 'greenwashing' when an environmental performance improvement has been delivered, and shared externally. 99
>
> *Xavier Houot*
> *SCHNEIDER-ELECTRIC*

The high rates of reporting and increased mandatory requirements certainly indicate sustainable reporting is here to stay. Therefore, the focus of attention has now shifted towards questioning the quality of reports which is yet far from the level expected. A survey conducted by KPMG on the quality of reporting among the world's largest 250 global companies,[1] showed that as of 2013, the quality of reports in some of the world's leading economies is remarkably low (Figure 1.4). Such is the case in the USA, where efforts put into communication seem to have exceeded those placed on CR processes (KPMG 2011; KPMG 2013) giving grounds to those who accuse firms of practicing corporate greenwashing.

> 66 Many sustainability reports are not really read by stakeholders, precisely because the information contained may not be what they are looking for. Organizations need to identify what is really important for their stakeholders, what is expected of them and act accordingly. 99
>
> *Luis Piacenza*
> *CROWE HORWATH*

---

[1] These were identified as the top 250 companies listed in the Fortune Global 500 ranking for 2012.

Even in the cases where CR processes are effectively implemented, very few companies publish well-balanced reports where setbacks and future challenges are discussed as often as successes. The main focus seems to be put on targets and indicators, which are also key aspects of effective sustainability practices, but lack value if their impact across the value chain is not reported upon (KPMG 2013). Transparency is therefore quite limited.

Moreover, the average quality score achieved by the group of companies as a whole amounted to little more than 55 out of a possible score of 100. If the largest global corporations with access to resources, both human and capital, are failing to deliver reliable and transparent accounts, how can we expect others to follow?

Figure 1. 4 Average Quality of G250 Reports by Country[2]

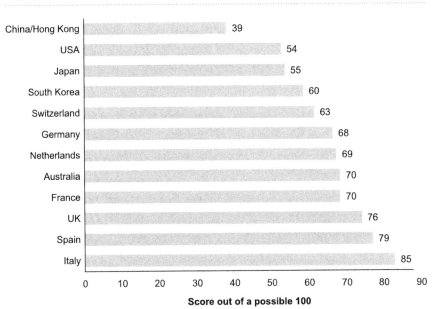

Score out of a possible 100

*Source:* KPMG Survey of Corporate Responsibility Reporting 2013. Copyright 2013 by KPMG International Cooperative.

---

[2] Average scores per country are only given for those countries that have five or more companies reporting on CR in the G250

Again, corporate reporting is only one of many responses, but its mixed results demonstrate the different levels of commitment that exist within the business community. The fact that all companies are waving the green flag doesn't necessarily indicate they all have a green heart. In fact, there are reasons to believe that a great deal of action is taken as a symbolic gesture, driven by the need to guarantee future legitimacy rather than born out of a real concern for society and the environment.

Unfortunately, this type of "corporate lying" has expanded rapidly as an easy response to mounting pressures on firms to operate in an environmentally responsible fashion. This behavior, also known as *greenwashing*, refers to the tools a given firm may use to deliberately send a message that its products, services and processes are environmentally friendly when in fact they are not. This might seem outrageous in the 21$^{st}$ century, the era of technology and information, but the truth is greenwashing works under the premise that the public really does have limited access to information on corporate performance. Hence, companies can very well manipulate public opinion by creating false images or providing fraudulent messages. They tell "green lies" to be able to continue with business as usual.

For example, when we consider the number of green products and services now available to consumers as an indicator of environmental commitment, the predisposition displayed by firms is indeed remarkable. According to TerraChoice, between 2009 and 2010 the percentage of "greener" products rose by 73%. On the other hand, when environmental claims made by firms on the same products were examined, over 95% were found to be committing at least one of the "Seven Sins of Greenwashing"(TerraChoice 2010). (We cover the "Seven Sins" in depth in Section 4.3.1.) Although this is surprising, it has become more and more common to find terms such as "green" or "environmentally friendly" sitting side by side with traditionally "dirty" industries.

So despite the explosion of green claims, and even though 93% of the CEOs identified sustainability as "critical to their company's success" (Accenture 2010), we know something is definitely wrong because environmental indicators just keep getting worse.

## 1.6 To Green or Not to Green

Although these indicators might seem discouraging, the accusation that firms are practicing greenwashing strategies cannot be generalized. In many cases, the gap between what firms say and do is a reality, but to be able to identify these companies correctly we need to determine the factors that define this behavior.

With this in mind, an organization's environmental performance can be classified depending on two variables; on the one hand the degree to which they advertise and communicate their environmental commitments (their "talk") and on the other, the extent to which said commitments are implemented (their "walk"). Consequently a company can fall into one of four categories (Figure 1.5): on one diagonal **Greenwashers** and **Green mutes**, and on the other, **Brown Firms** and **Sustainable Firms**.

Figure 1. 5  Walk or Talk Matrix

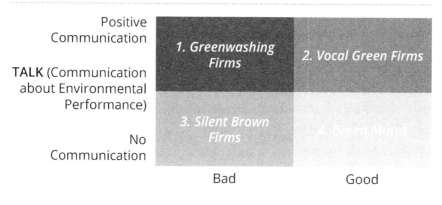

From the diagram above, we can easily deduce that greenwashing takes place at the intersection of two specific behaviors: 1) a firm's poor levels of performance coupled with 2) their paradoxically positive communication and branding regarding environmental and social impact. The bottom line is that greenwashing has become yet another strategy that has emerged in order to adapt to changes in consumer demands and external expectations.

As to why greenwashing has become a tempting option, the most obvious answer seems to be that the time required for a firm to alter or devise a communication campaign is nowhere near the time needed to actually develop, implement and monitor environmentally responsible strategies. Moreover, the potential benefits of sustainable policies are not always measurable in economic terms, further discouraging those firms preoccupied with obtaining immediate returns and short-term profits. The problems we face today prove that companies can no longer rely on economic and technology-driven efficiency gains to manage the environmental challenges ahead. However, trading short-term profitability for a long-term vision with uncertain probabilities of success is a risk few are willing to take.

Nonetheless, many global corporations have willingly accepted the role bestowed upon them, acknowledging the extent to which their actions have worldwide repercussions. In fact, many are setting examples by truthfully integrating sustainable practices into their everyday policies. Thus, a sustainable business model is a goal that can be met and not an impossible feat. We will discuss this in depth in the final chapters of this book.

## 1.7 Sustainability: Still Open for Debate

For many, improving environmental performance has become a duty rather than an option. They sincerely engage in sustainable practices and strategies to avoid, or at least minimize, their impact on the environment and society. However, corporate greenwashing is still happening on a large scale. Integrating sustainability into every day operations has proven to be far from easy and linking it to economic benefits is a difficult task to master.

Despite widespread recognition of the challenges and perils we face, if patterns do not change, many companies will still opt to do much less than what is expected and disguise minimal actions in green intentions. Unfortunately these practices are very difficult to recognize. However, in this book we prove that greenwashing is not a viable strategy as the risks are too great; short-term gains cannot thwart long-term necessities. Thus, we must fully understand the reasons behind greenwashing if we wish to eradicate it once and for all. We hope to foster the debate about sustainability and help companies focus on a goal that assures long-term public benefits.

In the chapters that follow we will address some of these questions:

▶ Why has sustainability become a central aspect of corporate life?

▶ How has greenwashing become an extended (and somewhat accepted) practice?

▶ What strategies do firms adopt that can be classified as greenwashing?

▶ Are there any key drivers that lead to or favor this kind of corporate behavior?

▶ What are the consequences both for firms and stakeholders?

▶ Is there a blueprint for a sustainable business model?

These are only some of the questions that will be discussed in the following chapters in an attempt to understand the antecedents and implications of this corporate misconduct which inevitably affects us all. What we do today, *will* affect our tomorrow.

# A Brief History of Sustainable Development

> 66 The one who does not remember history is bound to live through it again 99
>
> – George Santayana

Since it first appeared in the late 1980s, the term *sustainable development* has undoubtedly become one of the most influential concepts of our time, driving the environmental movement while becoming the core element of policy making and corporative measures, actions and decisions. Throughout the last 50 years, it has been the main reason corporations have had to deal with fast growing expectations and increasing pressures, redefining their role in society and the responsibilities that come with it.

Over the last few decades, the change in attitude displayed by corporations has indeed been remarkable, shaping governance principles and corporative values to face the challenge of integrating sustainability into everyday activities. This has proven to be a more difficult task than initially expected as the complexity and vagueness with which the term was first introduced has left its meaning open for interpretation.Sustainable development is fundamentally sustained on three basic pillars: economic, environmental, and social. On the one hand, this triggered the beginning of a new corporate culture aligned with all three aspects which has culminated in the establishment of measures directed towards environmental protection and social involvement. On the other, it has been the main source of the pressure companies have been subject to which in many cases has led them to practice greenwashing strategies. Since greenwashing is basically driven by the desire to seem environmentally friendly, it has ultimately emerged as a response to the urgent need to be seen as sustainable.

However, the relationship between one and the other can only be explained as a result of a long journey that started long before the concept of sustainability even existed. One cannot define greenwashing without fully understanding the evolution of sustainable development in general and its relationship with environmentalism in particular. Let's take a quick look at its history.

## 2.1 An Explosion of Public Awareness

The environmental crisis was initially introduced into the political arena towards the end of the 1960s and early 70s, driven by the publication of a series of scientific reports. The following table (Table 2.1) lists some of the most controversial and influential studies of the time, which raised the environmental alarm with catastrophic predictions of the future of the planet.

These reports exposed the severity of certain problems that up until then had been widely ignored by the public and governments. Based on the global trends present at the time it seemed pretty clear that humankind faced a rather bleak future. The studies all shared the same apocalyptic tone, advocating for immediate and drastic measures in order to prevent the global collapse that would inevitably take place should nothing change. In general, a neo-Malthusian[3] point of view was adopted where the key to understanding the environmental crisis and the depletion of natural resources resided in an accelerated demographic growth rate. Consequently, as a solution to the physical limits to growth, all conclusions converged towards one common proposal: zero growth, both economically and demographically, or the "limits to growth" theory.

Following is a review of three of the most controversial publications listed in Table 2.1, and the ripple effect they had on public opinion and corporate accountability.

### 2.1.1  Publication: "Silent Spring"

In 1962 Rachel Carson published Silent Spring, a compilation of research that proved nature was in fact vulnerable to human activity. This marked the beginning of an era, as Carson's research exposed the negative impacts agricultural pesticides were causing animal species and human health, focusing her attention on the use of DDT, the most powerful pesticide in the world. In her book, Carson explained how DDT could cause cancer and genetic damage as it entered the food chain and accumulated in the fatty tissues of animals and human beings. In other words, she proved that pesticides in general, and DDT in particular, were contaminating the world's food supply as well as causing irrevocable damage to the environment (NRDC 2013).

---

[3] Thomas Robert Malthus hypothesized unchecked population growth would exceed resource growth leading to naturally occurring catastrophes such as famine or disease to check the population. This would occur because population grew exponentially while food supply grew arithmetically.

Table 2. 1  Scientific Reports That Raised the First Environmental Issues

| | |
|---|---|
| 1950s | In 1949, Fairfield Osborn publishes Our Plundered Planet denouncing the immense risk humankind was creating by destroying the environment. It marked the beginning of the apocalyptic environmental literature that characterized these early studies, launching a Malthusian revival in the post War era that would inspire other authors such as Paul R. Ehrlich. |
| 1960s | In 1962, Silent Spring was published. It was considered by many to be the catalyst of the modern environmental movement. In it, Rachel Carson condemned the overuse of pesticides, drawing special attention towards DDT. |
| | In 1966, the economist Kenneth E. Boulding published the essay, The Economics for the Coming Spaceship Earth where he proposes to replace the past open economy of apparently illimitable resources, denominated the "cowboy economy," for an enclosed economy or "spaceman economy" with Earth acting as a spaceship with limited resources and finite space for pollution and waste. |
| | In 1968 Paul Ehrlich writes The Population Bomb claiming that the world's environmental problems are in fact a direct consequence of the earth's overpopulation. Following Osborn's trail of thought, Ehrlich made a series of catastrophic predictions, and even though they never came to pass, his apocalyptic point of view played an important role in raising issues such as family planning and contraception to the forefront of domestic and international politics. |
| 1970s | In 1971 Barry Commoner writes The Closing Circle, drawing attention towards the role played by industrialization and technology in the environmental crisis as well as their effect on our quality of life. |
| | In 1972, René Du Bois and Barbara Ward write Only One Earth, based on the findings of the UN 1972 Stockholm conference, warning about the impact of human activity on the biosphere. However it lacks the catastrophic tone present in its predecessors, suggesting that a collective and shared concern for the planet could in fact guarantee a brighter future for humankind. |
| | In this same year, the Club of Rome issued its first report, Limits to Growth, prepared by a team of scientists from MIT and directed by Dennis Meadows which supported the proposal of zero growth rate, as the earth would not sustain the increase in demand. It has been considered the most influential document in establishing contemporary environmental alarm. |

*Source:* Own based on the Sustainable Development Timeline http://www.iisd.org & The Environmental History Timeline http://www.environmentalhistory.org/

The uproar caused by the publication and diffusion of Silent Spring could not easily be ignored, and despite the chemical industry's attempts to discredit the book and Carson herself, the American government under President John F. Kennedy examined the issues raised and validated her conclusions. Shortly after, DDT fell under closer regulation and was eventually banned in 1972.

Prior to Carson's book, the conservation of nature had never really awoken public interest, however Carson's depiction of a lifeless American town annihilated by the effects of DDT caused an unprecedented reaction. For the first time technological progress was openly challenged as Carson's questions suggested closer scrutiny and control to ensure that progress was fundamentally compatible with natural processes. Even though Carson's stance was undeniably radical, the threats listed were too dangerous to ignore, igniting public concern and acceptance of the need to regulate industry in order to protect the environment.

Thus modern environmentalism was born, opening a larger national dialogue about the relationship between people and nature, and sparking a merge of the public health and conservation movements (Kovarik 1996).

### 2.1.2 Publication: "The Population Bomb"

Some years later, in 1968, Paul Ehrlich published *The Population Bomb*, in which he argued that the root cause of the world's environmental problems was overpopulation. He claimed demographic growth had increased at an alarming rate, having more than doubled in the past half century, a trend that would continue and ultimately cause mass starvation due to the lack of food supply. Consequently, he advocated for immediate and drastic measures aimed at limiting population growth, which were criticized by many for being too extreme. For example, with regards to foreign policy, he suggested adopting a system of "triage," based on the proposal made by William and Paul Paddock in *Famine 1975!* (Paddock 1967). This implied dividing countries into categories based on their ability to feed themselves in the foreseeable future. Therefore, the countries that could demonstrate they had sufficient programs in place to limit population growth and become self-sufficient would continue to receive food aid. However, countries such as India, which in Ehrlich's own words were "so far behind in the population-food game that there is no hope that our food aid will see them through to self-sufficiency" (Ehrlich 1968), would have their food aid eliminated, even if this meant mass starvation in entire countries at a time.

Despite the fact that his catastrophic predictions never came to pass, Ehrlich was not the only scientist supporting neo-Malthusian theories. Moreover, he alerted people to the importance of environmental issues and sparked an interesting debate regarding their relationship to world demographics.

### 2.1.3 Publication: "Limits to Growth"

The last controversial publication that needs to be discussed is *Limits to Growth*, commissioned and published by the Club of Rome in 1972. The report was produced by a team of systems scientists at the Massachusetts Institute of Technology (MIT), in which a number of scenarios were explored in regards to five variables: world population, industrialization, pollution, food production, and resource depletion.

Unlike *The Population Bomb*, specific predictions were not made, as the research was aimed at exploring how exponential growth intersects with finite resources. Since global resources cannot be quantified, the results obtained were based on general behavior modes, which the authors defined as "the tendencies of the variables in the system to change as time progresses" (Meadows 1974).

Although the final report included two scenarios where the global system did in fact collapse, a third scenario opened a door to hope, where a "stabilized world" was indeed possible. It concluded that unlimited and unrestrained growth in material consumption was obviously incompatible within a world of finite resources. Ultimately, it focused on a long-term vision, drawing attention towards the choices open to society to be able to reconcile sustainable progress within environmental constraints, supporting once again the "limits to growth" thesis.

The report left no one indifferent. On the one hand, Northern countries criticized the fact that the potential of future technological solutions was overlooked, while Southern countries denounced the fact that it favored the abandonment of economic development. Nevertheless, out of all the reports and publications mentioned, *Limits to Growth* had by far the greatest impact; environmental issues became the center of world debate almost overnight.

## 2.2 Worldwide Repercussions

Faced with this alarming reality, two parallel responses were developed and mutually influenced by one another. First of all, there was a notable expansion of the environmental movement propelled by the creation and establishment of national and international NGOs, predominantly in developed countries. Secondly, the first forms of institutional structures began to appear, both at international and domestic levels, designed to assess the situation and establish policies. This resulted in the celebration of international conferences and conventions led by the UN as well as the creation of specific international institutions. On a national level, the first environmental laws were enacted and government agencies were founded and empowered with a degree of authority to intervene in environmental matters (Deléage 2000).

### 2.2.1 Going green

Environmentalism caught on rapidly and strongly. The first ecological groups surfaced in the United States towards the end of the 1970s, as pressure groups such as Friends of the Earth (FOE) and Greenpeace were born, both of which are still very active today. FOE was founded in 1969 by David Brower after he abandoned the position of executive director of the Sierra Club, with the desire of becoming more politically engaged. Within two years, the FOE had reached 17, 000 members, a number which has grown to the current level of 50, 000 members (FOE 2015). Greenpeace was founded a year later at the initiative of a few Canadian citizens when they attempted to stop an atomic explosion by interposing their own boat. Since its foundation, Greenpeace has always stood out for taking direct action to stop certain damaging practices, especially but not exclusively, with regards to the aquatic ecosystem. It too spread rapidly as a worldwide organization and currently holds 30 national sections (Greenpeace 2015).

These concerns quickly crossed the ocean and extended to Europe, first in the Netherlands and Germany, and later on in the rest of the industrialized countries of Central and Western Europe. But the phenomenon was not exclusive to developed countries as underdeveloped countries such as India, Kenya and Brazil were also greatly influenced during the 70s, establishing organizations themselves. Nevertheless, these differed substantially, as it was not uncommon to link social causes to ecological protests and claims.

Moreover, on a national government level, particularly in Europe, this new social movement triggered the formation of alternative "green" parties which started to actively participate in national elections. In fact, by the mid-80s said parties had managed to become the third political force, displacing the old communist parties in western Europe in countries such as Germany, Belgium or Switzerland (Müller-Rommel 1998).

### 2.2.2  The United Nations: A step in the right direction

The first UN conference on environmental issues was held in New York in 1949. However, in the aftermath of the Second World War, attention was focused on rebuilding Europe, restoring food supply, and the beginning of the Cold War, and the conference went almost unnoticed. It was not until the International Conference of the Biosphere in 1968 that the UN decided to take matters into their own hands. It was at this event that the idea of promoting a global encounter was raised, a proposal which was unanimously supported by the UN members and the UN General Secretary, U Thant. As a result the General Assembly approved resolutions 2398 (XXIII) and 2581 (XXIV), deciding to convene in 1972 a global conference in Stockholm, whose principal purpose was "to serve as a practical means to encourage, and to provide guidelines ... to protect and improve the human environment and to remedy and prevent its impairment"(UN 1969). These intentions were also reflected in the report *Man and His Environment (UN 1969),* where U Thant stressed the need to present a united front against a "common global foe that required new planetary politics and concerted global action" (Alger 1998). Meanwhile, between 1969 and 1971 the United Nations Educational, Scientific and Cultural Organization (UNESCO) collected data on the condition of the environment according to region (Asia, Africa, Latin America, the Middle East, and Europe) which produced the report *Only One World,* serving as groundwork for the long-awaited conference.

## 2.3  The Road to Sustainability

### 2.3.1  The Stockholm Conference 1972

In 1972, the Global Conference on the Human Environment was finally held in Stockholm with the attendance of two heads of state, delegations from 113 countries, and representatives from 250 non-governmental organizations and UN specialized agencies (Alger 1998). It was a landmark event considered to be the single most important turning point in the history of Global Environmental Governance, introducing the issue into the political arena for the very first time with the purpose of forging a common outlook on how to address the challenge of preserving the human environment.

Consequently, one of the main goals was the elaboration of a declaration which would embody a set of basic principles and establish a framework for international action and cooperation. The resulting Stockholm Declaration was adopted by acclamation, with seven proclamations and 26 principles of environmental protection and enhancement. In addition, a Plan of Action was adopted that included 109 recommendations for environmental action as well as additional resolutions aimed towards banning the use of nuclear weapons and the creation of an international environmental database. Shortly after, the United Nations Environment Programme was established, creating a permanent forum for monitoring global environmental trends, convening international meetings and conferences, and negotiating international agreements.

To conclude, although the conference was focused on defining broad environmental policy goals and objectives as opposed to detailed normative positions, it succeeded in providing environmental policy with a sense of direction, establishing a framework that linked environment and development (Kannan 2012). This idea would be expanded in the years to follow, beginning with the introduction of **sustainable development**.

### 2.3.2  Publication: "Our Common Future" aka the Brundtland Report

Following Stockholm, global awareness of environmental issues increased dramatically as did the need to link environment and development. In response, in 1983, the UN decided to create a World Commission on Environment and Development chaired by Dr. Gro Harlem Brundtland, former Norwegian Prime Minister. The Commission spent three years investigating the relationship between environmental degradation and poverty, during which it conducted various public meetings throughout the world.

As a result, in 1987, the Commission published its findings and proposals under the name "Our Common Future"—also referred to as the Brundtland Report. By then, it had become clear that limiting economic growth was not an idea society was ready to accept, therefore the emphasis was placed on finding the balance between growth and environment. In Dr. Brundtland's own words, the aim was to begin "a new era of economic growth, growth that is forceful and at the same time socially and environmentally sustainable" (WCED 1987).

In it, the concept of **sustainable development** was introduced for the very first time. This was by far its biggest contribution, highlighting the intricate relationship that exists between development and environment. Moreover, it revealed that the economic inequalities and interdependencies that existed between industrialized and industrializing countries was in fact an important part of the problem.

Hence, the Commission recognized that the only way to achieve sustainable development was through the preservation of the environment which in turn depended upon policies aimed at poverty reduction, gender equity, and wealth redistribution. In other words, only by increasing productivity could the environmental crisis be addressed. As such, the report outlined a path for global sustainable development, where active participation from all sectors of society was of the utmost importance. This opened the door to the involvement of business organizations, whose leaders up until that point had remained skeptical and unconvinced there was a problem to solve (Ekins 1993).

Although the report left many questions unanswered, it became a major stepping stone to the 1992 Earth Summit and Development in Rio, recovering the spirit displayed in Stockholm a decade earlier and marking a definitive shift from the Malthusian point of view.

> *"Sustainable development is development that meets the needs of the present without compromising the ability of future generations to meet their own needs."*
>
> *"A world in which poverty and inequity are endemic will always be prone to ecological and other crises. ... Sustainable development requires that societies meet human needs both by increasing productive potential and by ensuring equitable opportunities for all."*
>
> *"Many of us live beyond the world's ecological means, for instance in our patterns of energy use. ... At a minimum, sustainable development must not endanger the natural systems that support life on Earth: the atmosphere, the waters, the soils, and the living beings."*
>
> *"In essence, sustainable development is a process of change in which the exploitation of resources, the direction of investments, the orientation of technological development; and institutional change are all in harmony and enhance both current and future potential to meet human needs and aspirations."*
>
> **From the Brundtland Report, "Our Common Future"**

### 2.3.3 The Earth Summit. Rio 92

In the years that followed the Brundtland Report, the concept of sustainable development continued to gain both popularity and supporters. Such was the case that by the time the UN Conference on Environment and Development (UNCED) was convened, it had become one of the central themes of the summit.

Despite international efforts, twenty years after Stockholm, some environmental problems seemed to be getting worse. New scientific data demonstrated that although UN efforts had managed to turn back some environmental threats and slow down the growth of others "the existing network of global institutions centered on the UN was inadequate for the urgent task of taking remedial action"(Vogler and Jordan 2003). The integrated and interdependent nature of the challenges and issues that had to be addressed, contrasted sharply with the nature of the institutions that existed then, which tended to be independent and fragmented. Clearly, the measures undertaken up until then had been too little, too late, too compromised, or too ignored.

It was in this context that the Earth Summit was held in June 1992 in Rio de Janeiro. With delegations from 178 countries, 118 heads of state, and thousands of NGO representatives it became the largest and most universally attended conference in the history of the UN. Expectations ran high, as it provided the perfect platform to launch sustainable development on a global level, giving the opportunity to reinforce international intentions through global consensus and binding political commitments.

Amidst the excitement generated by the summit, the Agenda 21 was approved. A program of action for sustainable development into the 21st century, it included more than 2,500 specific objectives and recommendations aimed at helping countries during the transition towards sustainable development. These covered four main categories: Social and Economic Dimensions, Conservation and Management of Resources for Development, Strengthening the Role of Major Groups, and Means of Implementation, marking an unprecedented endorsement of an environmental agenda (Kannan 2012). Additionally, the creation of a Commission on Sustainable Development (CSD) was recommended as a means to facilitate and monitor the implementation of Agenda 21, a proposal which was subsequently approved by the General Assembly. Lastly, the Earth Summit also led to the adoption of two conventions; on the one hand the Framework Convention on Climate Change and, on the other, the Convention on Biodiversity.

At first glance the summit appeared have been a complete success, when in reality the results were a mix of breakthroughs and disappointments. One of the original goals was to produce an Earth Chart to complement the UN Charter, with a defined framework of principles for global ecological security. This idea never came to pass as the "Declaration on Environment and Development" was approved in its place. This amounted to little as it closely resembled the Stockholm Declaration based on the principle of common but differentiated responsibilities, which once more lacked force due to the non-binding nature of the document.

The problem resided in the non-commitment demonstrated by many key governments. As a result, final measures ended up being watered down versions of the original proposals which prevented the consecution of the summit's initial goals. Most developed countries expressed their unwillingness to pay for past damages and even went as far as trying to limit the use developing companies could make of their own resources. Moreover, no interest was shown in funding the transition of the latter in a less conditioning way than the usual form of external debt. On the other hand, Southern countries protested that they had already been exploited by developed countries and should therefore be compensated for their economic losses and assisted in covering costs to protect their resources.

All in all, it became clear that "if the developed countries of the world wanted the environment to be secured for future generations, then they would have to radically assist the South in choosing a different road to development than the one they had been traveling on" (Rogers 1993), a sacrifice they were unwilling to make. In the years that followed, it became more and more clear that despite initial ambitions, the outcome of the summit had actually summed up to no more than a political declaration of intent.

### 2.3.4 The Earth Summit +5. 1997

Proof of the above was given only five years later, when the General Assembly called for a special session in order to monitor and evaluate the progress made up until then. Unfortunately, there was a widespread belief that even though both developed and developing countries had accepted the environmental challenge, Rio's fundamental purpose had not been reached. The fact that globalization continued to evolve at different rates meant that the gap between industrialized and industrializing countries was not being bridged. Developing countries were inevitably conditioned by industrial countries providing the means, and the truth was that aid was subsiding rather than increasing.

In the following years after Rio, 103 of the 178 participating states had taken promising steps, establishing governmental institutions with the purpose of integrating sustainable development concepts into national law and policy. However by 1996, 86 of these, mostly from the developing world, had stopped reporting on their efforts to meet Agenda 21 targets (Alger 1998).

The session's final document recognized the need to adopt legally binding targets to reduce emission of greenhouse gases leading to climate change, moving more forcefully towards sustainable patterns of energy production, distribution and use, and focusing on poverty eradication as a prerequisite for sustainable development (UN 2015).

The implementation of Agenda 21 had clearly been insufficient, either due to its complexity, the lack of resources suffered by many, or simple indifference on behalf of others. Consumption and production patterns remained unsustainably high, income inequalities had increased, and the state of the environment had continued to deteriorate. Almost every major problem discussed in Rio had grown worse. Empty promises were no longer an option.

### 2.3.5  The Kyoto Protocol 1997. Fighting Climate Change

One of the promises made in Rio in 1992 was to prevent and combat global warming. In this context, the United Nations Framework Convention on Climate Change (UNFCC) was adopted, through which industrialized nations had agreed to reduce their carbon dioxide emissions to 1990 levels by the year 2000. However, by 1997 it had become obvious that worldwide emissions were in fact rising, making it virtually impossible for industrialized countries to meet even their minimal commitment.

As a result, the Kyoto Protocol was drafted and adopted in Japan in December 1997, making it the world's first legally binding agreement with regards to climate change. The target set was fairly simple. On the one hand it established legally binding targets for industrialized countries which were obliged to cut their greenhouse gas emissions by 5% on 1990 levels by the years 2008–2012. To do so, Kyoto also offered a series of mechanisms aimed at offsetting emissions through investments in low carbon projects in underdeveloped parts of the world. On the other hand, developing countries such as China, India or Brazil would not have to face restrictions, but were encouraged to adopt policies that would promote greener growth (Henson 2011).

Originally adopted in 1997, Kyoto did not come into force until 2005, having suffered its ups and downs since then. Over the years it had been ratified by many states, reaching a total of 187 by 2009. Nevertheless the agreement's biggest setback has always been the non-ratification by the USA and China, the world's largest carbon polluters. This in turn has raised a lot of criticism, leading many to believe the treaty was defeated before it even started, as it only managed to cover a fraction of global emissions.

Finally, a year before the Kyoto Protocol was scheduled to expire, the UN Climate Change Conference was held in Durban in 2011. During said conference, the Kyoto terms were extended, and the promise of cooperation was made between developed and developing countries to work on a legally binding agreement to be written by 2015. This was undoubtedly considered a big step in the fight against climate change.

Nonetheless, the fact still remained that those willing to sign the extension of Kyoto still represented little more than 15% of global emissions. With this in mind, the resulting outcome of promises made is yet to be seen in 2015.

### 2.3.6  The Earth Summit +10. 2002

A decade after sustainable development was publicly embraced, the international community met once more at the World Summit on Sustainable Development held in Johannesburg. In attendance were 65,000 delegates from 185 countries including more than 100 heads of state, and unlike on previous occasions, this time the presence from multinational firms such as McDonald's and Nestlé was strong.

The summit's main focus was on the implementation and financing of Agenda 21, addressing successes and failures with the purpose of turning promises and goals into tangible actions. The new issues and challenges that had arisen since 1992 were also debated where once again the need to combat poverty was highlighted if sustainable development was to be achieved.

### 2.3.7 The Earth Summit +20. 2012

In 2012, the Conference on Sustainable Development took place, marking the 20th anniversary since the celebration of the Earth Summit, providing the largest international arena the world had witnessed up until then. This time however, reality seemed to have taken over the expectations and excitement demonstrated in Rio 92, as indicators continued to worsen, falling further away from the original targets announced 20 years before. To state an example, over the two interim decades, carbon dioxide emissions from developed countries had increased by 64%, and even though developing countries had only increased by 8% they still had the highest emissions per capita (UNEP 2011).

Figure 2. 1 $CO_2$ Emissions

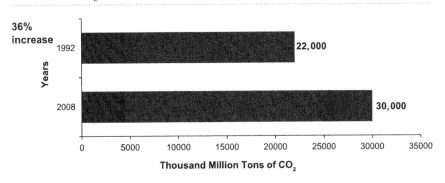

Source: Adapted from "Keeping Track of Our Changing Environment From Rio to Rio+20 (1992-2012)." Copyright 2011 by United Nations Environment Programme.

Figure 2. 2 $CO_2$ Concentration in the Atmosphere

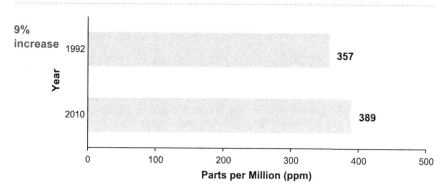

Source: Adapted from "Keeping Track of Our Changing Environment From Rio to Rio+20 (1992–2012)." Copyright 2011 by United Nations Environment Programme.

Nevertheless, despite the skepticism and frustration surrounding the summit, hope was not lost as society looked towards international leaders once more to give the necessary push everyone was waiting for.

In the end, the final document, presented under the name "The Future We Want," held no real or innovative breakthroughs, failing to satisfy the general public. It recognized sustainable development had three main dimensions—economic, social, and environmental—which in turn could only be fully and completely addressed by transitioning towards a green economy. As the General Secretary himself said, "Rio+20 has given us a solid platform to build on (…) it has reaffirmed fundamental principles, renewed essential commitments, and given us new direction" (UN 2012).

Despite the optimism shared by international leaders, the widespread disappointment was palpable. For many, the summit had been largely conditioned by the economic context of the world, the facts of short-term economic revival prioritized over long-term ecological challenges, thus wasting a valuable opportunity to change the trajectory of the future (Clémençon 2012).

### 2.3.8 COP21: Paris Climate Conference 2015

> ❝ The 12th of December 2015 will go down in the history of
> the planet. In Paris, we have seen a few revolutions over the
> last few centuries. But today, this is the most beautiful and
> peaceful revolution that has just been achieved, a revolution
> for climate change. ❞
>
> *– President François Hollande*

Finally, the most recent and promising international summit took place in 2015 in Paris where, for the first time in over 20 years of UN negotiations, an attempt had been made at signing a legally binding and universal agreement on climate in order to keep global warming below 2°C (SIF 2015). Maintaining the rise in global temperature below 2°C has been considered imperative for some time, as scientists have reached the conclusion that a further increase can result in catastrophic, and most importantly, irreversible consequences. The estimated threshold uses pre-industrial levels as a baseline, and the way we are headed it seems as though temperatures are likely to rise up to 5°C unless we curb current emissions "ASAP."

With previous commitments on greenhouse gas emissions expiring in 2020, the Paris conference was expected to produce renewed commitments beyond that date. Not only that, but a major change is in order, as despite best efforts and years of debate, temperatures have neither fallen nor stalled.

So why would we expect this agreement to be any different to those that came before? What has changed since the Kyoto Protocol that suggests this time we will not fail?

> " The Kyoto Protocol signed in 1997 has been revisited time after time to no avail. Now at last concrete measures have been agreed to and the conference of Paris promises to reflect these commitments in a legally binding agreement once and for all. "

*Antonio Fuertes Zurita*
*GAS NATURAL FENOSA*

Frankly, certain major obstacles have been removed since then which hint that a more effective result can be expected this time around. For starters, the world's biggest emitters seem to be on the same page for once, presenting a united front to tackle the pressing challenges at hand (including China, Russia and the USA). Second, unlike previous summits (like Copenhagen in 2009), the agreement reached in Paris was legally binding (at least partially), and over 190 countries committed to limiting their emissions in order to keep global warming "well below" 2°C and strive towards just 1.5°C. In other words, the main result of the Paris conference has been to materialize voluntary commitments agreed to in prior conferences. For the first time in history, everyone seemed willing to work towards one single goal. These elements allowed a move from historical skepticism to a moderate optimism.

But to what extent has it been successful? To begin with, instead of opting for a "one size fits all" approach, the agreement has been designed to drive global action and participation. All parties to the United Nations Framework Convention on Climate Change (UNFCCC) have been asked to present individual action plans establishing the way in which they intend to reduce their greenhouse gas emissions in the future, and unlike before, this includes major emerging economies such as India or China.

Hence more than 190 countries, accounting for more than 95% of global emissions submitted their national climate goals beforehand. However, despite best intentions, after evaluation, the UNFCCC declared these measures were still not enough to slow down the rate of global warming in order to avoid surpassing the above mentioned threshold of 2°C (Harvey 2015).

As a result, the Paris agreement requested countries to review their individual contributions every 5 years from 2020 onwards, encouraging higher targets where possible to ensure progress. Lowering targets however is not an option as the ultimate target is to lower the threshold to 1.5°C. In the long term, emissions should peak and countries have committed to achieve carbon neutrality in the second half of the century, which implies bringing the use of the most polluting fossil fuels to a halt at some point in the near future (UNFCCC 2015).

**Critical areas addressed:**

▶ **Mitigation** – reducing emissions fast enough to achieve the temperature goal

▶ **Transparency** – a transparent system and global stock-take – accounting for climate action

▶ **Adaptation** – strengthening the ability of countries to deal with climate impacts

▶ **Loss and damage** – strengthening the ability to recover from climate impacts

▶ **Support** – including finance, for nations to build clean, resilient futures

# PARIS2015

Furthermore, the agreement establishes an obligation for industrialized and developed countries to provide financial aid and fund the efforts of poorer, developing countries; this is a commitment that was long overdue. More specifically, $100 billion (in loans and donations) will need to be raised each year from 2020 (a figure that may gradually increase) to finance projects that enable countries to adapt to the impacts of climate change (rise in sea levels, droughts, etc.) or reduce greenhouse gas emissions,. Moreover, The Paris Agreement pledged to strengthen the existing Warsaw International Mechanism on Loss and Damage agreed in 2013, which helps address the financial losses that vulnerable countries incur (such low-lying islands countries).

Finally, the credibility of the agreement depends a great deal on how progress will be monitored and disclosed; above all countries need to be transparent and honest. To ensure these principles are respected, a legally binding accountability framework has been created to keep a track of individual and global efforts.

As of the writing of this book, the agreement is yet to be ratified as it will be open for signing in New York the 22nd of April 2016, so we can only predict its success at this point in time. Still, the mobilization is worthy of applause. And not only for governments and NGOs, but for the business world as well. Many companies have used this opportunity to show their support, and fight for global sustainability. In the UK several big retailers have demanded "more clarity and a long-term plan on clean energy," signaling the Paris conference as the perfect opportunity to respond (Schraum 2015). Yet, despite the question of follow-through, the COP21 was a turning point in the sustainability debate. For instance, the notion of putting a price on greenhouse gas emissions has become mainstream while it was barely a conversation a year ago.

Ahead of the conference, the *Carbon Disclosure Project* together with the coalition *We Mean Business* focused on collecting corporate commitments in several categories as a way of showing the business community's support and intention to move towards a low carbon economy (Figure 2.3).

A total of 540 companies and investors signed on, representing a range of industries, including large multinational corporations such as Nissan and Honda from the automotive sector, consumer goods conglomerates such as Nestlé and Unilever, and tech companies such as Autodesk and Hewlett-Packard, amongst others (Helper and Grady 2015; WMBC 2015).

Figure 2. 3 The *Carbon Disclosure Project* and *We Mean Business Coalition:* Range of Corporate Commitments

*Source:* Commit to business leadership on climate *https://www.cdp.net/en-US/Pages/commit-to-action.aspx.* Copyright 2015 by CDP.

Nonetheless, there has been no shortage of greenwashing accusations, as the choice of corporate sponsors has raised its fair amount of criticism. BNP, L'Oreal and Engie have been among those accused of using the event for publicity purposes due to the fact that their practices were not as in tune with the conference's spirit as expected. A survey of ten of the sponsors found that most did not report on their $CO_2$ emissions, half didn't track their lifetime carbon footprint and only one of them provided evidence it was reducing emissions according to the EU's targets (Neslen and Howard 2015).

However, all things considered, the fact that businesses have rallied together to ask for a clearer, smarter climate policy is a hopeful sign that this time, all relevant actors are on board and a change is possible. At the same time, binding commitments by national governments towards substantial reduction in greenhouse gases cannot be met without the full buy-in of the private sector. All we can do now is wait and see.

## 2.4 Where Do We Go from Here?

From a historical perspective, the steps taken have been extraordinary. Only 50 years ago, the environment was of little or no concern to most. Today, it is a motive for social unrest and preoccupation and is without a doubt on the top of all political agendas.

Nevertheless, the concept of sustainable development is nowadays far from being a novelty. It has already been around for over 20 years, and what was once a promising vision of the future seems to have become an empty promise we have been unable to fulfill.

But to say that the efforts made by the UN have been in vain would be going too far. Time and time again it has fought to keep environmental challenges and sustainability at the forefront of national and international policies, bringing together world leaders, providing public forums and ultimately giving voice to a much neglected planet.

On the other hand, despite having come a long way, the progress made up until now is clearly insufficient. Since the beginning, while governments and international leaders declared obvious successes, other sectors of society denounced the outcomes for falling short of what was deemed necessary. Establishing basic principles and publicly declaring the will to act has always been the first step towards change. But as they say, "the road to hell is paved with good intentions."

There is a huge gap between the multilateral processes, as the broad goals and policies established at international levels are not translated into national action, which are usually limited to reflect domestic political and economic realities (Drexhage and Murphy 2010). This comes to prove that talking about change is not the same as enacting that change, and global problems will never be properly addressed as long as they are not *assumed globally* by all sectors of society at all levels. We all have a shared responsibility towards the protection of our planet just by virtue of living on it, therefore active involvement and commitment are required to ensure that the promises and hopes expressed internationally become a reality.

# CHAPTER 3

# Industry: Friend or Foe?

> Earth provides enough to satisfy every man's needs, but not every man's greed.
>
> – *Mahatma Gandhi*

Since the beginning of the 90s, corporate action has definitely become one of the core elements of international expectations and initiatives. In this regard, the business sector can no longer ignore the part they play as, with or without their consent, the push for sustainability has ultimately transformed into the push for corporate sustainability. The increasing popularity of green campaigns is undeniable, and even though today most businesses and industries seem to be on board on the "Go Green" phenomenon, this was not always the case. In fact, in retrospect, the involvement of the industry and business sector has always been characterized by its reluctant attitude, as its commitment to the cause has been ever so gradual.

Over the years, private sectors have gradually opened up to the notion that business activities can cause irreparable environmental damage, as opposed to the shared skepticism that was common in the 1970s. Hence, having seen the evolution of sustainable development from an international point of view, we must once again turn back time to understand the reasons behind the reluctance and why business corporations seem to keep falling behind in the fight for a green and sustainable future.

## 3.1 Sixties: Silent Spring, Silent Industry

As we have already seen, the publication of *Silent Spring* in the early 1960s, constituted a fundamental turning point for modern environmentalism. It was the first time industry was openly challenged as the consequences of industrialization were brought to light, sparking public concern and awareness on a subject that, up until then, had been of little interest.

The age of modernism that characterized economic development in Europe and North America since the beginning of the 1900s, meant that for decades industry had not been confronted by external constraints. The only factors that could determine and influence production were human labor and man-made capital, whereas nature was treated both as an infinite supply of physical resources, and as a bottomless sinkhole for the by-products that resulted from consuming said resources (Colby 1991). This approach prevailed in most countries until the late 1960s, dominated by industry and the fixation on growth, as new machine technologies and modes of industrial production led to an unprecedented rise in material standards (Welford 1997). As a result, production activities were unregulated and the negative impacts of industrialization were completely unaccounted for. The environment was infinite in extent and therefore irrelevant to the economy (Colby 1991).

The facts and accusations contained in Carson's book changed everything. For the very first time, the economic perspective that had minimized environmental impact was challenged; the chemical industry was put in the spotlight, confronted with the need to defend itself from the public outcry. However, although the oil, chemical and automobile corporations began to suffer the first consequences of this movement, industry's stance in the matter remained unchanged throughout the 1960s. The concept of environmentalism was yet to be established, and despite new levels of awareness, public and societal interest continued to be significantly low.

While environmentalist concerns were considered exaggerated, lacking scientific grounds and influence, pollution and environmental degradation were viewed as collateral damage that could be solved independently. The fact that major environmental issues were associated with resource scarcities did not pose a threat. There was an unwavering faith in the power of human ingenuity and the potential of technological advancement to address such problems, creating the technological self-confidence that was common at the time (Hoffman 2001). Hence, environmental debates were regarded as anti-business, anti-industrialization and anti-civilization, and so the concept of corporate environmentalism was completely rejected (Menon and Menon 1997).

## 3.2 Seventies: Introduction of Command and Control Laws

The belief that nothing was wrong continued throughout the 1970s. But as the physical limits to economic growth continued to occupy the public arena in the form of pollution levels and resource degradation, government interference increased. Setting aside the exaggerated claims made in the 1960s, the environmental movement had begun to rally a significant amount of support as issues were internationalized with the celebration of the Stockholm conference in 1972 discussed in the prior chapter. Efforts were increasingly being put into creating enough legal pressure to change business practices through close collaboration with environmental agencies (Menon and Menon 1997).

As an inevitable response to public concerns, from the 1970s onwards, new laws and regulations focused on creating mechanisms and provisions to counter "market externalities."[4] The United States Congress enacted a series of environmental laws that established uniform technology-based and performance-based standards for corporations (Prakash 2000), while in Europe, this initiative was led by the EU which started to approve the first environmental directives. These legal provisions would later become known as *command and control* laws as they allowed relatively little flexibility in the means of achieving goals. Technology-based standards specified the method and in some cases even the equipment that businesses had to use in order to obtain legal compliance. Many viewed this approach as counterproductive, as they argued that it limited a firm's ability to respond to environmental issues in an innovative way.

This changed the panorama, as industry was now faced with unprecedented regulatory constraints, inaugurating a new period of environmental management. Nevertheless, within corporations, no major organizational or technological changes were made. Environmental health and safety departments were indeed created, but the attention given to environmental issues was still limited to obtaining the "technical compliance" needed to continue business as usual (Hoffman 2001). In fact, the mentality shared by most corporations back then was perfectly expressed in 1970 by Milton Friedman himself. Friedman believed that any company making pollution expenditures beyond what was "required by law in order to contribute to the social objective of improving the environment" was practicing "pure and unadulterated socialism"(Friedman 1970) mirroring the view that the social objective of business was solely to maximize shareholders' wealth.

---

[4] The unintended consequences of business activities.

Because of this, there was a widespread tendency for managers and directors to treat environmental management as a "threat" to economic growth. In 1974, a survey conducted by the Conference Board noted that corporations treated pollution control expenditures as non-recoverable investments, considered as the cost of doing business (Hoffman 2001). Environmentalism had become a temporary nuisance, a "necessary evil"; the fact that corporate environmental expenditure increased significantly throughout the 1970s was not triggered by a voluntary desire to act, but because they were forced to react, purely due to mandated corporate responsibility (Varadarajan and Menon 1988).

## 3.3 Eighties: The Beginning of Corporate Social Responsibility

Despite the resistance displayed by corporations, towards the end of the 1970s and throughout the 80s, a combination of external factors created the necessary climate to trigger a greater sense of corporate social responsibility.

### 3.3.1 Bursting the industrial bubble

The discovery of toxic waste dumps and a series of environmental disasters towards the end of the 70s and during the 80s, revealed the grave consequences business activities could cause when environmental risks and consequences were neglected or ignored.

The most relevant of these, included in the table below (Table 3.1), had both human and environmental implications, raising environmental liabilities to unprecedented levels. For example, following the Exxon Valdez oil spill, the Exxon Corporation was faced with fines and penalties mounting to $5 billion, a figure that would have bankrupted smaller corporations. Consequently, the threat of large fines forced firms to alter transport strategies (Hoffman 2000). However, the financial repercussions of the disasters were secondary aspects when we consider the immense reputational damage suffered by these corporations. Union Carbide, a corporate leader in the chemical industry, was held negligent and responsible for the irreversible effects caused by the gas leak in Bhopal. The entire company's moral integrity was also brought into question. The fact that the events took place in high technology industries with safety systems that seemed infallible at the time, served as a wakeup call.

In most cases, the root causes were actually traced back to management control and decisions and consequently, corporate management fell under strict examination. Many companies took their responsibilities to the next level, establishing self-regulating systems linked to performance indicators as well as activities to guide employees in the management of safety and environmental issues (Feyer and Williamson 1998).

Yet, it should be noted that until the mid-eighties, most corporate efforts were still directed towards achieving regulatory compliance and liability containment. Focus was placed on damage control rather than on methods of improvement, thus environmental management continued to be a cost of doing business and not a benefit (Colby 1991).

Nevertheless, one thing had become clear: the risk of industrial mismanagement was no longer limited to "invisible" environmental degradation. The cost of human lives and the hazardous effects suffered by entire towns had highlighted the need to make a substantial shift in the approach followed up to then, bursting the bubble of self-sufficiency displayed by the industry in previous decades.

## Table 3. 1  Industrial Accidents: 1970s & 1980s

| | |
|---|---|
| **1976** | **SEVESO DIOXIN CLOUD – ITALY**<br><br>On July 10, 1976, the town of Seveso, north of Milan, bore witness to the explosion of an Italian chemical plant that released a thick white cloud of dioxin. The devastating effects followed soon after as animals dropped dead and people, especially children, began feeling ill. Nausea, blurred vision, and a skin disease known as chloracne were some of the symptoms felt weeks before the town was evacuated. |
| **1978** | **LOVE CANAL – USA**<br><br>During the 1940s and 50s, many companies opted to get rid of toxic waste by burrying it underground. The dangers this could entail were made evident decades later. In 1978, Love Canal, a working class neighborhood located near Niagara Falls in upstate New York, experienced first-hand the consequences of sitting upon 21,000 tons of toxic industrial waste. By then the problem was unavoidable, leaving residents with no other alternative than to sell their houses to the federal government. This unprecedented scandal led to the creation of the Superfund Program in 1980, which held corporations accountable for the clean up of toxic sites. |
| **1984** | **UNION CARBIDE – INDIA**<br><br>In 1984, India suffered one of the worst industrial disasters known to man. A gas release in a plant established in Bhopal by the Union Carbide's Indian subsidiary, resulted in 20,000 deaths, and continues to create health problems for countless more. A cost cutting spree by the chemical corporation resulted in minimal safety measures which ultimately led to the unavoidable tragedy—mass exposure to the first world war gas MIC (methyl-isocyanate). |
| **1986** | **CHERNOBYL NUCLEAR PLANT – UKRAINE**<br><br>Only two years later, another industrial accident hit the Chernobyl nuclear power plant in the Ukraine. Once again the disaster was the product of a flawed reactor design operated by inadequately trained personnel. The steam that resulted from the explosion and subsequent fires released at least 5% of the radioactive reactor core into the atmosphere. Two plant workers died that very night, and out of the 237 people diagnosed with Acute Radiation Syndrome, 28 died shortly after. |
| **1989** | **EXXON VALDEZ OIL SPILL – ALASKA**<br><br>On March 24, 1989 an Exxon Valdez oil tanker ran aground on a reef in Prince William Sound, Alaska, producing one of the USA's worst environmental disasters to date. In total, an estimated 10.8 million gallons of crude oil was released before the spill was eventually contained, contaminating 1,300 miles of coastline. Hundreds of thousands of birds, fish, seals, otters, and other animals died in the aftermath. Exxon was openly criticised for its delayed and inadequate response to the accident. |

*Source:* Own.

### 3.3.2 "Going Green" becomes mainstream

By the beginning of the 1980s, the effectiveness and efficiency of *command and control* policies began to be questioned, with much evidence pointing towards their inadequacy and outright failure. As was expected, in the wake of these disasters, the environmental movement gained in strength. Its popularity and influence had continued to increase all through the 1970s, fueled by a growth in membership and budgets of the major environmental organizations. Dissatisfied and disappointed with the little progress, attention began to be redirected towards obtaining result oriented regulations as opposed to the centralized activity-oriented approach used until then (Portney and Stavins 2000). Interest groups began to view industry as a potential ally and not as an adversary, thus advocating for closer collaboration and flexible mechanisms that would give industry a bigger say in the way goals were to be accomplished.

In response to growing social concerns, by the mid-eighties, industry decided to adopt a more proactive and visible role, establishing environmental rules and norms to demonstrate their commitment towards society. They had been given the opportunity to become "part of the solution," broadening their influence in the establishment of future policies. This led to an increasingly collaborative attitude among business, regulators and environmental groups alike—at least on the surface—with the aim of seeking common ground and plausible solutions to the evident environmental challenges.

Within companies, environmental management gained visible importance as responsibilities were integrated throughout company departments. The gradual change in mentality became self-evident as corporate directives adopted a more strategic approach as opposed to the negative resistant attitude present in previous years. In some cases, objectives were now focused on redesigning processes to improve results, such as waste minimization, instead of regulatory compliance at the end of the pipe. In spite of this, for the vast majority, environmental concerns were still treated as problems to be solved and constraints that needed to be managed, implementing strategies to alleviate environmental problems and not as a way to seek competitive advantage.

> **"** There are three basic elements that have driven the 'sustainability' megatrend: conviction, convenience and coercion. **"**
>
> *Luis Piacenza*
> *CROWE HORWATH*

Nevertheless, the relationship between environmental protection and economic efficiency was beginning to be forged, driven by cost factors, liability concerns, public scrutiny and the indirect impact of regulations (Hoffman 2000).

### 3.3.3 Economic growth: The answer to sustainable development

Even though the mindset of most firms had already begun to change, the sole event that had the most impact during the 1980s was the publication of the Brundtland Report mentioned in section 2.3.2. Without a doubt, the transition towards positive business engagement was remarkable when compared to previous half-hearted initiatives.

This was mostly due to the redefinition of guiding principles which now pointed towards economic growth as a determinant factor in achieving the much needed levels of environmental protection.

As previously covered in chapter 2, the report introduced the term "sustainable development," with a focus on poverty reduction, technology investment, and economic growth as the way to tackle environmental issues efficiently. Because of this report, companies began to see that concern for the environment did not necessarily imply anti-development any more; on the contrary, sustainable development supported and encouraged further development and globalization. However, without active engagement on behalf of both business and government, the reconciliation between continuing economic expansion and the containment of environmental threats would not be possible (Ekins 1993).

Because of this new "evolutionary" vision, corporations were being further nudged towards actively engaging in environmental protection. Once again, firms demonstrated willingness to tackle the problem, only now they were open to the idea that solutions had to come from close collaboration with external interest groups such as governments, green organizations, and even investors. Firms also began to experience new forms of environmental pressures as environmental concerns and economic interests were integrated. This resulted in investors, insurers and competitors playing a bigger role in the move toward sustainable development (Hoffman 2001).

All in all, the 1980s represented the biggest step industry had taken up to that point. Replacing notable skepticism and evident resistance for a new found predisposition, corporations welcomed the 90s with a new era of corporate environmentalism in mind. In 1990, marking the 20th anniversary since the celebration of the first Earth Day, industry leaders could now be spotted among those advocating for the protection of our planet as opposed to the absence that had characterized previous celebrations (Piasecki 1995).

## 3.4 Early Nineties: Welcoming Sustainable Development

Following the Brundtland Report, the UN began to prepare for the next international summit in order to address the global sustainable development challenges. It was on the road towards the Earth Summit of 1992, that two important business initiatives were launched, signaling the remarkable change in attitude that was taking place among business corporations (Ekins 1993). These were the "Business Charter for Sustainable Development" for the International Chamber of Commerce (ICC) and the "Business Council for Sustainable Development" (BCSD).

The role of both initiatives was very significant, as they were formed to give advice and provide a business perspective in the UN Convention, giving corporations the kind of representation they had never had before; they were given a voice to express their own concerns.

### 3.4.1: The Business Charter for Sustainable Development

In 1990, the ICC formally acknowledged the newly found importance of environmental management, calling for an imminent change in traditional business practices. It recognized that economic growth provided "the conditions in which protection of the environment can be best achieved, and environmental protection, in balance with other human goals, is necessary to achieve growth that is sustainable"(ICC 1990). In this instance, it developed the Business Charter for Sustainable Development: the first environmental voluntary initiative proposed by a business organization for businesses of every economic sector and country.

The Charter contains 16 Principles for environmental management (Table 3.2) with the aim of assisting corporations in fulfilling their commitment towards the environment, providing appropriate framework and foundation on which to build an Integrated Environmental Management System (ICC 2000). Formally launched in 1991 at the Second World Industry Conference on Environmental Management in Rotterdam, it was based on the premise that "there should be a common goal, not a conflict, between economic development and environmental protection, both now and for future generations" (ICC 2000). In an attempt to reach a much broader audience, the Charter was presented once again during the UN Conference on Environment and Development in 1992. It was considered one of the biggest business contributions, gaining more than 2,000 supporters in the years that followed.

Table 3. 2  Business Charter for Sustainable Development: 16 Principles of Environmental Management

1. **Corporate Priority:** To recognize environmental management as among the highest corporate priorities and as a key determinant to sustainable development; to establish policies, programs and practices for conducting operations in an environmentally sound manner.

2. **Integrated Management:** To integrate these policies, programs and practices fully into each business as an essential element of management in all its functions.

3. **Process of Improvement:** To continue to improve corporate policies, programs and environmental performance, taking into account technical developments, scientific understanding, consumer needs and community expectations, with legal regulations as a starting point, and to apply the same environmental criteria internationally.

4. **Employee Education:** To educate, train and motivate employees to conduct their activities in an environmentally responsible manner.

5. **Prior Assessment:** To assess environmental impacts before starting a new activity or project and before decommissioning a facility or leaving a site.

6. **Products and Services:** To develop and provide products or services that have no undue environmental impact and are safe in their intended use, that are efficient in their consumption of energy and natural resources, and that can be recycled, reused, or disposed of safely.

7. **Customer Advice:** To advise and, where relevant, educate customers, distributors and the public in the safe use, transportation, storage and disposal of products provided, and to apply similar considerations to the provision of services.

8. **Facilities and Operations:** To develop, design and operate facilities and conduct activities taking into consideration the efficient use of energy and materials, the sustainable use of renewable resources, the minimization of adverse environmental impacts of waste generation, and the safe and responsible disposal of residual wastes.

9. **Research:** To conduct or support research on the environmental impacts of raw materials, products, processes, emissions and wastes associated with the enterprise and on the means of minimizing such adverse impacts.

10. **Precautionary Approach:** To modify the manufacture, marketing or use of products or services or the conduct of activities, consistent with scientific and technical understanding, to prevent serious or irreversible environmental degradation.

11. **Contractors and Suppliers:** To promote the adoption of these principles by contractors acting on behalf of the enterprise, encouraging and, where appropriate, requiring improvements in their practices to make them consistent with those of the enterprise; and to encourage the wider adoption of these principles by suppliers.

12. **Emergency Preparedness:** To develop and maintain, where significant hazards exist, emergency preparedness plans in conjunction with emergency services, relevant authorities and the local community, recognizing potential trans-boundary impacts

13. **Transfer of Technology:** To contribute to the transfer of environmentally sound technology and management methods throughout the industrial and public sectors.

14. **Contributing to the Common Effort:** To contribute to the development of public policy and to business, governmental and intergovernmental programs and educational initiatives that will enhance environmental awareness and protection.

15. **Openness to Concerns:** To foster openness and dialog with employees and the public, anticipating and responding to their concerns about the potential hazards and impact of operations, products, wastes or services, including those of trans-boundary or global significance.

16. **Compliance and Reporting:** To measure environmental performance; to conduct regular environmental audits and assessment of compliance with company requirements, legal requirements and these principles; and periodically to provide appropriate information to the board of directors, shareholders, employees, the authorities and the public.

*Source:* Own adapted from ICC Business Charter for Sustainable Development https://www.iisd.org/business/tools/principles_icc.aspx. Copyright 2013 by IISD.

### 3.4.2 **The Business Council for Sustainable Development**

In spite of taking the first fundamental steps to elevate environmental management to the next level, the ICC was not the predominant business voice at Rio 92. While preparing for the Earth Summit, Maurice Strong, appointed secretary general for the UN Convention, decided that the ICC was not the right platform to develop and support the corporate vision that was expected and needed from the business world.

Instead, Stephan Schmidheiny, a Swiss businessman, was given the task of bringing together a group of CEOs to represent the perspectives of global business at Rio. As a result, the Business Council for Sustainable Development was born with a total of 48 industrial sponsors. From then on, it became the platform for the business input at Rio, taking over the responsibility which had once only belonged to the ICC.

To introduce its participation at the UN Convention, an official report was published just before the celebration of the summit providing the world with an unprecedented corporate view on sustainable development. In it, the Council advocated for a change in practical terms, which for the first time focused on what *business* had to gain from this new ecological awareness (McDonough and Braungart 1998), thus presenting the term "eco-efficiency."

The origins of this concept can be traced backed to the previously mentioned Brundtland Report as it called for the adoption of industrial operations "that are more efficient in terms of resource use, that generate less pollution and waste, that are based on the use of renewable rather than non-renewable sources, and that minimize irreversible adverse impacts on human health and the environment" (WCED 1987). Building on this same idea, Schmidheiny and the BCSD came up with the term as a way of defining the connection between economic and environmental performance. In essence, it recaptured the spirit of industrialization, "doing more with less," as by making processes more efficient companies would not only succeed in reducing negative environmental impacts, but could obtain economic benefits while doing so. Environmental concerns needed to be internalized and made a central part of corporate governance and policy making (Redclift 2005).

Thus, the report *"Changing Course: A global business perspective on development and the environment"* marked the beginning of a new approach, reflecting a significant shift in mindset; corporate environmentalism had evolved from strictly managing environmental concerns to viewing environmentalism as a strategic opportunity that could be exploited (Schmidheiny 1992). It stressed the importance of eco-efficiency in competitive terms, considered the only way of guaranteeing both sustainability and success in the long term. There was so much excitement surrounding the Earth Summit that Schmidheiny himself made an adventurous prophecy: "I predict that within a decade, it is going to be next to impossible for a business to be competitive without also being 'eco-efficient,' adding more value to a good or service while using fewer resources and releasing less pollution"(Schmidheiny 1992).

In the aftermath of the Earth Summit, eco-efficiency became a widespread practice, supported by industry as it offered a means of integrating economic, environmental and ethical concerns without having to alter economic and organizational structures or jeopardizing further economic growth (McDonough and Braungart 1998). In the end, profit-maximization firms will always work towards maximizing the efficiency of operations. Therefore, as opposed to Friedman in 1970, the "strategy guru" Michael Porter argued in 1994 that "emissions are a sign of inefficiency and force a firm to perform non-value-creating activities" thus reducing pollution levels voluntarily could increase profits by "improving the productivity with which resources are used" (Porter and Linde 1995). This idea heralded a paradigm shift in the way companies started to deal with the notion of sustainable development.

> **"** It is not possible to comply with legislation and become the leader of the 'cleanest' from one day to the next, and pretend it will not affect a company's bottom line. However, managers must become aware that one can be green and be profitable at the same time. **"**
>
> *Valentín Casado*
> *ELMET S.L.U*

### 3.4.3 The World Business Council on Sustainable Development

Building on the optimism that emerged from the UNCED, the BCSD and ICC continued, committed to helping enforce the agreements reached during the summit. Acting as advocates for self-regulation and market mechanisms, both organizations have carried on promoting alternative regulations to encourage the voluntary implementation and enhancement of environmental policies and management systems.

As such, in 1993 the ICC created the World Industry Council for the Environment (WICE), which among other things, collaborated closely with the UNEP to produce the *Environmental Management System*

*Training Resource Kit* with the purpose of helping companies implement the Environmental Management System (EMS) successfully.

However, by 1995, the BCSD and the WICE had decided to merge in order to form a unified global business platform: the World Council for Sustainable Development (WBCSD). As of today, WBCSD is supported by more than 200 CEOS of some of the largest companies in the world, coming from over 35 countries and 20 major industrial sectors (Drexhage and Murphy 2010).

With regards to international cooperation, both the ICC and the WBCSD have continued to work closely with the UN, providing the Commission on Sustainable Development with the business input needed, and officially supporting the United Nations Global Compact launched in July 2000 which will be further discussed below.

## 3.5 Beyond Rio 92 – "Win-Win" Strategies

Aside from these independent initiatives, the Earth Summit was seen as a major turning point in the relationship between industry and the environment. Although no binding agreement was produced, the role of the business community was undoubtedly reinforced.

Internationally, corporate sustainability was promoted as the result of three basic pillars: economic growth, ecological balance, and social responsibility. However, in the first years after Rio, efforts were mostly placed on enhancing the economic and environmental dimensions of sustainability (as opposed to the social dimension), investing in cleaner technologies within the aim of redirecting everyday operations to more sustainable practices. Product certification also became a usual practice. Industries encouraged corporations to make use of resources in a more sustainable manner, and in exchange provided accreditation to those who met defined standards of compliance. Green products were therefore adopted in an attempt to transform benefits of environmental protection from public to private goods (Prakash 2000). Businesses were ultimately seeking "win-win" situations where economic growth was stimulated without increasing pollution levels. This was based on the belief that as economies develop they become more sustainable and produce less waste (Redclift 2005). In other words, they were balancing legitimate legal and regulatory needs with moneymaking (Piasecki 1995).

The implementation of sustainable development was therefore conditioned by policies that focused on pure economic growth. It was seen as the only way of achieving development and the ecological balance everyone was expecting. Consequently, the early 1990s was characterized by a period of accelerated globalization where priority was given to trade, investment and expansion of capital markets (Drexhage and Murphy 2010).

Nevertheless, in the latter part of the 90s the much forgotten social dimension was suddenly subject to a great deal of attention. Globalization had produced new issues and concerns as international corporations fell under public scrutiny, accused of violating labor and human rights at some point in their supply chain. Setting environmental claims aside, activists were now demanding global organizations to urgently reform operating policies to guarantee compliance with basic human rights (Welford 2002).

On top of this, a new wave of corporate scandals and failures began to take place in the late 90s and early 2000s, bringing to light the unethical conduct of many corporate leaders, which resulted in massive job losses and wiped out life-long retirement plans (Christofi, Christofi et al. 2012). The 1980s had already been a decade plagued with corruption, fraudulent reporting, insider trading and junk-bond schemes, however, in light of the new prominent role assigned to business corporations, the reputational damage experienced by companies such as Enron was much greater than it had ever been before (Rockness and Rockness 2005).

The lack of responsibility demonstrated by these multinational corporations fueled new demands for corporate responsibility, as it had become clear that business practices and strategies were intrinsically related to all three dimensions: economic, environmental, and social. On the one hand, stakeholders were creating new pressures driven by technological and communication advancements—including, most prominently, the internet—which allowed them to hold companies responsible for their impacts. On the other, the value of intangible assets such as a company's perceived brand integrity, reputation, and human capital became self-evident, pushing corporations to rethink traditional business models.

## 3.6  Business Sector Initiatives – Shaping Corporate Responsibility

Since then, the initiatives aimed at promoting responsible and sustainable business approaches have been numerous, challenging the dominant market logic of free trade and profit maximization (Waddock 2008). This has signaled the transition from shareholder theory oriented policies to stakeholder theory based approaches, concerned with layers of corporate accountability, transparency, and responsibility.

Although corporate responsibility as such was not a new term, the implications around it were substantially different than those sought in the past. While the global business community had fixated on product and consumer safety as the extent of their commitment, they finally began to understand the importance of stakeholder relationships if they were to retain their "license to operate."

Business sector responses vary in nature, ranging from the establishment of mechanisms designed to assure certain levels of responsibility, to the creation of associations aimed at diffusing best practices.

### 3.6.1 Corporate guidelines

First of all, the use of **standards, codes of conduct, and principles** has become a prime means of influencing corporate behavior (Waddock 2008). Having expanded the nature and scope to include new explicit responsibilities, many business associations and multi-stakeholder coalitions have adopted them as a major tool to publicly endorse and foster the "right" kind of behaviors. They serve as guiding principles, outlining external expectations and providing specific and precise outcomes companies should aim for. All in all, they give corporate responsibility a sense of direction as more and more behaviors fall under examination and become classified as acceptable or unacceptable, which ultimately limits a firm's discretionary power.

Box 3. 1   The United Nations Global Compact: Codifying Corporate Responsibility

The UN Global Compact (UNGC) was established in July 2000 and symbolizes an important milestone as it was the first international business oriented initiative, launched with the hope of creating closer ties with the business community (Waddock 2008). The desire to increase collaboration with corporations, as opposed to only governments, was warmly welcomed and triggered immediate support. To this day, it continues to be the largest corporate sustainability initiative in the world, with more than 12,

000 signatories from over 140 countries (UNGC 2013). As a result, the "Ten Principles" of the UNGC have become one of the best known and most followed sustainable frameworks. Focused on consecrating human rights, labor rights, environmental sustainability, and anti-corruption conduct, it was the first step towards comprehensively integrating all dimensions of sustainability into business organizations and practices.

On a personal note, in 2011 I was invited by the UN Global Compact to act as a keynote speaker in a conference in Atlanta, GA. For the first time in my career, I was able to "feel" that the need for a better world was a sincere concern for many policymakers, corporate leaders, and academics around the globe. Perhaps the main takeaway I got from that conference was that if we, as a society, want to eliminate "grand challenges" (large, unresolved societal problems such as environmental degradation), we need to recognize that no single organization can provide a solution to the issue and collaboration is the name of the game. However, I couldn't help but feel that words were bigger than actions.

**The Ten Principles of the United Nations Global Compact**

**HUMAN RIGHTS**

1. Businesses should support and respect the protection of internationally proclaimed human rights; and

2. Make sure that they are not complicit in human rights abuses.

**LABOR**

1. Businesses should uphold the freedom of association and the effective recognition of the right to collective bargaining;

2. The elimination of all forms of forced and compulsory labor;

3. The effective abolition of child labor; and

4. The elimination of discrimination in respect of employment and occupation.

**ENVIRONMENT**

1. Businesses should support a precautionary approach to environmental challenges;

2. Undertake initiatives to promote greater environmental responsibility; and

3. Encourage the development and diffusion of environmentally friendly technologies.

**ANTICORRUPTION**

1. Businesses should work against corruption in all its forms, including extortion and bribery.

### 3.6.2 Corporate reporting practices

The above mentioned principles, standards and codes have certainly been a step in the right direction, but lack value when adopted on their own. Since the introduction of sustainability, stakeholders have constantly advocated for reassurance that corporations are not making empty claims of recognition and compliance, and are actually implementing what they openly support. Because of this, from the mid-1990s, leading companies have opted for publicly disclosing their policies and practices as a way of demonstrating how social and environmental issues were being addressed, sparking the use of corporate reporting; a practice that to this day constitutes an essential part of corporate sustainability.

The origins of environmental and social reporting can be traced back to John Elkington who introduced the concept *triple bottom line* (TBL) in 1994 by defining sustainability as the sum of three separate dimensions: profit, people, and planet (Elkington 1998) (Figure 3.1). Consequently, corporate sustainability could only be measured by evaluating the financial, social and environmental performance of a corporation in a given period of time. This could only be done if social and environmental aspects were monitored with the same scrutiny as corporate profit since what you measure is what you are likely to pay attention to. Under the premise of "you cannot manage what you cannot measure," the new era of corporate social reporting was born.

Figure 3. 1  Triple Bottom Line

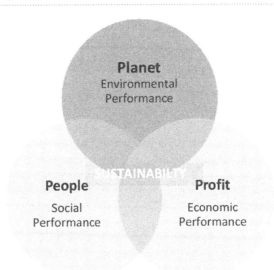

    Corporate sustainability is much more than just the environment. Corporate sustainability is also human rights, ethics, health and safety, risk management, human resources etc. Thus, the three pillars of sustainability must be embedded into a company's strategy, that is, environmental, social and economic aspects must all play a critical role in management.

*Ángela Sáenz de Valluerca*
*EDP RENOVAVEIS*

Eager to prove the effectiveness of new operational practices, firms turned to corporate reporting which gradually gained popularity as a voluntary instrument for TBL disclosure. However, there was growing criticism regarding the veracity of what was being reported. Firms could easily choose to focus on positive activities and ignore those which reflected badly on the organization. There were no specific guidelines to follow or requirements to comply with.

In this context, a series of initiatives and organizations emerged, some with the purpose of standardizing reporting, others as independent verifiers in order to give corporations the credibility they clearly lacked (see Box 3.2 for some examples).

Box 3. 2 Institutions Promoting Standardized Reporting

### THE GLOBAL REPORTING INITIATIVE

In 2000, the combined efforts of the UNEP, the Coalition for Environmentally Responsible Economies (CERES) and the Tellus Institute produced the Global Reporting Initiative. Aimed at standardizing corporate practices, it provided the first international framework to guide sustainability reporting. Based on the principles of transparency and accountability it has become a world leader in the matter, producing standards and guidelines to report environmental and social impacts. In total, as of today, more than 1,500 companies have voluntarily adopted GRI guidelines (GRI 2015), submitting hundreds of reports on an annual basis.

### THE U.K.'s ACCOUNTABILITY

The U.K.'s Accountability is one of the many examples of how NGOs have been pioneers, acquiring assurance responsibilities with regards to corporate reporting. In 2003 the AA1000 Responsibility Assurance Standard was launched with the aim of promoting accountability innovations that advance sustainable development. It became the first of its kind to assure the credibility and quality of sustainability performance and reporting. It has recently been republished in 2008 to build on the experience gathered since its inception (AccountAbility 2008). The motivation behind these types of initiatives is two-fold: to help businesses improve corporate responsibility whilst giving stakeholders a means of checking and monitoring their progress.

### 3.6.3 Corporate responses to investors

Communicating sustainability-driven practices has also become increasingly important with regards to investors, who have started to get vocal about the social impact of firms and who have become the primary consumers of information on the matter. Over the years, a responsible investment movement has developed incorporating the stakeholder performance of firms as a fundamental criterion to determine the profitability of potential investments (Christofi, Christofi et al. 2012). For example, the assets under management by responsible funds in the US rose from $639 billion in 1995 to $6.57 trillion in 2014 (USSIFF 2014). Likewise, in Europe, socially responsible asset management rose from €1 trillion in 2005 to €7 trillion at the start of 2014 (Eurosif 2014).

Responsible investment emerged as the approach by which investors explicitly acknowledge the relevance of Environmental, Social, and Governance (ESG) factors, and the long-term health and stability of the market as a whole at the time of deciding their portfolio composition (PRI 2015). Focus is beginning to be put on long-term investment returns rather than short-term gains, pushing corporate strategies in the same direction. In this regard, a series of initiatives have been launched reinforcing the role played by investors, the most important of which is supported by the UN: The Principles for Responsible Investment Initiative (PRI). On the other hand, the new demands for information on ESG issues have been met through the creation of several indices that track environmental, social and governance aspects of given firms to aid and encourage responsible investors (Box 3.4). In addition, investors can now turn to specialized research firms such as *KLD Research and Analytics* based in the USA, in order to access sustainability related data (Waddock 2008).

Box 3. 3  The Principles for Responsible Investment Initiative (PRI)

This UN supported initiative is composed of an international network of investors focused on integrating the six *Principles for Responsible Investment* into investing practices. Its main purpose is to understand the implications of ESG issues for investors and help signatories incorporate these issues into their investment decision-making and ownership practices. To this day, it is supported by more than 1, 300 signatories with combined assets under management worth around $45 trillion (Mycoskie 2008; PRI 2015).

**PRINCIPLES:**

1. We will incorporate ESG issues into investment analysis and decision-making processes.

2. We will be active owners and incorporate ESG issues into our ownership policies and practices.

3. We will seek appropriate disclosure on ESG issues by the entities in which we invest.

4. We will promote acceptance and implementation of the Principles within the investment industry.

5. We will work together to enhance our effectiveness in implementing the Principles.

6. We will each report on our activities and progress towards implementing the Principles.

> **❝** Investors have gradually become more sensitive to sustainability issues and expect greater transparency. They demand proof, expecting concrete environmental policies and initiatives that sustain corporate claims. This also applies to rating agencies who have become increasingly strict and rigorous [with] exhaustive assessments and very detailed questionnaires, which is very positive. **❞**

*Gael Gonzalez*
*SUSTAINABILITY EXPERT, LUXURY SECTOR*

Moreover, responsible investors have recently started to use their equity stake in a corporation to put public pressure on its management. This form of shareholder activism has gained popularity in publicly traded companies during recent years and has shifted focus from standard corporate governance issues (such as management pay) to environmental and social-related aspects. My own work in this area has shown that shareholder proposals presented at shareholder meetings not only act as a reflection of minority shareholders discontent (Gomez-Mejia, Martin et al. 2015), but also as an effective mechanism for responsible investors to start dialogue with senior executives and board members about firms' social and environmental behaviors (Rousseau, Berrone et al. 2015).

Box 3. 4  Tracking ESG Performance

**THE DOW JONES SUSTAINABILITY INDEX (DJSI)**

After the environmental disasters of the 80s and financial scandals of the 90s, the link between adequate sustainability programs and better corporate performance began to be forged. As a result, the DJSI World was born in 1999, under the assumption that leading sustainability companies display the top level managerial skills needed to address global and industry challenges. The DJSI tracks the top 10% of the biggest 2,500 sustainability driven companies in the Dow Jones Global Index. Corporate sustainability is defined as *"a business approach that creates long-term shareholder value by embracing opportunities and managing risks deriving from economic, environmental and social developments."* (DJSI 2015). The DJ Index creates a set of performance indicators used to report on the financial performance of such companies to demonstrate the long-term economic benefits of successfully integrating sustainability in the business model, which makes them an attractive option for investors.

Companies included in the Index over the years include *Repsol* (Oil and gas; Spain), *Unilever NV* (Food, Beverage and Tobacco; the Netherlands) and *Siemens* (Industrial Conglomerates; Germany). However, the recent *Volkswagen AG* greenwashing case has cast doubts about the extent to which DJSI accurately tracks actual environmental performance. In early September, 2015, DJSI awarded a sustainability prize in the "Automobiles & Components" category to Volkswagen, only to find out one month later that the German carmaker's motors were producing over 1 million tons of illegal pollution each year. Despite the fact that DJSI eventually removed VW from the index, the negative impact is expected to affect ratings in general (not only DJSI), especially those that are based mostly on voluntary reporting by companies rather than on due diligence from independent third parties.

## 3.6.4 Corporate responses to consumers

Aside from increasing levels of transparency, an important part of effectively introducing sustainable practices are the outputs obtained at the end of the line. Ultimately, the direct impact firms have on consumers lies within the range of services and products offered in the market that effectively satisfy their expectations. With the introduction of sustainable development came new levels of public awareness, and with new levels of public awareness came a change in consumer preferences.

In 2014, Nielsen conducted a *Global Online Environment and Sustainability* study that revealed that around 55% of respondents claimed they would be "willing to pay more for products and services provided from companies that are committed to positive social and environmental impact"(Nielsen 2014). Not surprisingly, these preferences have culminated in the expansion and establishment of a "green" market that has pushed for a new category of goods and services aligned with sustainable principles and long-term objectives.

As a result, businesses have redirected efforts to produce innovative eco-friendly and sustainable goods, or redesign existing products. This shift in focus has been identified across all major sectors, as the increase in "greener" product offerings has been tracked and monitored over the years. To state an example, a report issued by TerraChoice on the state of the Canadian and US markets, found that the percentage of green products rose by 79% between 2008 and 2009, and again by 73% from 2, 739 products in 2009 to 4, 744 products in 2010 (TerraChoice 2010). Moreover, as of 2011, a survey conducted by KPMG reported that 62% of the G250[5] companies were offering green or sustainable products, recognizing that their availability increases brand reputation and thereby market share and revenue (KPMG 2013).

---

[5] These were identified as the top 250 companies listed in the Fortune Global 500 ranking for 2010.

> " Although consumers are more aware, they usually do not
> choose sustainable products out of solidarity (even if they
> know that buying a certain product is indirectly enabling poor
> working conditions) as people continue to be individualistic. "

*Gael Gonzalez*
*SUSTAINABILITY EXPERT, LUXURY SECTOR*

Furthermore, the demand for greener products has also generated a set of voluntary green labels and certifications used to communicate environmental traits to consumers. To this day, there are more than 300 labels present in the market which can be categorized according to the scope, certification and final use of the given label.

Nevertheless, there is also evidence that suggests that "consumers' uptake of green products has not kept pace with their growing concern for the environment" (Johnstone and Tan 2014). This is evident when, despite consumers stating their willingness to pay more for environmentally friendly products, this is not reflected in market trends. In other words, there is a significant inconsistency, or what has been denominated as a "green gap" —a gap between consumers' green intentions and green actions (Bennet and Williams 2011).

For example, in 2013 consumers in the UK expressed their desire to purchase greener cleaning products (Butler 2013) but conventional brands, not promoted as environmentally friendly, continued to dominate the market between 2008 and 2013 (Euromonitor International 2013). This is not a unique phenomenon, and although to this day we have limited knowledge as to why consumers do not "walk their talk," most research seems to agree that price, perceived performance and trust are amongst the main reasons that explain such behavior (Pickett-Baker and Ozaki 2008; Gupta and Ogden 2009; Gleim, Smith et al. 2013). For example, the success of the Tesla Model S is not just that it is a zero emission vehicle. It is also the highest-scoring car Consumer Reports ever tested, and set a new record for safety in tests conducted by the National Highway Traffic Safety Administration.

This, of course, poses a problem when businesses seek to placate demands and fulfill expectations, yet do not actually reap the expected benefits of their efforts due to extenuating circumstances. For now, we can conclude that consumers want to see the evident added value of purchasing greener products and they want to go green without compromise or sacrifice. We'll explore this issue further on in the book.

> **"** The world is well aware of the challenges posed by climate change, as all agents involved no longer have doubts regarding what drives global warming. This offers a wide range of opportunities; [there are] new business models, new energy sources, new projects regarding energy storage or sustainable transportation…there are a broad number of opportunities. **"**
>
> *Antonio Fuertes Zurita*
> *GAS NATURAL FENOSA*

### 3.6.5 Beyond corporate: Green entrepreneurs

Finally, green product initiatives have not been limited to the efforts of existing corporations. Given the projected potential of the green market which is poised to reach \$2.74 trillion by 2020 (Conner 2012), and a new social consciousness, a growing group of "green" entrepreneurs have emerged.

They have recognized the potential that lies in giving back to society and thinking "green." This "green" thinking has proven to be a profitable opportunity and as such simply makes good business sense. As a result, the examples of green ventures are as numerous as they are varied, ranging from simple smartphone apps targeting responsible consumers (Table 3.3), to organizations that have built their whole corporate strategy around the concept of sustainability.

Table 3. 3 Smartphone Apps That Fit into Your Daily Routine

| Instead |
| --- |
| "Micro donations, macro impact" is the philosophy behind the app Instead. The app displays the impact of your choice, so instead of buying a $3 dollar coffee one can provide a South Sudanese child with clean water for a year. |
| **I Can Go Without** |
| When you make a pledge to reduce daily consumption you can choose to give that money away via this app. Pledges are then converted into donations. Just as Instead, the app connects conscious consumers with trusted causes. |
| **Take a Photo, Make a Difference** |
| Johnson & Johnson has found a way to tap into the photo-sharing mania. By downloading this app, the company donates $1 to a chosen cause for every photo shared. |

*Source:* Own based on "6 Apps That Fit Into Your Daily Routine" by S. Ang, 2014, Mashable.

Many of these young entrepreneurs are not only producing sustainable products but are revolutionizing the entire value chain. Such is the case of Kyle Berner, the CEO of *Feelgoodz*, and Blake Mycoskie, the creator of TOMS. (see Box 3.5). Both have created business models that integrate money making with society's best interests and that add value along every aspect of the supply chain. Both companies are extremely successful, which goes to show that making a living while helping preserve and protect the world is actually *possible* and *profitable*. Of course, in certain circles, the debate about these "hybrid" organizational forms is still open on two fronts. On the one hand, a large percentage of endeavors of this sort perish rather quickly and this high failure rate is often neglect by the business press. On the other hand, it is not clear whether successful cases do well *because* of their environmental and social commitment or *in spite* of it.

Box 3. 5 Possible and Profitable

### TOMS – Shoes for Tomorrow Project

During a trip to Argentina, Blake Mycoskie was amazed at the number of children who didn't have shoes. Putting his entrepreneurial skills to work, he came up with the idea of TOMS (short for *tomorrow*) a business which has introduced the traditional Argentinian shoe, the *"alpargata,"* as a fashion item in the US. However, the striking feature of the organization is the "one for one" philosophy behind it; for every pair purchased in the developed world, the business helps a person in need.

Owning a pair of shoes is actually a big deal in disadvantaged communities as it becomes a passport into other things that are very important such as education. Without a proper uniform, which includes shoes, most children are not allowed to access schools. Moreover, foot infections and diseases are not uncommon among these young generations, problems which can be easily avoided by wearing proper footwear. The company depends on word of mouth, thus redirecting all possible resources towards their commitment instead of investing in advertising campaigns.

Originally, the company started by donating a pair of shoes to children in Ethiopia and Argentina for every pair purchased, but has expanded over the years to providing sight, water and safer birth services in more than 70 countries around the world.

To this day, TOMS has given more than **35 million pairs of new shoes** to children in need.

### FEELGOODZ

Inspired by Mycoskie, Kyle Berner founded Feelgoodz, another way of making money and giving back with shoes. Committed to creating a sustainable business, the company has a triple corporate mission based on a "Farm to Foot" model; 1% for the Planet, 1% for the People and 1% for Phitsanulok.

**1% for the Planet:** The company uses natural rubber, hemp and bamboo to make the shoes as well as using recycled paper flip flop hangers. Moreover the company's contribution to 1% for the Planet allows them to support environmental organizations worldwide.

**1% for the People:** Guaranteeing fair wages and proper working conditions are of the utmost importance which is why profits are invested in creating the necessary systems and processes to establish fair trade programs.

**1% for Phitsanulok:** Starting in the community of Phitsanulok, Thailand, Berner's long-term goal is to develop infrastructures that focus on creating and sustaining healthy economies for the people in Southeast Asia.

### 3.6.6 Corporate peer pressure

Leaving external expectations to one side, it is worth noting that a great deal of business membership organizations established in recent years are oriented towards corporate sustainability and responsibility. This has successfully created a new source of pressure within the business world itself, guiding those who want to keep up with leading companies, as these are usually the first to get on board (Waddock 2008).

These organizations act as platforms and forums to diffuse knowledge acquired on the matter by sharing successful practices and discouraging those practices deemed unacceptable. The means used range from dialogues to conferences which allow companies to share their learning experiences while generating public interest and pushing for further engagement. Membership allows companies to demonstrate the will to improve existing practices through cooperation and collaboration, providing them with some degree of reputational benefit. On the other hand, they also assume the risk of being publicly exposed when expectations are not met, adding on to existing external demands.

> 66 Many industries still find it extremely difficult to 'monetize' good environmental management, and as such many sustainability related aspects are seen as a cost as opposed to an investment. Experience (in addition to regulations) has proven in numerous cases that sustainability is critical to the survival and success of any business project. 99
>
> *Carlos Salvador*
> *SUSTAINABILITY EXPERT, OIL & GAS SECTOR*

In this regard, the most prominent efforts have been made in Europe where many influential and successful business associations have been established to provide clear leadership in a wide range of responsibility-related issues. Some efforts are country or industry specific while others are launched by companies or stakeholder groups and oriented towards a broader general public (Table 3.4).

Oil & Gas U.K. is an example of how an association has become a prominent figurehead in its domain. Despite being oriented towards companies operating in the UK continental shelf, it has become a reference of good practices to the offshore industry as a whole promoting open dialogue within and across all sectors of the industry, developing and delivering industry-wide

initiatives and programs, and engaging with governments and other external organizations in order to shape and guide the industry's future (OGUK 2015).

## Table 3. 4  Examples of Leading Business Oriented Organizations

| BUSINESS MEMBERSHIP ORGANIZATIONS | |
|---|---|
| Business in the Community (UK) | UK based membership organization with more than 700 leading companies seeking to improve their positive impact on society. |
| CSR Europe | European business network with more than 60 leading multinational firms as members. |
| Fundación Empresa y Sociedad (Spain) | Membership business network based in Spain that aids companies in integrating community involvement as part of their business strategy. |
| Institutional Investors on Climate Change | Global Forum for collaboration between pension funds and institutional investors on climate change issues to deal with risks and opportunities associated with climate change and shifting to a lower-carbon economy. |
| International Business Leaders Forum (UK) | UK based organization that works with businesses, governments and civil society to improve companies' contribution to sustainable development. |
| Oil and Gas UK (OGUK) | Membership-based organization that acts as the representative body for the UK offshore oil and gas industry, providing a leading platform to diffuse industry related knowledge and establish best practices. |
| World Business Council for Sustainable Development (BCSD) | Global association that brings together CEOs from 200 companies to address business and sustainability issues by sharing knowledge and best practices. |
| World Economic Forum | Independent international organization that promotes partnerships among industry leaders to shape policies that deal with global, regional and industry concerns. |
| **BUSINESS-RELATED CR INSTITUTIONS** | |
| Carbon Disclosure Project | Independent not-for-profit organization which acts as a platform between shareholders and corporations to discuss the relevant implications derived from climate change. It brings together almost 300 Institutional investors managing more than $41 trillion. |

*Source:* Adapted from "Building a New Infrastructure for Corporate Responsibility." Copyright 2008 by Academy of Management.

The idea that firms within industries can voluntarily associate in order to control their collective action (i.e., industry self-regulation) has been proposed as a nice complement to government regulation. However, scientific research in the area has shown for the most part that firms' association in this type of organization is more symbolic. My colleagues King and Lennox conducted a study that suggests that effective industry self-regulation is difficult to maintain without explicit sanctions (King and Lennox 2000). A later study by Short and Toffel tempered these results by showing that firms are more likely to follow through on their commitments to self-regulate when they (and their competitors) are subject to heavy regulatory surveillance, but in the absence of an explicit threat of sanctions (Short and Toffel 2010). The authors also found that historically poor compliers are significantly less likely to follow through on their commitments to self-regulate, suggesting a substantial limitation on the use of self-regulation as a strategy for reforming struggling organizations. All in all, these studies show that industry self-regulation cannot replace traditional deterrence-based enforcement.

### 3.6.7 Corporate responses to employee expectations

From a different perspective, another source of pressure that has increasingly incentivized business sustainable efforts has emerged within the company itself; employees are increasingly advocating for a change in business practices.

> **"** Employees do not like it when they perceive their own company is exaggerating or telling half-truths. It is both disappointing and shameful when you feel you belong to a group that 'lies' to you. The same applies to consumers. **"**
>
> *Gael Gonzalez*
> *SUSTAINABILITY EXPERT, LUXURY SECTOR*

The reason behind this phenomenon can be explained once again by the shift in expectations that characterizes new generations. Nowadays, having a job is no longer viewed as a means to an end but as an integral part of the lifestyle one hopes to lead. In 2010, a survey conducted by Johnson Controls found that 96% of Generation Y respondents (18 to 25 age group) were highly concerned about the environment and consequently expected employers to take steps towards becoming sustainable by making real commitments (Puybaraud 2010).

Among other factors, corporate culture and value has become a determinant factor when deciding for which job to apply to. These same preferences were reflected in yet another survey directed at college students and recent graduates; 80% of young professionals look for jobs that impact the environment in a positive way, and 92% give preference to environmentally conscious companies when submitting job applications (Dunn 2007). So individuals now value jobs which enable them to give back to society in their day to day activities. Thus, the need to become an environmentally friendly and sustainable business is not limited to satisfying external stakeholders and achieving regulatory compliance, but necessary for those companies who wish to attract and retain future talent.

The importance of employee engagement has traditionally been recognized as an invaluable practice within business organizations. It serves firstly as a way to attract workers to the company, and secondly as a way to generate high levels of job satisfaction, helping workers achieve their full potential through appropriate levels of motivation.

Training, empowerment and in many cases financial bonuses or incentives, have long been used as motivational methods, however, as time goes by, it seems as though these methods alone will not be enough to retain and attract top talent (Lovins 2012). What motivates workers today has effectively changed, hence companies unable or unwilling to address these changes will find themselves at a clear disadvantage with regards to competitors who do.

Evidence suggests that sustainable companies benefit from increased profitability (22%), productivity (21%) and customer loyalty (10%), as well as reporting lower levels of employee turnover (25%), safety incidents (48%) and absenteeism (37%) (Gallup 2014). Clearly, employee engagement does make a difference.

Because of this, over the last years, new methods of employee engagement have been adopted, and the benefits widely documented. In many companies, Green Teams have been established to drive internal initiatives focused on specific aspects such as reducing energy consumption, while others tie employee bonuses to the achievement of sustainability goals. Training programs related to environmental stewardship, social outreach and leadership have also become very popular, providing employees with the opportunity to develop professional and personal skills, while giving the company a competitive advantage through well-trained, proactive employees (Lovins 2012).

In addition, employee engagement can also affect external stakeholders. Workers with a positive perception about their employers will explicitly and implicitly "sell" the company they belong to, inspiring customer trust and enhancing perceived brand value. This is important in many aspects, as effective communication of a company's sustainability has become more and more critical. On the one hand, customers are more likely to trust a firm's intentions if their employees reflect and vouch for their outward commitments, while on the other, the company can gain a competitive advantage when recruiting as top talent will be attracted to join the firm, and those already in will not want to leave (Odell 2007).

All in all, studies have proven that sustainable leaders are outperforming competitors in the same industry, showing better financial results, lower risks and happily engaged employees (NCS 2012). These companies are synchronizing their sustainability strategies, using employee engagement as a key driver in the transition towards building a business model that endorses environmental responsibility and social commitment. These types of strategies advance company initiatives by aligning company values with employees' personal interests. There is definitely more to gain by focusing internally on effective employee engagement programs.

Box 3. 6  Engaging Employees

### THE KIMBERLY-CLARK CORPORATION (Kimberly-Clark 2013)

An example of employee engagement is the Crystal Tree Award for leadership in sustainability, introduced by the Kimberly-Clark Corporation in 2010. The award honors outstanding contributions in three categories: employees, mills and business units. Within each category a series of objectives are established in relation to the three pillars of sustainability: People, Planet and Profits.

For example, all mills are evaluated annually by the firm's Global Sustainability Team. During the evaluation, the Team identifies those who have achieved specific targets related to occupational safety, energy efficiency, water use reduction and waste elimination throughout an entire year. Winners receive a Crystal Tree Award made out of recycled glass, a donation to the nonprofit of their choice and an opportunity to participate with one of Kimberly-Clark's NGO partners on a project such as tree planting or water replenishment. This program combines employee satisfaction with a sustainability strategy, as well as boosting the company's public image.

**INTEL (McCullough 2014)**

Intel is another company that provides a clear example of how employee engagement can drive company objectives. Since 2008, the company has linked environmental performance to every employee's compensation. Thus, sustainability has become a part of everybody's job. Annual bonuses has been calculated based on the company's performance and effectiveness in sustainability related aspects, considering measures such as product energy efficiency, the completion of renewable energy projects and the company's reputation for environmental leadership. By 2012 Intel had reduced its greenhouse gas emissions by 35%, showing the initiative has certainly paid off.

## 3.7  The Danger of Green Semantics

All in all, the progress made by the business community is self-evident. In little more than 50 years, corporate industry has gone from strongly resisting environmental concerns to openly embracing sustainable development. Whether reactively as a result of external or internal pressures, or proactively to seize a market opportunity, the journey has not been easy. But it seems that businesses have finally adapted to their new role in society and accepted the critical part they play in the future of the world. Or have they?

The voluntary initiatives that have emerged over the past two decades have revealed a willingness to endorse and promote a corporate culture in which social responsibility is prioritized. For instance, while in the early 90s only a few companies practiced sustainability reporting, today, the number has grown to literally thousands. This shows the transition is underway, as things that were once unthinkable have now been established as standard business practice. Moreover, "green" strategies have become common praxis, with aims to reduce the environmental impact of operation across all organizational areas.

Nevertheless, at the end of the day, it feels as though corporations are still far from reaching their full potential. Many consider that although sustainable development has been universally adopted, the attempts to implement it correctly have been thwarted time and time again. Efforts have been significantly conditioned by the importance given to economic growth, where key players have fought to preserve a market based, shareholder oriented business approach in ways that have not always been visible (Drexhage and Murphy 2010). Industrial accidents and scandals that once caused public outcry and sparked the beginning of an era, are still taking place today. We don't need to go too far to find examples of companies that have externally made commitments they haven't been able to live up to (Table 3.5). So why do companies risk making promises they cannot keep? The obvious answer seems to be social pressure.

Table 3.5 Industrial Accidents of the 21st Century

| | |
|---|---|
| **2010** | **DEEPWATER HORIZON OIL SPILL – USA**<br><br>In April 2010, tragedy struck the Gulf of Mexico as the Deepwater Horizon, an offshore oil drilling rig operated by BP, suffered a catastrophic explosion, claiming the lives of eleven workers and injuring many more. In total more than 200 million gallons of crude oil was pumped into the sea for over 80 days, making it the biggest oil spill in US history. 16, 000 miles of coastline have been affected and over 8,000 animals were reported dead just 6 months after the spill, many of them included in the endangered species list. Inmediate cleaning costs were estimated at $14 000 million, a figure which to this day has amounted to more than $30 000 million. |
| **2013** | **SAVAR BUILDING COLLAPSE – BANGLADESH**<br><br>The 24th of April 2013, an eight-story commercial building named Rana Plaza collapsed in the outskirts of Dhaka. It was considered the deadliest garment-factory accident in history. Warnings to avoid using the building had been previously ignored by management, and even though other floors had been evacuated, garment workers were ordered to return the following day. The building collapsed that same morning during rush hour causing the death of 1, 129 people and injury to approximatelty 2, 515 others. |

| | |
|---|---|
| **DAN RIVER PLANT – USA** | |
| 2014 | That same year, the third largest spill in US history took place, as coal ash leaked into the Dan River after a storm water pipe burst at a steam station owned by Duke Energy. The cost of damages rose to an estimated $70 million. In the aftermath, accusations were made that Duke Energy had been contaminating the water supply in violation of state standards since 2011, resulting in cancer, birth defects and heavy-metal contamination in the affected population. |
| **CHERNOBYL NUCLEAR PLANT – UKRAINE** | |
| 2014 | Only two years later, another industrial accident hit the Chernobyl nuclear power plant in the Ukraine. Once again the disaster was the product of a flawed reactor design operated by inadequately trained personnel. The steam that resulted from the explosion and subsequent fires released at least 5% of the radioactive reactor core into the atmosphere. Two plant workers died that very night, and out of the 237 people diagnosed with Acute Radiation Syndrome, 28 died shortly after. |
| **KUNSHAN ZHONGRONG METAL PLATING FACTORY – CHINA** | |
| 2014 | In August 2014, a metal plating factory that supplied wheels to General Motors, Volkswagen and Mitsubishi suffered a build-up of aluminum dust on the premises causing a lethal explosion that killed 146 people. The factory allegedly ignored repeated warnings from local work safety authorities regarding the risk posed by metal particles. |

*Source:* Own.

## Box 3. 7 BP – The "Beyond Petroleum" Fiasco

BP has done a good job of demonstrating the dangers that lie behind green rebranding. The company fell under public scrutiny in 2010 in the wake of the DeepWater Horizon oil spill disaster, which claimed human lives as well as causing irreparable environmental damage and devastating economic losses.

The fact that BP had spent millions of dollars on a rebranding campaign in the years leading up to the catastrophe only made matters worse. In the early 2000s the oil and gas giant renamed itself "Beyond Petroleum" symbolizing its commitment to broadening its vision and strategic objectives *beyond* fossil fuels. The sunflower became their logo, green became a corporate color, and clean energy technology became a N°1 priority. And in spite of the scepticism expressed by a few, the wider public believed in the firm's good intentions based on evidence that indicated an internal transformation was in place.

However, this public approval was short-lived, as in the aftermath of the USA's biggest oil spill, investigations revealed the evident failures and deficient safety methods employed by the company. BP's actions were described as "reckless" and the firm was apportioned with more than 60% of the blame for the spill. In the end, there was a general consensus that the disaster could have been avoided if only BP had done its homework. Previous claims were also questioned and the company lost all credibility in a matter of days through an anti-BP campaign and accusations of greenwashing.

The truth of the matter is that the organization's core activity is fundamentally "dirty" and no amount of marketing can change that. However, instead of wasting $650 million on green branding, the company should have been concerned with operating as safe and environmentally responsible as possible. Appropriate blowout preventer technology would have been a start. In the end, the reputation and brand value the company had worked so hard to build was shattered. Everyone could see BP had spent millions on "looking green" while being brown—a betrayal not easily forgiven.

Since the appearance of the first environmental movements, social forces have persistently pushed for the adoption of responsible practices and firms have responded by shaping their policies to mirror these expectations. Nevertheless, these corporate actions have mostly been characterized as reactive rather than proactive, with a preference for mechanisms that guarantee minimal organizational changes. Hence, the pressure to "Go Green" has already been acknowledged, but to what extent have companies really internalized these demands?

Over time, businesses have indeed identified the potential economic benefits of being environmentally friendly and socially responsible. Moreover, sustainability has permeated social behavior, with active penalization meted out to those perceived as irresponsible.

On the one hand, we have seen how cost reduction, increased efficiency, exploiting new market opportunities and reinforcing brand value are all possible perks of establishing a sustainable business model. On the other, the value of intangible assets such as a firm's reputation is now as important (or even more so) as tangible ones. This has made sustainability more than just an implicit obligation because the future legitimacy of the company relies on it. Obtaining a "license to operate" is now just the bare minimum.

Both factors have definitely inspired numerous corporate responses and initiatives loaded with sustainable intents, some of which are included in this very chapter. But when we consider cases such as the one described in Box 3.7, we find there is reason enough to believe some might be used as a means to an end; to reduce external demands and criticism by *appearing* to act as they are expected to.

Take "eco-efficiency" for example. At the time it seemed as though the idea was full of good intentions. However, when taking a closer look, its effectiveness is questionable. In the long run the measure lacks depth, as the system that caused the problem in the first place remains fundamentally unaltered. The process will effectively be slower, but the bottom line is industry can continue causing irreparable damage "quietly, persistently and completely," presenting "little more than an illusion of change" (McDonough and Braungart 1998).

Voluntary initiatives also pose difficult questions. International programs, such as the UN Global Compact (UNGC), have actually generated a great deal of skepticism and mistrust amongst the general public, not because of the organization in itself, but because of the hidden agenda of many of its members. There are those who challenge the effectiveness of the initiative since there are no screening or enforcement mechanisms in place that ensure corporations are complying with the established principles. Consequently, critics argue that corporations might join the UNGC solely for the opportunity to look good without having to make internal changes. In other words, the partnership is reduced to a public relations ploy aimed at improving the corporate image (GPF 2007).

Unfortunately, there are hints of evidence that give these claims valid grounds. The UNGC's own annual report has recently highlighted the clear gap that exists between what firms "say" and what they "do" to implement the organization's management model; "while **65%** of signatories are committing to sustainability at the CEO level, only **35%** are training managers to integrate sustainability into strategy and operations" (UNGC 2013).

Another good example is the minimal efforts companies are putting into tracking supplier's compliance or helping them reach goals; "while **83%** of companies consider adherence to the Global Compact principles by suppliers [to be necessary], only **18%** assist them with setting goals, and just 9% take steps to verify remediation"(UNGC 2013). There seems to be a widespread tendency to hang back and wait to be sure that actions will reap short and long-term benefits before investing the time and money needed to implement real changes. And where changes are made, tracking systems seem to fail.

In conclusion, corporate motives are clouded by doubt. In spite of the many signs of progress shown throughout this chapter, a lot of corporations still prefer to "do the talk" rather than "walk the walk." In many cases, sustainability strategies are driven by the desire to improve profit margins through external approval, which can easily be obtained just by looking the part. Or at least that's what they think. Experience has shown that sooner or later greenwashing backfires, causing more harm than good.

Moreover, the hypocritical stance of a few has served to undermine the credibility and good faith of the business community as a whole. Practically any corporate response can be dismissed as greenwashing nowadays regardless of whether it is or isn't true.

The problem lies in how difficult it has become to distinguish the "real deal" from the rest. Many global organizations are on the right track, having successfully redirected their corporate visions and long-term strategies, while others are still finding their way. Indeed, not all companies have responded in the same way or at the same pace, but progress has been made in a relatively short period of time.

It may be that sustainability simply hasn't reached the "tipping point," a point after which change is inevitable, irreversible, and imminent, where all companies see the need for truly sustainable business practices. In the long run, corporations that fail to grasp the social and economic benefits of sustainability will end up falling behind, unable to maintain a competitive edge. What is worse, those found guilty of being deceitful may not ever recover.

Real change can only come from the inside out, not from the outside in. Therefore the question we must ask is "Why?" Why are some companies choosing to "Go Green" publicly but not privately? Why has "greenwashing" become as popular as "sustainability"? And more importantly, why do some firms think they can get away with it?

# CHAPTER 4

# The Origins and Types of Greenwashing

> For every good reason there is to lie, there is a better reason
> to tell the truth.
>
> – *Bo Bennett*

Green has definitely become the official theme of the corporate image, with companies falling over backward to demonstrate their commitment towards the planet. Turning into an environmentally friendly, socially responsible business has clearly become the goal of CEOs all over the world, a fact that has been corroborated by the numerous corporate actions taken in recent years. Green advertising for one, has gained significant ground, having increased almost tenfold over the last twenty years and tripled since 2006 (TerraChoice 2007; Fell, Downing et al. 2009) (Figure 4.1).

Figure 4. 1  Green Ads on the Rise[6]

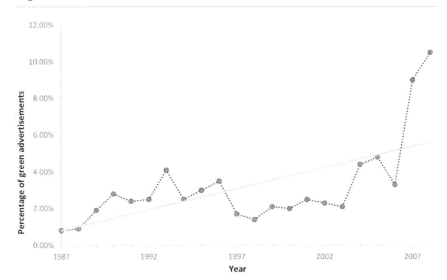

Moreover, amongst certain industries the popularity of green advertising has been greater than in others. For example, a study released by the Department for Environment, Food and Rural Affairs (DEFRA) (Fell, Downing et al. 2009), revealed significant insights into how green claims and advertisements are distributed across industries in the UK.

From the research conducted, DEFRA concluded that green advertising was most prominent in the automotive, energy and public sectors (Figure 4.2) with companies such as British Gas, BP and Lexus ranked among the top 20 brands making the most green claims. Furthermore, with regards to the private sector, around 61% of green claims were found to promote specific products or services (automotive sector), while 21% related to a company's broader brand and CSR messages (energy sector).

[6] TerraChoice researchers surveyed more than 18, 000 advertisements in the back of issues of Time, Fortune, National Geographic, Forbes, Sports Illustrated, and Vanity Fair. Advertisements that made environmental claims were counted and described as a percentage of the total number of advertisements.

Figure 4. 2 Percentage of Ads per Sector

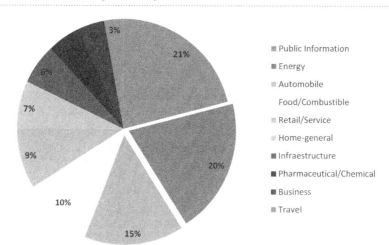

The study strongly suggests two things: 1) more effort is put into making end products more desirable for consumers, and 2) some industries show a greater tendency towards making green claims than others.

But how much of what is claimed really true? Evidence has poked some serious holes in many an environmental story showing that while some firms are genuinely committed to making the world a better and brighter place, others seem to view the environment as an exploitable marketing opportunity. At best, companies are making exaggerated environmental claims, playing up accomplishments or stretching the truth. At worst, they are using green as a way to hide their true colors, covering up questionable or even dangerous practices. How come traditional dirty industries such as energy or automobiles are investing more resources into green advertising than others? Does this mean they are more environmentally friendly?

The line between good green advertising and blatant greenwashing is indeed very fine. So fine in fact, that it has become almost impossible to distinguish between companies committed towards "doing good" and those concerned in just "doing green."

## 4.1 Greenwashing: Origins of the Term

The term greenwashing was first coined in the mid-1980s by an environmental activist named Jay Westerveld. While staying in a South Pacific hotel room, he learned about an initiative that had been launched in order to protect the environment. A card decorated with the recycling symbol read the following: *"Save Our Planet: Every day, millions of gallons of water are used to wash towels that have only been used once. You make the choice: A towel on the rack means, 'I will use again.' A towel on the floor means, 'Please replace. ' Thank you for helping us conserve the Earth's vital resources."*

At first glance, the idea might seem well intentioned, but after careful consideration, Westerveld realized the hypocrisy of it all. When we consider the amount of resources consumed and waste generated in hotels, the towel movement pales in comparison, constituting a miniscule and perhaps even irrelevant effort. Nonetheless, it was being promoted as a huge environmental accomplishment, when in reality it was probably providing more benefits to the hotel and its reputation than to the planet itself.

Westerveld noted how the word "green" was being hijacked by corporations, used indiscriminately in an attempt to create environmentally friendly reputations with the sole purpose of increasing profits (Motavalli 2011). They were giving "whitewashing" a green spin, or as Westerveld put it, they were "greenwashing."

The term caught on almost immediately, becoming the war cry of NGOs and interest groups involved in correcting corporate misbehavior. His contribution didn't lie within the actual idea; many before him had spent years pointing out the hypocritical stance adopted by many corporations. However, it was he who materialized the latent problem, giving it a catchy and identifiable name for the very first time.

In reality, awareness of greenwashing started the moment environmentalism became a "thing," a side effect triggered by a new social consciousness.

### 4.1.1 Corporations: Under closer scrutiny

Back-tracking to approximately two decades earlier towards the end of the 1960s, (long before the term "greenwashing" was coined) green was on the rise and the environmental movement could no longer be ignored. Corporations suddenly found themselves regarded as a public enemy. Something had to give and so companies began flooding the media with an unprecedented level of "greenness." Millions were spent on campaigns touting the industry's renewed commitment towards the planet, while under the surface everything remained more or less the same.

Jerry Mander, a former advertising executive, denominated this first wave of greenwashing "*ecopornography*." He found that contaminating sectors such as the oil and gas, automobile or chemical industry, were spending an average of $1 billion a year on green advertising, with visualizations that included animals like dolphins and seals, while investing next to nothing on pollution control (Mander 1972). In 1969, public utilities alone spent more than $300 million on publicity, a figure eight times higher than the amount invested in the anti-pollution research that figured in their ads (Karliner 1997).

Throughout the 1970s and 80s matters only got worse. In the wake of disasters such as the Bhopal gas leak, protecting the environment became a primary concern. With corporations under closer scrutiny, and market studies revealing a surge in green consumerism, companies focused on rebranding products to appeal to the socially conscious consumer. The market was suddenly full of "biodegradable," "recyclable" and "ozone-friendly" products, to the point that by 1990 around 25% of all household products introduced in the USA market were advertised with at least one identifiable green attribute (CorpWatch 2001).

Greenwashing during this era was fundamentally based on capitalizing on consumer concerns by touting environmentally friendly aspects of products and services, while proactive processes were completely ignored. Thus, during the 80s and early 90s, developed countries experienced rapid and substantial growth in both the supply of and demand for products claiming to have a reduced environmental impact (Lane 2013).

With environmental claims being made left and right, the public became wary, questioning the motives behind such big branding shifts. These misgivings were often confirmed as products failed to provide the advertised benefits, proving companies were sending misleading messages and in some cases even making false claims. Hidden agendas were revealed, and as a result, the industry was accused of exploiting the social consciousness to their benefit; they sought to profit from the expansion of the green market only by looking the part. It became clear that symbolic actions were decoupled from actual implementation, a decision that ultimately backfired as skepticism amongst consumers and NGOs extended rapidly, shattering business credibility along with it.

### 4.1.2 Society demands corporate accountability

This general feeling of betrayal pushed society to mobilize against these corporate giants. Legal actions were initiated by and on behalf of individual consumers, who represented the overall victims of false advertising. The efforts of governments and NGOs alike were focused on protecting consumers from the existing flow of false or misleading information, and publicly undermining and challenging dubious corporate claims. Even Hollywood reacted by bringing two real-life stories to the big screen (see Box 4.1).

In the USA, these efforts culminated with the publication of the Green Guides developed by the Fair Trade Commission (FTC) in 1992. With it, the FTC sought to provide a clear framework for acceptable green marketing, establishing the rules corporations should follow if they wished to avoid suspicion. To do so, four general principles were introduced (FTC 1992):

1. Wherever qualifications and disclosures are needed to support a given claim, these must be sufficiently clear and understandable to prevent deception;

2. Any environmental claim should clearly indicate as to whether it applies to a product, its packaging, a service, or to a portion or component of the product, package or service;

3. Claims should not overstate their environmental attribute or benefit, expressly or by implication; and

4. Any ad that compares a product to another must be clear about the baseline for comparison.

Far from being merely a symbolic gesture, the presentation of the "Green Guides" was accompanied by an aggressive campaign against deceptive environmental advertising, with the FTC undertaking up to 37 cases between 1990 and 2000. Products targeted by the FTC during this time included ads for biodegradable plastic bags and diapers, ozone-friendly aerosols, and automobile related products carrying claims of fuel efficiency or reduced emissions.

Box 4. 1  Stories Worth Telling

### REALITY OUTDOES FICTION

In the 2000 Academy Award-winning film Erin Brockovich, Julia Roberts played the American legal clerk Erin Brockovich, who constructed a case against the $28 billion Pacific Gas and Electric Company (PG&E) of California in 1993. The case voiced the complaints of 648 residents in the small Southern California town of Hinkley who suffered high incidences of cancer and respiratory ailments due to contamination of their drinking water. Erin Brockovich proved that PG&E's Hinkley Compressor Station, part of a natural gas pipeline that connected to the San Francisco Bay Area, leaked hexavalent chromium, known to be toxic and carcinogenic, into the water supply. The case was settled in 1996 for $333 million, the largest settlement ever paid in a direct action lawsuit in US history until that day. PG&E's bad reputation as a big polluter was consolidated. The environmental message of Erin Brockovich echoed an earlier film called A Civil Action (1998), in which John Travolta played a lawyer representing families from Woburn, Massachusetts whose children had mysteriously died from leukaemia. Travolta proved that environmental toxins had leaked into the town's drinking supply. The film depicted the landmark federal case of Anderson vs. Cryovac.

### THE US POSTAL SERVICE AGAINST NATIONAL FUELSAVER CORPORATION

In the early 1980s the US Postal Service attempted to ban National Fuelsaver Corporation from using their services to sell its mail-order

Gasaver product, accusing the company of making false claims about its potential benefits. The ads launched by the corporation claimed the product in question had passed an EPA test proving it could improve fuel economy by up to 48.3 %. The US Postal service argued National Fuelsaver Corporation was guilty of making profit based on false representations since there was not enough evidence to support such a claim.

## NATURAL GAS: THE EARTH'S CLEANEST FUEL?

In 1989, British Gas launched a series of ads where natural gas was portrayed as "the earth's cleanest fuel." In response, the Association for the Conservation of Energy (ACE) rallied against the company, complaining the ads failed to properly inform consumers. The use of natural gas releases methane, a greenhouse gas that contributes to global warming; this fact was intentionally omitted in the campaign as were the alternative energy sources that are cleaner than the one in question. The ACE maintained that the claim made by British Gas was an obvious exaggeration, and as such both misleading and deceitful.

As for the general public, consumers remained largely unconvinced of such a sudden change in attitude. Most initiatives were seen for what they were: a tactic used to divert attention from recent industrial accidents and overall corporate irresponsibility. They actively joined the fight, expressing their discontent and anger through numerous private actions.

An example of an individual lawsuit or consumer class action filed against companies during this time was the Mobil Chemical Company. It was sued for advertising a range of "degradable" garbage bags with claims they would break down into harmless particles even after they were buried in landfills. The plaintiffs alleged that consumers were being misled into thinking they were acting favorably towards the environment if they purchased the product. The company was charged with failure to provide sufficient scientific basis for its claim that the bags would completely break down into "harmless particles" when disposed of under normal conditions, as in fact they would simply break down into smaller pieces of plastic (Commissioner 1991).

Many of these early examples seem obvious and easy to identify, but unfortunately, the fight is far from over. The indiscriminate use of environmental claims in product marketing was only the beginning, a mere glimpse of the lengths to which many companies have been willing to go at the expense of others. Despite countless efforts and what seemed like an early head start, it continues to be a very real, very dangerous problem that has managed to persist over time.

## 4.2 Fifty Shades of Green...washing

In short, greenwashing has been around for quite a while. First introduced in 1986, Westerveld defined it as **"marketing or PR intended to deceive consumers into believing that a company is practicing environmentally friendly policies and procedures"** (Lane 2013).

Since then, countless definitions have emerged, the most popular of which have been provided by NGOs such as Greenpeace, TerraChoice or Sourcewatch (Table 4.1) who have coined the term as if it were their own, or scholars attempting to decode such a pervasive dilemma. Although the use of the term tends to be somewhat vague, true to Westerveld's original idea, you can note the common ground between every definition available: greenwashing is the act of making false or misleading claims regarding environmentally friendly products, services or practices to obtain a series of benefits.

Table 4. 1  Fifty Shades of Definition

| Source | Definition |
|---|---|
| Oxford Dictionary (1999) | Disinformation disseminated by an organization, etc. so as to present an environmentally responsible public image; a public image of environmental responsibility promulgated by or for an organization etc. But perceived as being unfounded or intentionally misleading. |
| **ACADEMIC RESEARCH** | |
| Polonsky et al. (1997) | Marketing hype to a give a firm a green tinge, without reducing the firm's detrimental environmental impact. Occurs when firms make fewer substantive claims and more posturing claims in environmental advertising. |
| Laufer (2003) | Disinformation from organizations seeking to repair public reputations and further shape public images. |
| Gillespie (2008) | Advertising or marketing that misleads the public by stressing the supposed environmental credentials of a person, company or product when these are unsubstantiated or irrelevant. |
| Delmas and Burbano (2011) | The intersection of two firm behaviors: Poor environmental performance and positive communication about environmental performance. |
| Lyon and Maxwell (2011) | The selective disclosure of positive information about a company's environmental or social performance, without full disclosure of negative information on these dimensions, so as to create an overly positive corporate image. |
| Walker and Wan (2012) | A strategy that companies adopt to engage in symbolic communication of environmental issues without substantially addressing them in actions. The difference between symbolic and substantive actions. |
| Forbes and Jermier (2012) | A superficial corporate environmentalism that is all style and no substance; a green ceremonial façade that focuses attention on one or small number of highly visible green criteria and neglects all others. |
| Marquis and Toffel (2012) | A form of selective disclosure in which companies promote environmentally friendly programs to deflect attention from an organization's environmentally unfriendly or less savory activities. |
| **INSTITUTIONS** | |
| Greenpeace (1992) | When transnational corporations are preserving and expanding their markets by posing as friends of the environment. |

| | |
|---|---|
| Sourcewatch | The unjustified appropriation of environmental virtue to create a pro-environmental image, sell a product or a policy, or to try and rehabilitate their standing with the public and decision makers after being embroiled in controversy. |
| Greenwashing Index | When a company or organization spends more time and money claiming to be "green" through advertising and marketing than actually implementing business practices that minimize environmental impact. |
| TerraChoice (2007) | The marketing tactic of misleading consumers about a product or service's environmental friendliness. |

As shown in Table 4.1, from an academic point of view, greenwashers have been defined in various ways. Walker and Wan (2012) focused on those who adopt symbolic gestures decoupled from actual implementation, while Marquis and Toffel (2014) described greenwashing as a company that enhances and exaggerates environmental performance by selectively disclosing positive information while ignoring negative aspects of their business activity.

From another perspective, Delmas and Burbano consider corporate greenwashing *per se* as the result of a series of specific factors (Delmas and Burbano 2011). To this end, we must first revisit the Walk or Talk Matrix introduced in chapter 1 in greater depth (Figure 4.3). Based on this matrix, corporate greenwashing can be defined as the intersection of two corporate behaviors: poor environmental performance coupled with positive communication about said performance. To simplify matters, even though a firm's environmental performance can fall along a wide spectrum, the matrix divides firms into one of two environmental performance categories across the walk axis: poor environmental performers are classified as "brown" firms, while good environmental performers are classified as "green" firms.

Figure 4. 3  Walk or Talk Matrix

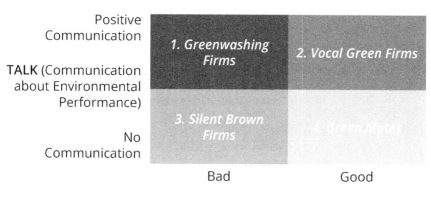

Positive
Communication

**TALK** (Communication
about Environmental
Performance)

No
Communication

Bad                    Good

**WALK** (Environmental Performance)

*Source:* The Drivers of Greenwashing. Copyright 2011 by Delmas & Burbano.

For obvious reasons, brown firms are expected to choose between remaining silent (quadrant 3) or attempting to present their bad environmental performance in a positive light (quadrant 1). Again, although there are varying degrees of positive communication, for simplicity, the matrix classifies a firm's communication on environmental performance into one of two categories: no communication and positive communication (Delmas and Burbano 2011).

> ❝ What bothers me about the term greenwashing is that due to the pejorative meaning of the word, many companies prefer to avoid green talk altogether, and restrain from developing sustainable strategies or implementing practices, out of fear of being accused of greenwashing. ❞
>
> *Gael Gonzalez*
> *SUSTAINABILITY EXPERT, LUXURY SECTOR*

Essentially, greenwashing firms are brown firms who decide to hide beneath layers of positive, green-colored, communication strategies. They manipulate and disseminate misleading information based on the assumption that the public has limited information about corporate environmental performance (Lyon and Maxwell 2011).

At the same time, communication strategies can also fall into one of two categories: 1) **Firm-level greenwashing**, focused on the environmental practices of a given company or 2) **Product-level greenwashing**, focused on the environmental benefits of a given product or service (Delmas and Burbano 2011), whereas the environmental claims made on one or both subjects, can be broadly categorized as *unsubstantiated* (a green lie) or *irrelevant* (a green distraction) (Futerra 2008).

To add more to it, each industry, company, and even managers have their own definition of the concept of greenwashing. Testament of this statement, is the following table (Table 4.2) that compiles a few definitions gathered during the interview process conducted for this book.

Table 4. 2 Greenwashing: Further Nuances of Definition

*Greenwashing appears when companies regard environmental initiatives purely as marketing strategies and as such do not integrate them into the values and core of the business.*

**Ángela Sáenz de Valluerca, Sustainability Director, EDP RENOVAVEIS**

*Although the term greenwashing historically emerged to address corporate environmental behavior, it now applies to corporate social responsibility efforts as a whole. When companies fail to fulfill expectations regarding both social and environmental claims, these can be accused of greenwashing. Therefore it encompasses both environmental and social claims, when referring to corporate commitments that do not match the reality of the company in question.*

**Antoni Ballabriga Terreguitart, Global Director of Responsible Business, BBVA**

*Greenwashing is when companies can claim positive achievements to the world around them, while remaining silent about the externalities (pollution, $CO_2$ emissions, upstream, downstream) so willingly misguiding a target audience using partial or inaccurate environmental information. Definitely, revealing only part of the actions implemented by the company.*

**Xavier Houot, Senior Vice President – Group Environment, Safety, Real Estate, SCHNEIDER-ELECTRIC**

*One can actually draw a parallel between the definition of corruption (given by Transparency International) and greenwashing. If we consider corruption as "the abuse of entrusted power for private gain," we can also understand greenwashing as a form of corruption where companies abuse their power to communicate in order to profit from a private gain that is probably harming an interest group... one is generating an asset for oneself and a liability for others.*

**Luis Piacenza, Managing Director Global Sustainability Services, CROWEHORWATH**

*Greenwashing means implementing an environmental practice/communication campaign that seeks to portray a false image of environmental commitment when the reality of the firm does not match the practice/communication in question. This includes measures that may be true, but are hiding a broader negative impact of the company, that make people fall for a false positive "halo" effect; inconsistency with supposed green image (without really having to commit a felony).*

**Antonio Fuertes Zurita, Reputation and Sustainability Senior Manager, GAS NATURAL FENOSA**

*Greenwashing is advertising, in the clearest and most obvious way, the environmental benefits of a given product that ultimately, isn't as environmentally friendly, which... can be considered a misleading marketing practice.*

**Pablo Bascones Ilundain, Director, PwC**

*Greenwashing describes an attitude, a situation where a company communicates, with much exaggeration, information on corporate actions, usually related to the product or service it offers where environmental benefits are enhanced, or claiming more actions and better results that do not match the company's reality.*

**Gael Gonzalez, sustainability expert, Luxury Sector**

*Greenwashing can be understood as a company that uses a marketing policy that emphasizes the environmental benefits of a given product or service, when said benefits either: a) do not exist b) are actually less than those claimed, or c) there is a legal obligation to fulfill certain requirements, but the company takes all the credit.*

**Ernesto Lluch Moreno, Senior Manager in Environmental Innovation, G-ADVISORY**

*I understand greenwashing as intentionally building an image of a "sustainable business model" which isn't based on real facts and data, but is based purely on an exercise of "marketing and fictional image building."*

**Carlos Salvador, sustainability expert, Oil and Gas Sector**

*Greenwashing is "selling" of environmental policies. While a green image is sold externally, internally practices continue to be rather gray. Thus, the image projected regarding "good environmental conduct" does not correspond to the internal approach awarded to environmental matters.*

**Valentín Casado, CEO, ELMET S.L.U**

Greenwashing has been defined in many ways depending on the aspects considered in each case, which when put together explain the broad use given to the term. This includes selective disclosure, decoupling, misleading advertising, and marketing tactics just to name a few. Furthermore, no one denies many companies actively take part in numerous greenwashing activities. The real problem lies in distinguishing how firms attempt to do so. Not surprisingly, the demands for a "richer conceptual understanding of how, when, and why" firms pursue this strategy are constant (Bromley and Powell 2012; Marquis and Toffel 2014) as an in depth understanding of the problem is deemed necessary.

## 4.3 Greenwashing Strategies and Trends

Whenever the word greenwashing pops up, the first images that come to mind are primarily green: cars driving along green sceneries, oil giants with green logos, and shops full of green products. But what more is there? We are constantly bombarded by corporations wishing to rise above the rest, and although deep down we know much of it is just a green screen, sometimes we fail to recognize when and where greenwashing is actually present.

This has opened the door to a new field, in which extensive research has been conducted with the purpose of understanding the nature, structure and content of green advertising. Consequently to this day, there are a number of different approaches to choose from which describe greenwashing strategies from various perspectives. Nonetheless, there are three general trends which are common to most: vague words, suggestive pictures and communication aimed at creating superficial impressions in the absence of proof (Demmerling 2014). As mentioned at the start of this chapter, most environmental claims are usually made in relation to specific products or services, so it comes as no surprise that most of the efforts displayed by governments and NGOs seem to focus on product-level greenwashing, as opposed to broader firm-level greenwashing. Nevertheless, over the years, the latter has adopted many new forms which are not as easily identified and are equally detrimental, all of which will also be discussed in the following sections.

### 4.3.1 Product-level greenwashing: Seven sins

One of the first and most notable efforts made by companies in order to capture the green market has always been the supply of green products. Businesses have jumped on board, redirecting their efforts to produce innovative eco-friendly and sustainable goods or to redesign existing ones. However, although many have worked towards enhancing their product's environmental performance, marketing environmentally friendly products has always been the easiest and fastest way of window dressing. Not surprisingly, traditional greenwashing has always been associated with intentionally misleading consumers into thinking one product is greener than another.

This sudden surge in green product supply has inevitably brought with it increasing levels and ways of product greenwashing, prompting organizations such as TerraChoice, Futerra and Greenpeace to raise red flags, providing criteria to better understand greenwashing methods.

> **"** Customers expect products of the highest quality, which to some extent implies certain levels of sustainability. When these high expectations are not met, say the product has been manufactured in poor working conditions or with great environmental impact, the customer is bound to feel disappointed—even cheated on—and brand loyalty is broken. **"**
>
> *Gael Gonzalez*
> *SUSTAINABILITY EXPERT, LUXURY SECTOR*

To state an example, in 2007 TerraChoice, an environmental marketing firm, conducted the first of many studies that evaluated the environmental claims on 1,018 products sold in "big box" retailers in the United States and Canada. Out of the 1,018 products analyzed, *all but one* had undergone some sort of greenwashing. After considering the list of false and misleading claims, TerraChoice was able to identify certain patterns in how these products were being marketed. This culminated in the creation of the popular "Six Sins of Greenwashing," which was later revised to include a seventh (Figure 4.4).

Figure 4. 4 TerraChoice: The Seven Sins of Greenwashing

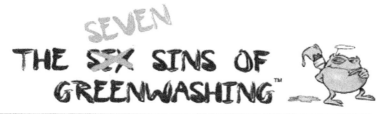

*Source:* Sins of Greenwashing: Home & Family Edition http://sinsofgreenwashing.com/games-tools/index.html. Copyright 2013 by UL LLC.

By far, the most commonly committed Sin was "The Sin of the Hidden Trade-Off" committed in 57% of the products (Figure 4.5) and defined by TerraChoice as:

> **"** The Sin of the Hidden Trade-Off is committed by suggesting a product is 'green' based on a single environmental attribute (the recycled content of paper, for example) or an unreasonably narrow set of attributes (recycled content and chlorine-free bleaching) without attention to other important, or perhaps more important, environmental issues (such as energy, global warming, water, and forestry impacts of paper). Such claims are not usually false, but are used to paint a "greener" picture of the product than a more complete environmental analysis would support. **"**
>
> *(TerraChoice 2007)*

Figure 4. 5  Sins Committed by Category

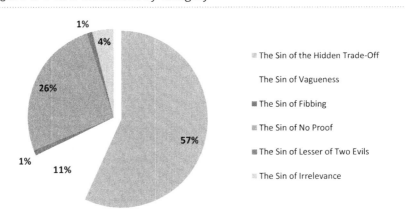

*Source:* The Six Sins of Greenwashing. Copyright 2007 by TerraChoice Environmental Marketing Inc.

This first study was followed by another two in 2009 and 2010, which found that the percentage of green products rose by 79%, and again by 73% (from 2,739 products to 4,744 products) respectively (TerraChoice 2010). In 2009, a total of 2,219 products making 4, 996 green claims were tested against best practices, of which **over 98% were found to contain at least one of the previously defined six sins.** Furthermore, the report also bore witness to the birth of a seventh sin; the "Sin of Worshiping False Labels." The latter is defined as the use of words or images that intentionally give the impression of third-party endorsement where no such endorsement actually exists (TerraChoice 2009). In other words, corporations use false labels that resemble third-party certifications in order to enhance the credibility of their own environmental claims.

Figure 4. 6. Sin Free Products as of 2007, 2009 & 2010

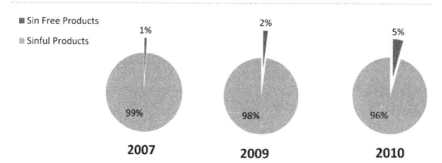

Source: The Sins of Greenwashing: Home & Family Edition. Copyright 2010 by TerraChoice Environmental Marketing Inc.

Essentially, the "seven sins of greenwashing" break down product-level greenwashing into smaller categories, providing a simple and comprehensive framework to work with. Furthermore, the firm's most recent report identified which four sins deserve greater attention, (Figure 4.7), and as such will be explained in greater detail in the following section.

Figure 4. 7 Percentages of Occurrence of Sins in 2007, 2009, 2010

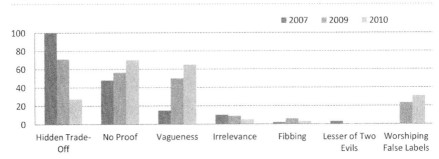

Source: The Sins of Greenwashing: Home & Family Edition. Copyright 2010 by TerraChoice Environmental Marketing Inc.

## 1) Sin of the hidden trade-off

**THE SIN OF THE HIDDEN TRADE-OFF: Are you being Bamboozled?**

The sin of suggesting a product is "green" based on an unreasonably narrow set of attributes without attention to other important environment issues. (TerraChoice 2010)

Even though the Sin of the Hidden Trade-Off has decreased dramatically since 2007 (Figure 4.7), one of the most commonly cited examples used to illustrate its meaning has been the controversy surrounding products derived from bamboo.

The bamboo plant is one of the planet's most sustainable resources. As such, its use has skyrocketed in recent years as a solution to the increasing threat of deforestation, and it has become one of the most popular materials amongst manufacturers in an attempt to placate social demands. The industry promotes products derived from bamboo as a sustainable alternative that helps to preserve the environment. But does it really?

As a woody grass, bamboo is one of the fastest growing plants in the world, able to grow as much as a meter per day and maturing in only four years, whereas its hardwood counterparts need as long as 30 to 50 years before they can be harvested. Unlike other plants, it does not need replanting as its root network keeps reshooting. It also requires little to no irrigation or fertilizers (cotton plants require 25% of the world's insecticides and tons of fertilizers), and absorbs greenhouses gases, and produces more oxygen than a forest of similar size (Barrios 2009). All in all, the facts certainly suggest it's the perfect material from which to draw sustainable products, so why so controversial?

As always, not everything is as it seems, and even though the growth and cultivation of bamboo is very much sustainable, the process by which it is converted into usable products is anything but green.

Take fabric for example, where the most often used process, hydrolysis-alkalization, is followed by a multi-phase bleaching which requires a series of harsh and toxic chemicals that release hazardous air pollutants (FTC 2009; Ring 2013). Despite there being a more sustainable alternative through the implementation of a mechanical process, it is both time and labor intensive and increases the costs of production significantly, which means that most manufacturers opt for the higher contaminant yet less costly option.

The bottom line is that the chemical processing for bamboo results in a celluloid fabric much like rayon, a man-made fabric that is far from natural. The end product is thus neither sustainable nor eco-friendly, regardless of the beneficial properties offered by the plant to begin with. This however, has not stopped the textile industry from touting its environmental stewardship by claiming bamboo as an eco-friendly fabric while hiding the truth behind its production. Many manufacturers are intentionally committing the Sin of the Hidden Trade-Off, marketing their products as environmentally friendly based on the raw material it comes from with labels such as "Pure Bamboo" or "ecoKashmere," while completely omitting mention of the harmful manufacturing process (FTC 2009). Consumers are misled into believing they are purchasing a green product and are misinformed about the integrity of the process from plant to product.

## 2) Sin of no proof

**THE SIN OF NO PROOF: Where does this come from?**

*An environmental claim that cannot be substantiated by easily accessible supporting information or by a reliable third-party certification. (TerraChoice 2010)*

**THE SIN OF VAGUENESS: What does this mean?**

*A claim that is so poorly defined or broad that its real meaning is likely to be misunderstood by the consumer. (TerraChoice 2010)*

In contrast to the Sin of the Hidden Trade-Off, (which Figure 4.7 shows decreased over a three year period) the popularity of both the Sin of No Proof and the Sin of Vagueness (next point) has only increased. Although they describe two different behaviors, it is not uncommon to find them side by side.Regarding the "Sin of No Proof," the last report issued by TerraChoice focused on toys and baby products, where 89% of the products tested were found to fall under this Sin (TerraChoice 2010). The use of BPA-free claims and phthalate free claims were especially prominent in this category, most of which were not supported by any type of evidence. This does not mean the claims are necessarily false, but with no way of verifying the facts, they might as well be.

## 3) Sin of vagueness

The "Sin of Vagueness" is also a persistent problem, present in all the categories evaluated by TerraChoice. Words like "natural," "recyclable" or "eco-friendly" are familiar to us all, but what do they really mean? Unless the claim is specified, these terms are open to interpretation and as such are too vague to be meaningful. For example, the term "natural" is commonly found among products regardless of the category they belong to. Its popularity lies in the positive attributes consumers commonly associate it with. "Safe," "good," or "green" are all words that come to mind when a product is perceived as natural, but as TerraChoice pointed out, arsenic, cyanide and mercury are as natural as they are hazardous.

Claiming a product is made from recycled material is also a commonly cited example. How much of the product has been made from recycled material? 10%? 50%? 0.01%? Bottom line: unless a claim is specific and self-evident, the use of "buzz words" or "fluffy" language (Futerra 2008) is definitely a tactic used to mislead consumers (Table 4.3).

Some of these buzz words have been around for quite some time, while others are relatively new. With the threat of climate change looming over society, new words such as "carbon-neutral," "carbon zero" or "carbon negative" have also become recurring terms. Although many have clear defined meanings, here, the element of vagueness lies with the use of words that are still not widely understood and therefore constitute a source of confusion for the broader public. This is a clear example of what Futerra considers "gobbledygook"— jargon and information that only a scientist could understand (Futerra 2008)—as consumers are not as familiar with what constitutes a carbon footprint or what offsetting entails.

Table 4. 3 Buzzwords: Frequently Used Greenwashing Words in Marketing

| | |
|---|---|
| Biodegradable/ de-gradable | The words on their own mean nothing. All products break down eventually but that doesn't mean they are eco-friendly. There are no independent agencies that certify the accuracy of the claim. |
| Eco-friendly/ earth friendly/environmentally preferable/ eco-safe | They are all broad and generic terms used for products and services that reduce negative environmental effects on the environment. They lack any meaning if not accompanied with some sort of specification and proof as to what it is referring to. |
| Organic | Unless the definition is regulated by law (USA or elsewhere) it means nothing. Moreover, even where regulated, if not supported by third-party certification it holds no value. |
| Ozone friendly | If a company claims its products are "ozone friendly" or "ozone safe," it should have proof that the products do not harm the upper ozone layer and the air at the ground level. |
| Natural | A product or material which does not come from man-made origins. This can be especially confusing since there are harmful substances that are also all-natural. Furthermore, unless the meaning of the claim is clear and has been verified, the term is easily confusing. |
| Non-toxic | Another pointless label that is neither legally defined nor certified. |
| Recyclable | A product claiming to be recyclable does not necessarily mean one can find a place to recycle it. |

| Recycled | Once again, this term require further clarification, such as the % of the product made from recycled materials. |
|----------|-----------------------------------------------------------------------------------------------------------------|
| Sustainable | Even today, there is no clear consensus as to the meaning of "sustainable" in relation to consumer products. The term is too broad and generic and as such can be dramatically misleading. |

*Source:* Adapted from "Beyond Identity Washing: Corporate Social responsibility in an Age of Skepticism." Copyright 2011 by Elving & Vuuren. "Compilation of Terms Marketing Green Products: A 'green' Glossary Version 1.0" retrieved from http://www.greenchemistryandcommerce.org/downloads/MarketingTerms110110.pdf.

## 4) Sin of worshiping false labels

### THE SIN OF WORSHIPING FALSE LABELS

A product that through either words or images, gives the impression of third party endorsement where no such endorsement exists.(TerraChoice 2010)

The confusion created by increasing levels of unchecked claims and vague messages has led to new "truth-in-advertising" requirements. Consequently, companies are experiencing notable difficulties when attempting to provide credible green products as most customers now seek some sort of verification.Aside from substantiating claims with easy-to-access information (which avoids the Sin of No Proof), companies have also resorted to voluntary labels and certification schemes. Eco-labels allow firms to easily provide clear and direct information on the environmental attributes of a given product.

Not surprisingly, the use of labels has skyrocketed in a matter of years, and recent data indicates there are more than 300 present in the market (WRI 2010). However, although this might seem like a good sign, not all labels are as legitimate as they should be. In fact, many companies are guilty of "worshiping false labels," making claims seem as though they are verified and certified by independent third parties when in reality they are self-awarded.

To provide a much needed frame of reference, ISO defined the main categories eco-labels may fall into depending on their scope, certification and overall purpose (see Table 4.4 and Table 4.5). While the sudden surge of numerous and varied labeling schemes has proven to be problematic *per se*, the greatest potential for greenwashing occurs with Type II schemes, better known as self-declaration claims which as of 2010 amounted to almost 40% of the eco-labels in the market (WRI 2010).

Self-declarations are not inherently bad since they can be submitted to independent verifications. The difference lies within the standards set for compliance, as in this case they are usually established internally by the company in question. Moreover, even when self-awarded, so long as the labels are clear and able to be properly substantiated through easy access to relevant information, there is no reason to doubt their validity.

Once again, the problem resides with claims which are too vague and difficult to check—much like in the Sin of Vagueness—which ultimately renders them useless. But the False Labels sin takes things to the next level by implying legitimacy and credibility as well as third-party verification where there is none. TerraChoice highlighted the increasing popularity of this practice, as more than 32% of the products evaluated in 2010 carried a fake label, compared to the 26.8% in 2009.

Table 4. 4  Eco Label ISO Definitions

| Classified attending to | Subcategory | Definition | Examples |
|---|---|---|---|
| Scope (ISO defined voluntary label schemes) | Multi-attribute labels (Type I) | Voluntary compliance with pre-determined, multi-attribute criteria. Identifies environmentally preferable products within a product category based upon life cycle considerations. | EU Ecolabel |
| | Self-declaration claims (Type II) | Self-declaration claim focused on one environmental aspect such as the % of recycled content, biodegradability or energy efficiency of a given product. | 65% |
| | Environmental Product Declaration (Type III) | Provides comprehensive product information based on quantitative life cycle assessment (Business to Business). | N/A |
| | Single-attribute label (Hybrid) | Focus on one environmental claim such as the % of recycled content, biodegradability or energy efficiency of a given product. | ENERGY STAR |

Table 4. 5  Certified Eco-Labels and Eco-Labeling Framework

| Characteristics | The company needs to perform an LCA[7] | Certification by 3rd party | The eco label communicates |
|---|---|---|---|
| Multi-attribute labels (type I) | No | Required. | Better environmental performance with same quality. |
| Self-declaration claims (type II) | No | Not required but enhances credibility. | Improvement of one environmental aspect. |

---

[7] Life Cycle Assessment of the product.

| | | | |
|---|---|---|---|
| EPD (type III) | Yes | Not required but enhances credibility. | Plain LCA data for comparison with other EPD. |
| Single-attribute labels (hybrid) | No | Required. | Improvement of one environmental aspect. |

*Source:* Certified Eco-Labels and Eco-labeling Framework http://www.ecosmes.net/cm/navC ontents?l=EN&navID=ecoLabels&subNavID=1&pagID=1. Copyright 2003 by EcoSMEs.

*Note:* Adapted from Environmental Labeling and Declarations: How ISO standards help. Copyright 2012 by International Organization for Standardization

## Certified: Officially fake green product

Common examples of fake labels are those carrying buzzwords such as "eco-friendly" or "sustainable" which mimic the design and logos of legitimate and recognizable certification programs. Many of these false labels can be easily accessed through the internet and downloaded for next to no cost. In appearance they seem appealing when in actual fact they are meaningless. Furthermore, fake eco-labels have also been distributed by profit-hungry independent companies claiming to provide credible verification and external approval for a fee. Companies don't need to provide proof or meet specific standards–they just have to pay a fee. Hence the overall goal of both parties has nothing to do with enhancing environmental performance.

Other greenwashing accusations are made for entirely different reasons. While some self-declaration labels lack meaning and context, others follow self-regulated standards which in many cases are communicated through the firm's own eco label. This in itself does not constitute greenwashing. The controversy is sparked when such labels give the impression of third-party approval where there is none.

## Greenlist or green trick?

In 2009, a class action suit was filed against SC Johnson & Son, Inc. (SC Johnson) accused of misleading consumers regarding the "environmental safety and soundness" of the cleaning product Windex. The controversy was sparked by the company's Greenlist trademark which had been placed on the Windex product labels, stating "Greenlist is a rating system that promotes the use of environmentally responsible ingredients."

The complaint alleged that the mark and statement falsely implied a neutral third-party endorsement, when it was actually owned by SC Johnson itself. The term "greenlist" is easily found amongst environmental group certifications, implying that SS Johnson was intentionally seeking to convey third-party approval.

In truth, the company's Greenlist program is a rating system designed to promote the use of "environmentally friendly ingredients." However, even though the company does not explicitly hide the fact that the system is developed and implemented by them, the label used was enough to trick consumers into believing it was a credible independent or neutral third-party label.

To sum up, product-level greenwashing can be identified by spotting certain symptoms. We have focused on the "Seven Sins of

Greenwashing" as it provides a simple yet comprehensive framework that embodies the main trends and mechanisms corporations resort to when attempting to promote green products. Nevertheless, there are many others ways of approaching this dilemma.

Moreover, the number of initiatives aimed at putting a stop to this corporate misbehavior continues to grow. Regulators have worked towards establishing a legal framework that has gradually evolved to respond to increasing levels of greenwashing. We have already highlighted the efforts of national agencies such as the FTC in the US and the Advertising Standards Authority (ASA) in collaboration with DEFRA in the UK, countries which have published guides to avoid deceitful marketing tactics such as the "Green Guides" and the "Green Claims Guidance" respectively.

At a European level, the *Unfair Commercial Practices Directive*[8] constitutes the main body of horizontal legislation used to assess environmental claims and establish whether a claim is misleading either in its content or in the way it is presented to consumers. Although it does not regulate greenwashing directly, the Directive clearly states it "prohibits traders from creating a false impression of the nature of products," ergo protecting consumers from misleading or false green claims and thus avoiding greenwashing.

Various directives have also been approved for the regulation of specific product labels such as "bio" or "eco"[9] labels or energy standards,[10] as well as sector-specific regulation. An example within

---

[8] EUROPEAN UNION (EU). Directive 2005/29/EC of the European Parliament and of the Council, 11 May 2005, concerning unfair business-to-consumer commercial practices in the internal market ("Unfair Commercial Practices Directive"). OJ L 149 p. 22-39.

[9] EUROPEAN COUNCIL (EC). Council Regulation No 834/2007 of 28 June 2007 on organic production and labeling of organic products and repealing Regulation (EEC) No 2092/91, OJ L 189, 20.7.2007, p. 1-23.

[10] EU. Directive 2010/30/EU of the European Parliament and of the Council of 19 May 2010 on the indication by labeling and standard product information of the consumption of energy and other resources by energy-related products.

the energy sector is the Third Energy Package Directive 2009/72/EC regarding electricity, and Directive 2009/73 relative to natural gas, both of which stipulate that the consumer must receive transparent information concerning the generation mix of their supplier. Another related directive is the Renewable Energy Directive 2009/28/EC which refers to the certification of green electricity.

The EU recently proposed the *Single Market for Green Products* initiative which seeks to provide a harmonized legal framework within Europe which, among other things, seeks to provide principles for communicating environmental performance with transparency and clarity as well as establishing clear methods of measuring environmental performance.

A variety of tools and platforms have also become available for concerned buyers who wish to make informed purchasing decisions, or at least avoid where possible, falling for greenwashing tactics. Reports and guides such as the ones issued by TerraChoice or Futerra raise society's level of awareness, provide consumers with warning signs to watch out for, and serve as a deterrent for greenwashing activity. EnviroMedia, another environmental marketing firm, has launched the Greenwashing Index in collaboration with the University of Oregon, where consumers can report and rate the truthfulness or perceived greenwashing in ads promoting environmental benefits (EnviroMedia 2015). All in all, advertisers must be made accountable.

### 4.3.2 Firm-level greenwashing: Five transgressions

The other main category greenwashing strategies fall into, are related to firm-level messages. These can range from advertising campaigns to PR events that seek to enhance a company's overall environmental performance.

In this case, the most commonly cited criteria for firm-level transgressions belongs to Greenpeace (Table 4.6) which looks beyond specific product claims to assess a broader set of corporate environmental actions. These will be covered in the following sections in addition to a fifth transgression, namely, fuzzy reporting.

Table 4. 6 Greenpeace's Four Greenwashing Criteria

| Greenpeace Greenwash Criteria | | |
|---|---|---|
| | Definition | What it looks like |
| Dirty Business | Touting an environmental program or product, while the firm's core activity is inherently polluting or unsustainable. | Playing up green R&D projects while most spending is directed towards reinforcing old, unsustainable, polluting practices. |
| Ad Bluster | Using targeted advertising and PR campaigns to exaggerate an environmental achievement and divert attention from environmental problems; investing more money in environmental claims than the cost of actual implementation. | A company that invests in a million dollar campaign about a clean up that actually cost less. |
| Political Spin | Advertising or publicly speaking about corporate "green" commitments while lobbying against pending or current environmental laws and regulations. | Advertising and public statements used to emphasize corporate environmental responsibility in the midst of legislative pressure or legal action. |
| It's the Law, Stupid! | Advertising or branding a product with environmental achievements that are already required or mandated by existing laws. | A company that has been forced to change a product, clean up its pollution or protect an endangered species that then uses PR campaigns to make the action look proactive and voluntary. |

*Source:*  Own, adapted from http://stopgreenwash.org/criteria. Copyright 2015 by Greenpeace.

## 1) Dirty Business

Think of an example of a "dirty business." Now think of an example of a company known for its green advertising. Are both answers related? It shouldn't come as a surprise if they are.

> **"** There is a barometer/scale of 'greenwashing excellence' ... from lying/hiding to promoting genuine or enhancing green qualities, though partial. Companies may generally claim things that they actually do right, even though they do not do everything right. **"**
>
> *Xavier Houot*
> *SCHNEIDER-ELECTRIC*

Companies known for touting green commitments have traditionally belonged to what most of us consider dirty industries. The energy or automotive sectors are usually first on the list with examples such as Shell and BP, or Lexus and Ford. As we already pointed out at the beginning of the chapter, we can see that both industries invest heavily in green advertising (Table 4.7), together amounting to 35% of all green claims made in the UK.

Table 4. 7 Top Ten Companies Sponsoring International Adverts

| Advertiser Profile Company name | Total (n=473) % (percentage out of a total of 473) |
| --- | --- |
| Shell | 7,0% |
| Asea Brown Boveri | 5,7% |
| BP | 5,3% |
| Bayer | 4,2% |

| | |
|---|---|
| TOTAL | 3,4% |
| Degussa | 3,2% |
| BASF | 3,0% |
| General Electric | 2,3% |
| Chevron | 2,1% |
| Opel | 2,1% |

Source: Evaluating the Green advertising practices of international firms: a trend analysis. Copyright 2011 by Emerald Group Publishing Limited.

Since these companies are typically multinationals, the same trend can be observed at an international level. A study evaluating 473 international adverts sponsored by 193 firms, found that companies belonging to both sectors dominated the top ten companies responsible for 38% of the total amount, represented by Shell, BP and TOTAL on the one hand, and Opel (closely followed by Lexus) on the other.

Furthermore, the study found that top advertisers share two common traits: 1) they handle products that depend on natural resources, and 2) the consumption of these products seriously affects the environment (Leonidou, Palihawadana et al. 2011).

In an increasingly environmentally aware society, companies with inherently dirty activities are displaying a greater inclination towards enhancing their environmental performance and overall image. Demonstrating their commitment serves as a way of offsetting their negative impacts. Again, the fact that these multinational corporations communicate their efforts with regards to environmental issues is not in itself the problem. Greenwashing only occurs when such statements are used as a distraction from what goes on behind the scenes, in other words firms that are guilty of "touting an environmental program or product, while the firm's core activity is inherently polluting or unsustainable"(Greenpeace 2015).

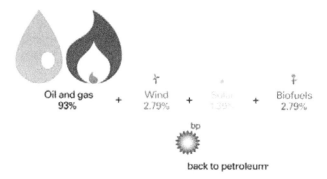

**Energy mix or PR fix?**
BP's actual investments in 2008

Oil and gas 93% + Wind 2.79% + Solar 1.39% + Biofuels 2.79%

bp
back to petroleum

*Source:* BP wins coveted ‹Emerald Paintbrush› award for worst greenwash of 2008 http://www.greenpeace.org.uk/blog/climate/bps-wins-coveted-emerald-paintbrush-award-worst-greenwash-2008-20081218. Copyright 2008 by Greenpeace.

### BP: "Beyond Petroleum"?

In this case, the easiest examples are companies that use green R&D projects as a screen to hide that most spending is directed towards reinforcing old, unsustainable and polluting practices. Consider BP. Some years back the company launched a campaign focused on the millions that were being invested in alternative energies. Slogans like "We can't put all our energy in one barrel" or "There's energy security in energy diversity" were used to tout their long-term sustainability campaign, dubbed "Beyond Petroleum." In numerical terms, BP proudly boasted their bet on cleaner energy sources by announcing they were investing $1.5bn a year in "alternative energy."

This might seem impressive for the regular consumer, but when we consider the bigger picture, the presence of greenwashing becomes far too obvious. First of all, BP's alternative energy division included not just wind and solar and biofuels, but natural gas as well (Pearce 2008). And although natural gas may be less polluting than oil or coal, at the end of the day it's still a fossil fuel, and is not among what a regular consumer would think of as alternative. Secondly, $1.5 bn dollars may seem a big commitment on an individual level. However, when compared to the total investment the company planned for 2008— an astounding $21 bn—the figure amounted to little more than 7% (Walker 2010). The remaining 93% belonged to their main attraction: oil.

BP was indeed telling the truth, thus showing claims do not need to be false to be misleading. It's the context that matters.

*Source:* BP wins coveted "Emerald Paintbrush" award for worst greenwash of 2008 http://www.greenpeace.org.uk/blog/climate/bps-wins-coveted-emerald-paintbrush-award-worst-greenwash-2008-20081218. Copyright 2008 by John Cobb/Greepeace.

Furthermore, by 2011, BP Solar had been closed down after Mike Petrucci, chief executive of BP Solar, stated that "the continuing global economic challenges have significantly impacted the solar industry, making it difficult to sustain long-term returns for the company" (Macalister 2011). In other words, solar energy was simply not making enough money. Previously BP had already shut down its separate London headquarters for BP Alternative Energy, and by 2013 had started to sell all the company's wind power assets as investments were redirected towards carbon-heavy tar sands operations as well as its traditional oil and gas fields (Macalister 2015). Beyond Petroleum? It sure doesn't seem the company has been able to follow through on its promise.

## 2) Ad Bluster

While the definitions of "Dirty Business" and "Ad Bluster" differ in theory, in practice their distinction may be a bit confusing. The latter is defined as "using targeted advertising and PR campaigns to exaggerate an environmental achievement and divert attention from environmental problems; investing more money on environmental claims than the cost of actual implementation." Hence, the main difference between one and another is that "Dirty Business" is limited to traditional industries that aggressively contaminate the environment, while "Ad Bluster" applies to companies in general, regardless of their core activities. Nevertheless, most examples of ad bluster are related (surprise surprise) to the same industries.

### General Motors: Gas-Friendly to Gas-Free

In 2007 General Motors (GM) launched the *Gas-Friendly to Gas-Free* marketing campaign which featured its bestselling brand, Chevrolet. The $750 million campaign advertised five ways Chevrolet was "greening" its fleet including increased fuel efficiency, the production of vehicles that ran on E85 Ethanol, and the development of hybrids, plug-in hybrids and fuel cells. Shortly afterwards, they were accused of greenwashing. Why? Because while the claims included on their ads were true, the extent to which GM had used their green technologies to promote this new green image was definitely misleading.

Vehicles with improved efficiency actually represented a minimal amount of the 9.3 million cars GM produced in 2007. The ads focused on seven vehicles yet failed to acknowledge that the remaining 51 models sold were not nearly as fuel efficient. According to Greenpeace, no GM car was first in its class with regards to fuel economy, and at that point in time the company was the leading producer of "gas guzzlers."

Another key element of the campaign was promoting the Chevy Volt plug-in Hybrid and the Chevy Equinox, neither of which were available at that point. The viability of both was yet to be seen, which along with other factors suggested that GM's rebranding was in fact ad bluster, based on future promises that inflated the company's green credentials.

### Shell: Flower power

The same year that GM painted the town green, Shell ran a national press ad in UK that pictured industrial smokestacks emitting multi-colored flowers beneath the headline "Don't throw anything away. There is no away."

Shell claimed that the company's $CO_2$ waste was being used to grow flowers, a bold statement that implied most or all emissions were used to this end. Considered too good to be true, the company was openly challenged by environmental groups, including Friends of the Earth, and after further investigation Shell was found guilty of greenwashing.

Behind the flower power façade, the percentage of total emissions used to grow flowers amounted to little more than 0.325% of the company's total $CO_2$ output. This ad bluster was a textbook example of greenwashing, too obvious and ridiculous to be ignored. Ultimately, they had used a bit of good environmental practice to make a big claim about themselves and their products, and as such the ASA concluded the ad was misleading by omission (ASA 2012).

## 3) Political Spin

The third greenwashing transgression Greenpeace highlights refers to companies that advertise or make corporate "green" commitments in public, while actively lobbying against environmental laws and regulations. This is perhaps the most hypocritical stance a firm can adopt: touting environmental achievements, while attempting to halt or delay the introduction of new laws.

Frequent examples of "Political Spin" greenwashing include lobbying efforts, sponsorships, or the creation of "front groups." The latter involves so-called independent scientists or green-sounding groups that are actually funded by corporations to challenge issues such as climate change. They seek to deflect the blame and persuade the public they can continue business as usual.

### General Electric: "Eco-Imagination" or "Eco-Lobbying"?

A commonly cited example of firm-level greenwashing is the Eco-Imagination initiative launched by General Electric in 2005 (Delmas and Burbano 2011). With it, GE wished to reflect the company's commitment towards the environment, and establish itself as a dominant player in environmental technology.

The campaign advertised the progress made in the environmental arena but, while these efforts were indeed visible, it came at a time when GE's environmental practices were being openly questioned. The fact that in 2000 GE had gone as far as the Supreme Court to fight the new clean air Environmental Protection Agency (EPA) requirements had not been forgotten. Furthermore, while Eco-Imagination was being announced on one front, the company was still fighting an EPA-ordered cleanup of the Hudson River on the other (Sullivan and Schiafo 2005).

In short, despite the company's good intentions, the public accused GE of trying to hide other environmentally harmful attitudes behind a smoke screen; a rather obvious green distraction.

### General Motors: Gas-free, law-free?

GM has already been mentioned as an example of "Ad Bluster," but their *Gas-Friendly Gas-Free* campaign also falls under "Political Spin" because it was launched while the US Congress was debating on whether to increase Corporate Average Fuel Economy (CAFE) Standards.

What seemed like quite a coincidence of course wasn't. The company was already lobbying against further federal mandates. GM sought to use their "green" reputation to undermine efforts, declaring that automakers were already working to increase fuel economy and reduce emissions as much as possible. They argued that new legislative requirements would do more harm than good, cutting into revenues and limiting the funds available for innovation (Greenpeace 2008).

To this end GM spent more on lobbying than any other automotive company, with a record setting figure of $14.28 million in 2007 (CRP 2007). Hence the campaign had more to do with supporting their argument than anything else.

Furthermore, GM is a founding member of an industry lobbying group, the *Alliance of Automobile Manufacturers (AAM)*, alongside other industry heavyweights such as Toyota, Ford and BMW, that aim "to develop and implement policies that enable the introduction of new technologies needed to support sustainable mobility" (AAM 2015).

However, during 2007, the group ran radio and print adverts in states with high percentages of truck and SUV owners which contradicted the official sentiment the AAM had promoted. The $1 million campaign targeted pick up drivers and "soccer" mums who drive larger vehicles and are especially concerned with safety, with the idea that increasing fuel economy standards would ultimately decrease the safety and functionality of cars (Korzeniewski 2007). By implying consumer priorities were at risk, the industry sought to stall stringent legal requirements that funnily enough, would "support sustainable mobility." At the same time this would ensure the survival of "gas guzzlers" and protect their market share.

As if this were not enough, a year later, GM joined the *U.S. Climate Action Partnership (USCAP)*, a group of businesses and environmental groups alike that advocate for the establishment of federal laws to reduce greenhouse gas emissions, quite the opposite of what they were doing a year before. As a result, the USCAP has repeatedly been accused of enabling greenwashing since many of its members are also working behind the scenes to undermine greenhouse gas regulations (SourceWatch 2010).

All in all, images may speak louder than words, but no amount of greenwashing can hide the fact that GM's main concern is to maintain business as usual. The actions speak for themselves.

## 4) It's the Law, Stupid!

The fourth and final greenwashing transgression defined by Greenpeace refers to "a company that has been forced to change a product, clean up its pollution or protect an endangered species that then uses PR campaigns to make the action look proactive and voluntary." In other words, they use legal mandates to look good, boosting their green image by giving the impression they took the first step, when in most cases the company was probably falling short of acceptable environmental standards.

### Dirty coal: "Green" little lies

With climate change on the front page of international agendas, the coal industry has been forced to adapt to increasing levels of pressure and criticism. It seems as though this energy source is facing gradual extinction. Nevertheless, key players in the sector have rallied together to present a united front, resisting constant attacks aimed at preventing their future survival.

To this end, the coal and electricity industry has funded the front group "American Coalition for Clean Coal Electricity (ACCCE) with the mission "to advance the development and deployment of advanced clean coal technologies that will produce electricity with near-zero emissions."

Although the ACCCE proclaims it is a non-profit organization, its list of supporters shows otherwise. All 43 are prominent corporations belonging to the coal, rail and electricity industries which casts a serious shadow over the group's neutrality. Rather than promote coal as a source for clean or green energy, it seems a though the end game is to ensure the United States continues to depend on coal as an energy source.

For example, in 2008, ACCCE spent more than $35 million in a public relations campaign that focused on coal as the only way of guaranteeing America's energy independence under slogans of "clean coal." Among the benefits included in the ads, ACCCE claimed that its "coal-based generating fleet is 70% cleaner than before," a rather impressive accomplishment. But was it theirs to begin with? In actual fact, the statement was made in reference to reductions in sulfur oxide and nitrogen oxide emissions, which lose relevance when compared to $CO_2$ emissions. Moreover, the reason coal plants were cleaner, had little to do with the industry's voluntary efforts, and a lot to do with mandated changes and court decisions. The perceived improvements had been achieved through no merit of their own, a fact that did not prevent the industry from exploiting governments actions to their own benefit.

### 5) Fuzzy Reporting

Finally, this section on firm-level greenwashing would not be complete without mentioning the corporate sustainability reporting frenzy that seems to have invaded the business world. As anticipated at the very beginning of the book, the use of social and environmental reporting has skyrocketed at an astounding rate, having become a standard business practice in less than a decade.

Nevertheless, despite this sudden surge of information, stakeholders remain uninformed about the social and environmental performance of many companies. The lack of harmonization in reporting frameworks has led to significant variations in content and comprehensiveness, making it nearly impossible to effectively compare reports belonging to different companies. Furthermore, many fear that fuzzy reporting on sustainability has become another greenwashing tool used by firms who merely wish to present their environmental performance in a positive light, casting serious doubts over its true value to society. How much corporate sustainability reporting is just greenwashing? In theory, the use of reporting has been constantly endorsed as a critical pillar in the transition towards sustainable business models, but in reality, its usefulness has been challenged time and time again.

Scholars have debated on whether increasing the flow of environmental information "is an increase in actual corporate transparency and accountability or merely symbolic action"(Marquis and Toffel 2011). Do reports actually provide a full and accurate picture of a company's operations? Or do they selectively disclose information that will positively impress the public? For the most part, reports depend upon the extent to which a company willingly shares information, thus allowing them to exaggerate green credentials while omitting less positive aspects of their activities.

> **“** When a firm chooses to be ethical and transparent with regards to sustainability efforts there is no turning back. Once you have decided to believe it and to pursue it a new factor comes into play...accountability. **”**
>
> *Valentín Casado*
> *ELMET S.L.U*

Indeed, companies can excel at reporting and the utilization of environmental management systems, while still emitting notable amounts of pollution. Moreover, corporate reporting in general places more focus on *processes* used to enhance environmental performance, than on actual *outcomes*. It would not be surprising to find that companies established these processes as a form of window dressing as opposed to implementing solutions directed towards improving end results.

These misgivings are present in various environmental reporting studies. For instance, Kim and Lyon (2011) explored the effect of the Voluntary Greenhouse Gas Registry program launched by the US Department of Energy whereby companies could register their voluntary reductions of greenhouse gas emission. Their research concluded that while participants of the program reported specific emission-reduction projects, they conveniently neglected to report that their overall emissions were increasing. Firms were clearly greenwashing, exploiting the flexibility of the reporting system which allowed companies to disclose positive results and ignore negative information, which could harm their corporate image; a problem present in most reporting systems.

In addition the subject of most, if not all reporting policies, are large corporations. And although multinational and large companies have a great impact, SMEs can still be exempted from reporting obligations leaving an important part of global business activities unregulated. Thus, SMEs may find it easier to boast about environmental commitments and achievements if there is no way of holding them accountable to their word.

While organizations may very well be paying attention to environmental issues, the general public still believes that the reports fail to accurately reflect an organization's behavior (Marquis and Toffel 2011). It is interesting to note that most (if not all) of the companies mentioned in previous examples engage in some sort of environmental reporting. After taking a look at what happens behind the scenes, there is reason enough to believe that fuzzy corporate reporting can be used as one of many symbolic actions and manipulated to look "greener."

As Kim and Lyon pointed out in *Strategic Environmental Disclosure. Evidence from the DOE's Voluntary Greenhouse Gas Registry,* "There is no academic consensus on whether voluntary environmental disclosures and environmental performance are even positively correlated" (Kim and Lyon 2011)

Some researchers suggest there actually is a positive relationship, as firms that perform better are more likely to disclose their positive results (Milgrom 1981; Shin 2003; Sinclair-Desgagne and Gozlan 2003; Al-Tuwaijri, Christensen et al. 2004; Clarkson, Li et al. 2008). Yet others argue that firms conveniently increase their corporate disclosures right after industrial accidents or negative events take place as a way of repairing and minimizing damages (Patten 1991; Patten 1992).

Not surprisingly, voluntary disclosures are somewhat controversial, seen by many as a tool to paint over a "dirty" company's public image and therefore considered less trustworthy as corporate environmental claims (Bennear and Olmstead 2008).

## 4.4 The Shape-Shifting Green Monster

Unfortunately, greenwashing can shape shift into many different forms. Although most of the examples included in this chapter may seem obvious, in many cases exposing a firm's corporate misbehavior requires both time and effort. As a result, it has become easier to discard any type of green claim as greenwashing, even if it is not the case, which negatively affects the industry as a whole.

So greenwashing can also have profound secondary negative effects on consumer and investor confidence in truly green products and genuine environmentally responsible firms, making stakeholders reluctant to reward companies for environmentally friendly performance. Consequently, improving environmental performance requires more than just improving communication. It is about undertaking substantive organizational changes and investments that might be initially costly.

> " When it comes to greenwashing and external communications, we can distinguish between two types of companies: 1) those that use it as a way to minimize damage or radically change their corporate image while maintaining existing practices, or 2) those that actually use it as a starting point that [instigates] a profound change within ([in other words] the campaign also used internally as the first step towards changing the way things are done). Hence, in both cases external actions are adopted, but the real difference lies in how they are assumed internally. "
>
> *Pablo Bascones Ilundain*
> *PwC*

But is cost the only aspect that is driving greenwashing? The obvious answer seems to be yes. However, the truth of the matter is much more complex, as the drivers behind such an approach are as numerous as they are varied.

# Temptations and Drivers of Greenwashing

> " Since most corporate competitors have the same problems with sustainability and social reputation, it's worth trying to solve them together. "
>
> – Simon Mainwaring

Clearly, greenwashing has emerged for a reason. Up to now, we have hinted at some of the possible motives for which corporations seem to lean towards this practice, but many more are still unexplored. Not surprisingly the number of studies and papers addressing the factors, circumstances and characteristics affecting which companies are more likely to greenwash than others has grown notably. Understanding the reasons why corporations take such risks is crucial on the way to finding a solution and decreasing the incidence of greenwashing practices, which is why we must ask what shapes an organization's behavior in the first place.

Essentially, greenwashing is a reactive response. Greater public scrutiny for environmental wrongdoing coupled with growing concerns of stakeholders regarding corporate environmental practices have put firms under strong pressure to conform to social expectations and environmental standards. However, because conformity often comes at a price and conflicts with the challenge of maintaining organizational efficiency, many firms may create the appearance of conformity by engaging in greenwashing policies that usually involve some sort of "misleading" communications (Lyon and Montgomery 2015). Fundamentally, the belief that conformity to social norms holds advantages for firms, is what incites misbehavior in the first place.

This idea has thus been echoed in various disciplines, especially organization theory, economics and marketing that have focused on identifying the factors and circumstances that ultimately drive a company to greenwash. For example, institutional scholars argue that external actors exert coercive and normative pressures that induce firms into adopting environmental policies as a demonstration of their environmental commitment. Thus, companies decide to greenwash as a way of responding to institutional pressures.

Nevertheless, institutional theory falls short in explaining the varying degrees of response among corporations which is why many academics have focused on other aspects that influence and shape organizational behavior. In this regard, Delmas and Burbano proposed a broad theoretical framework that examines a series of factors that explain greenwashing according to three levels: external (both institutional and market), organizational, and individual drivers (Figure 5.1).

Figure 5. 1  Drivers of Greenwashing

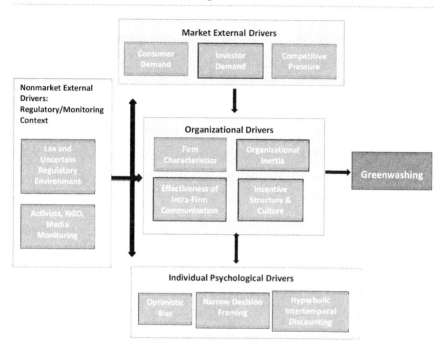

*Source:* Adapted from *The Drivers of Greenwashing.* Copyright 2011 by Delmas and Burbano.

In this chapter, we focus on what drives brown firms to communicate positively despite their poor environmental performance. Based on the Walk and Talk Matrix introduced in previous chapters (Figure 4.3), the question is: what leads a firm to go from quadrant three (silent brown firms) to quadrant one (greenwashing firms)?

## 5.1  External Drivers: Nonmarket and Market Actors

Most companies have opted to bring green into the equation as an answer to a change in external expectations. This is not in question. We have repeatedly argued the critical role society plays in exerting enormous pressure on companies and expecting them to operate in an environmentally sustainable fashion. However, the pressure comes from a varied number of sources which interact with corporations in different ways. These include both nonmarket actors such as regulators and NGOs, and market actors such as consumers, investors and competitors (see Figure 5.2). And although we have already mentioned some examples, further discussion of particular external drivers is necessary.

Figure 5. 2  Nonmarket and Market External Drivers

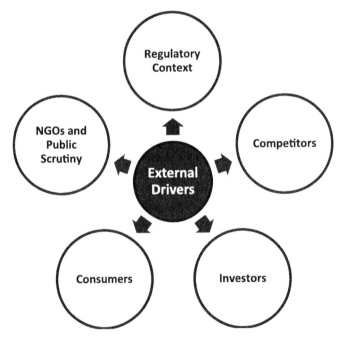

*Source:* Own.

## 5.1.1 Nonmarket external drivers

### 1) Regulatory Context

Regulatory pressure typically refers to the level of involvement of governments, manifested through the legal requirements and activity monitoring that inevitably shapes business practices. With this in mind we must ask ourselves, how has policy-making affected the emergence and survival of greenwashing? Has it acted as a deterrent? Or on the contrary, has it enabled corporations to actively adopt greenwashing strategies?

Although legal frameworks have evolved over the years, regulation regarding corporate greenwashing is still quite limited. In most countries, efforts have been directed at controlling the increasing number of environmental claims made in product and service advertising since environmental marketing constitutes the most visible form of greenwashing. Moreover, the way such regulation is enforced is highly uncertain, as the legal consequences of greenwashing are still rather unclear.

As a result, most scholars have argued that the most important antecedent of greenwashing is lax and uncertain government regulation. For instance, Delmas and Burbano focused on regulatory context as the most critical driver of firm greenwashing, arguing that weak legal requirements and uncertain sanctions enable firms to manipulate consumer and investor demands with a low chance of being punished.

**THE GREEN GUIDES (USA)**

For example, in the USA the FTC has the power to apply Section 5 of the FTC Act that prohibits unfair or deceptive acts or practices in relation to environmental claims. In theory, if an advertisement is deemed to fall under such a definition, the FTC can issue a cease and desist order to the firm responsible, which can result in a fine of $10, 000 or up to a year in prison if the violator does not comply. In practice, the FTC has only investigated and charged companies in 42 cases since the beginning of the 1990s, a figure that suggests enforcement has been notably limited (Pellus 2014).

On the other hand, firms face the difficulty of determining whether an environmental claim may or may not fall under Section 5 and result in an FTC charge. Although there have been cases where the FTC's intervention was both logical and straightforward, in most cases, determining what constitutes an acceptable environmental claim can be difficult for both firms and government agencies.

It is in this context that the Green Guides become relevant. First published in 1992, they provide firms with a series of general principles and guidelines which should be followed in order to avoid making claims the FTC might find deceptive. However, even though this constitutes a valuable tool, the Guides are neither rules nor regulations, and as such lack legal force. Furthermore, because they are voluntary they do not preempt state regulations, which results in a lack of national uniformity. Because definitions can vary greatly depending on which state the company is operating in, this can result in confusion and possible additional costs for manufacturers which can ultimately prevent advertiser compliance.

In short, the FTC can only review environmental claims on a case by case basis, based on subjective interpretations of how they understand the general "deceptive" standard to be applied; this approach is both time consuming and resource intense. Not surprisingly, only the most blatant attempts of greenwashing have been effectively prosecuted which explains the significantly low amount of cases undertaken by the agency to this date.

From a firm's perspective, directors are faced with the dilemma of knowing beforehand whether a given environmental claim will set off the FTC's radar. In fact, many companies have complained that the Green Guides fail to provide "clear rules on what they may or may not claim about their products" as manufacturers are "left to interpret the definitions and examples" when assessing whether their claims are valid or not (Pellus 2014). Indeed, the terminology and standards defined in the Green Guides are based on what the agency perceives as greenwashing. The lack of scientific basis makes it difficult to establish objective criteria with which to compare green claims, and although previous cases may provide some sort of guidance, there are no clear or reliable standards firms can turn to when looking to market environmentally friendly products.

As a result, we can conclude that the current regulatory framework in the USA can provoke one of two negative reactions: 1) risk-averse manufacturers may stop making environmental claims altogether to avoid accusations of false or misleading advertising, or 2) manufacturers may take advantage of and exploit the legal loopholes caused by the Guides' subjectivity in regards to greenwash. Anecdotal observation and evidence suggest that the latter is the dominant corporate behavior.

Finally, the FTC has traditionally adopted a more reactive approach towards corporate misbehavior, taking action only after greenwashing signs have been spotted instead of preventing misleading claims to begin with. As a result, the agency has not been able to keep up with the marketing context it aims to regulate. This has inevitably given space for companies to market products in ways that have not been considered by the agency yet. In the absence of guidelines and norms, companies may be tempted to adopt unprecedented greenwashing strategies until they catch the FTCs attention. In fact, companies may even engage in accidental greenwashing, unaware their actions could possibly result in accusations of greenwashing in the future.

Overall, since it is impossible to predict when and where a claim may be prosecuted, and due to the FTC's limited resources to properly enforce sanctions, we can conclude many a firm may be inclined to greenwash. The general confusion, lack of criteria and weak enforcement, makes it that much easier for brown firms to communicate positively about their environmental performance without fear of being punished.

## OTHER DEVELOPED NATIONS

Although the USA is just one example, most developed countries have taken similar steps and as such face similar problems. In the UK, the Advertising Standards Authority (ASA) is empowered to prosecute misleading and deceptive marketing claims, including those which involve environmental issues, while in Australia and Canada, such violations are addressed by the Australian Competition and Consumer Commission (ACCC) and the Canadian Standards Association (CSA) respectively. Both Canada and the UK have elaborated guidelines that parallel those published by the FTC, with the latter also taking into consideration the international standard of environment claims, the ISO 14021.

While adherence to the standards are indeed voluntary, a few countries such as France, Norway and Australia, have actually made the international norm legally binding by establishing fines and penalties to ensure compliance.

## THE EUROPEAN UNION

In the EU, the main body of legislation used to assess environmental claims, is the Unfair Commercial Practices Directive (UCPD). Article six[11] of the UCPD applies to claims such as text, logos, pictures and symbols used in marketing and product packaging, which are assessed by national authorities on a case by case basis. Similar to the FTC, claims are evaluated depending on the impact they will likely have on the average consumer. Furthermore, Annex I of the UCPD includes a list of forbidden practices which includes:

1. The unauthorized use of logos;

2. False approval or endorsement by public or private bodies;

3. Falsely claiming to be a signatory of a code of conduct;

4. Falsely claiming that a code of conduct has been endorsed by a public or private body.

National self-regulatory organizations have also flourished, in specific reference to environmental claims. However the scope and competences of these organizations varies between EU member states. While some only regulate advertising practices, others have extended their scope to cover information on product packaging. Moreover, national authorities may back up these organizations through recognition by law or agreement, turning their advice into mandatory requirements for certain products.

---

[11] EU. Directive 2005/29/EC of the European parliament and of the Council of 11 May 2005 concerning unfair business-to-consumer commercial practices in the internal market and amending Council Directive 84/450/EEC, Directives 97/7/EC, 98/27/EC and 2002/65/EC of the European Parliament and on the Council and Regulation (EC) No 2006/2004 of the European Parliament and of the Council ("Unfair Commercial Practices Directive")(200%) OJ L 149/22, art 6.

Once again, the UCPD represents many challenges, most of which have been identified by the EU itself (EC 2013). In general, most problems arise in relation to the application of its provisions especially because member states hold discretionary power when enforcing EU directives (Table 5.1).

The differences among countries is indeed notable, which only makes matters worse for multinational corporations, especially when we consider that on the other side of the spectrum, regulation is virtually non-existent in most developing countries.

Delmas and Burbano made a strong point of highlighting the difficulties firms face due to the complexity and uncertainty "regarding which practices are legally subject to which countries' regulations" when it comes to possible greenwashing activities. Again, this can result in accidental greenwashing, as appropriate environmental claims in one country may be considered greenwashing in another. Firms may apply the same standards in all of their facilities, unaware of the existing differences among regulatory frameworks. However, it also gives companies the opportunity to greenwash, investing resources and efforts in applying strict standards to achieve compliance in some places, while saving costs in countries with weaker regulatory requirements.

Table 5. 1 Challenges Arising From Existing EU Regulatory Framework

| Challenges related to the knowledge base | Need for consistent and comprehensive data throughout the EU |
|---|---|
| Challenges related to definitions, terminology and methodology | Vague and not well-defined environmental claims |
| | Poor understanding of product life cycle impact across some business sectors |
| | Different methods for assessing environmental performance |

| | |
|---|---|
| **Challenges related to confusion and understanding** | Difficulties for companies to find the "right language" |
| | No standardization of labels |
| | Trademarks: "green" terms in brand names |
| | Business concerns about unsubstantiated complaints on (genuine) green claims |
| | Confusion between green claims and mandatory (information) requirements |
| **Challenges related to achieving a coherent enforcement** | Verification of environmental claims |
| | Accessibility and reliability of data |
| | Applicability of court decisions |
| | Enforcement in absence of agreed standards |
| | Enforcement of "implicit" claims |
| | Sanctions: Need for more coherent approach |
| | Different national interpretations and variations in guidelines |
| | Company decision making, reporting and marketing |

*Source:* Own adapted from "Environmental Claims: Report from the Multi-Stakeholder Dialogue." Copyright 2013 by EU.

Finally, and as previously mentioned in Chapter 4, international and global initiatives such as the GRI Guidelines have recognized the role of corporate reporting with regards to corporate accountability. However since adherence to most reporting programs and initiatives continues to be voluntary, in most cases there is little to no monitoring on behalf of a supervisory body. And while mandatory reporting policies are on the rise, the risk of overlapping, conflicting, and even competing standards is even greater than before. Just like with green marketing, clarity and consistency at an international level is urgent since the absence of global standards and requirements, along with practically close to no sanctions, creates a landscape where greenwashing becomes a tempting strategy.

Indeed, the role of external regulatory and political environment has been the focus of several empirical papers which have arrived at different yet supporting conclusions (Table 5.2).

Table 5. 2  Key Findings: External Greenwash Drivers

| External Drivers | Relevant Academic Research |
| --- | --- |
| Lax regulatory environment | Delmas and Burbano (2011) |
| Weak political pressure | Delmas and Monte-Sancho (2010) |
| Threat of regulation | Kim and Lyon (2011) |
| Weak pressure from environmental groups | Kim and Lyon (2011) |
| Weak relationships with government agencies | Delmas and Monte-Sancho (2010) |
| Weak connections to industry trade groups | Delmas and Monte-Sancho (2010) |
| Weak connections to global economic system | Marquis and Toffel (2013) |

Source: Adapted from "The Means and End of Greenwash." Copyright 2015 SAGE Publications.

Key findings have concluded that greenwashing is more likely to happen among firms that experience less regulatory pressure, particularly because they are less dependent upon regulatory agencies (Delmas and Montes-Sancho 2010). If regulatory pressure is weak, firms will find it easier to obtain social approval with symbolic actions without having to undergo real changes.

In general, green marketing and corporate reporting continues to be significantly under-regulated. The lack of regulatory harmonization due to the absence of global standards makes it that much easier for firms to obtain social compliance through symbolic actions that merely paint a green picture. Furthermore, because the legal consequences of misbehaving are still unclear and enforcement has proven to be weak, firms are led to believe such actions can go unpunished. At the same time, greenwashing has also become a tool by which companies seek to avoid the establishment of stricter environmental standards.

In order to satisfy political and regulatory pressures, companies may often turn to either international or government-initiated voluntary programs whereby they voluntarily commit to actions that might improve their environmental performance (Delmas and Terlaak 2001). However, many scholars have already warned against the underlying motives of what at first glance looks like a sign of corporate "goodness."

Firms might participate to gain favorable publicity, greater flexibility in complying with existing regulations, or as mentioned above, to deter the imposition of new regulations. This "free-riding" behavior, a.k.a. greenwashing, is possible precisely because of the voluntary nature of the initiatives.

Indeed, costs associated with membership are in many cases negligible and firms are not required to achieve certain goals or objectives, or comply with a given set of criteria. They are not monitored or controlled, and most of the information provided depends on the company's willingness to share.

In addition, there are no penalties in the case of not reporting environmental achievements, and participants can publicize their membership regardless of their environmental record. Firms can enter voluntary programs not only to communicate their previous environmental initiatives in order to get governmental recognition, but also as a vehicle for interacting with governmental officials in an effort to obtain an "insurance" against risks such as claims of negligence and costly regulatory sanctions.

Likewise, industry self-regulation and self-imposed codes of conduct within organizations may be adopted for similar reasons. They act as a signal to public institutions, a sign that appropriate measures are being taken and therefore government intervention is not necessary. And while many companies may actually enforce these codes, others may be tempted to decouple, announcing such measures without the intention of implementing them.

On the whole, greenwashing in all its forms, be it through symbolic actions, selective disclosure, or decoupling, may be tempting since it allows companies to deflect attention from their actual environmental performance, and comply with regulatory pressures without having to undergo any real changes. The above is also a reminder that regulation might be a strong tool to stop greenwashing practices, as long as it is clearly specified, penalties are strong, and it is strictly enforced. Otherwise, regulation is of little use.

## 2) Activist, NGO and Media Pressure

From the beginning, activist groups and NGOs have driven the green movement. Not surprisingly, in light of a weak legal framework, the importance of their role has only increased. In an era where information is easily accessed, they have become informal monitors of corporate activity, spreading information and launching aggressive campaigns against those considered greenwashers. In other words, they constitute a means by which firms are held publicly accountable for their actions even when regulations fail.

Websites such as the Greenwashing Index, or Greenpeace's "stopgreenwash" site, directly target companies in order to raise consumer awareness and unveil what are considered socially unacceptable practices. While the first provides a platform where consumers themselves can rate any ad promoting the environmental qualities of a product or company, the second also includes a list of case studies providing information about greenwashing incidents. Both websites point fingers at corporations, making them the subject of undesirable and unwanted attention in an attempt to influence both public opinion and corporate behavior.

Nevertheless, these sites have limited reach as they depend on the interest of a given individual.

Then there are activist and NGO-led campaigns. These usually reach a much wider audience, constitute more aggressive pressure tactics, attract more media attention, and consequently have wider social repercussions. As a result, many a corporation has been "persuaded" to change existing practices in an attempt to prevent further protests and attacks.

Such was the case of Boise Cascade, one of North America's biggest wood product corporations. For years the corporation was called out by environmentalist groups (with little result) for declines in old-growth forests across the world. Then the Rainforest Action Network decided to abandon gentler tactics to endorse a full-on public boycott. A 30 meter inflatable dinosaur was strategically placed to tower near the headquarters of the company, proclaiming Boise Cascade "a dinosaur of the timber industry." This label was echoed in media headlines across the country, rapidly capturing social attention.

Shortly thereafter, the company agreed to "phase out all of its old-growth wood products," and despite publicly denying any relationship between the decision and the activist campaign, it seems plain they were finally forced to yield to environmental pressure.

Throughout the years environmental activism has managed to achieve impressive results. To state an example, the fight against deforestation seems to have advanced significantly in recent years, with four of the world's biggest forest destroying corporations (APP, APRIL, Wilmar and Golden Agri Resources) announcing no-deforestation policies, a change driven mostly by public pressure. One of these, Asia Pulp & Paper, has even gone as far as to publicly thank Greenpeace— one of its most ferocious critics—for pushing them towards changing environmentally harmful policies.

Friends of the Earth launched the Pinocchio awards in 2008 to focus expressly on anti-greenwashing tactics. The popularity and attention given to the awards has grown notably since then, as the NGO uses the awards to point out perceived corporate duplicity. They exert pressure on companies to close significant gaps between corporate messaging on sustainable development and actual corporate practices.

All in all, NGOs have become an active representative of civil society, focused on bringing attention to the social and environmental impacts of business activity. Since information on corporate environmental performance is limited due to weak formal regulation on the matter, NGOs have stepped in to fill in the gap. Moreover, their power is enhanced by the advances in communications technology, most especially the emergence of social media, which allow NGOs to share and reveal broadly and quickly information that would otherwise pass unnoticed.

Twitter, Facebook and YouTube enable activists to access the public fast, diffusing information in a matter of seconds. Thus, firms developing misleading marketing campaigns can be spotted quickly and exposed through blogs, YouTube videos or what has been dubbed "tweetjacking" (Lyon & Montgomery, 2013).

> 66 Only a few years back, communication was just a one way street; the general public could only access the information that companies chose to disclose. Obviously this is no longer the case as the internet and social media allows information to be within reach of anyone who is interested. Consequently, a company's real behavioral conduct can now come to light much more easily, and greenwashing becomes much more obvious and easy to spot. 99
>
> *Antonio Fuertes Zurita*
> *GAS NATURAL FENOSA*

Ultimately, campaigns and boycotts manage to get the attention of large corporations who are forced to listen when their credibility and reputations are at stake. Severe damage to reputations can even affect market share as consumer perception of the company turns negative. In short, greenwashing becomes counterproductive, as the ever lingering threat of being denounced and exposed by activists cannot be ignored. In fact, several empirical papers have found that strong environmental groups act as a deterrent by providing information that influences consumers' purchasing decisions (Lyon 2011).

Nevertheless, the relationship between these nonmarket external actors and corporate greenwashing is two-sided. As stakeholders in their own right, they constitute a source of incentive that drive firms towards social compliance. On the other hand, the regulatory context also determines the extent to which accidental and intentional greenwashing may actually take place. To summarize key points, limited greenwashing regulation, weak enforcement of penalties and sanctions, and the lack of global norms and standards, create a confusing and uncertain regulatory context which increases the likelihood of greenwashing in any of its forms.

### 5.1.2 Market external drivers

"Nonmarket" external contexts such as the legal requirements and the presence of environmental groups can make greenwashing more or less attractive. However, they are not the only reason firms consider greenwashing. Market external drivers including consumers, investors and competitors, are usually the reason that companies choose to disclose information about their environmental performance in the first place.

Firms have been faced with the need to satisfy consumer demands and investor expectations that now factor in new levels of social awareness. In actual fact, the advantages obtained through satisfying either group of stakeholders, provide incentive enough for firms to pursue strategies that will enhance their green image.

In this context, brown firms may be tempted to greenwash in order to enjoy the benefits derived from investor and consumer satisfaction, most especially when the chances of being punished are low. Not surprisingly, the greater the pressure to become environmentally friendly, the stronger the incentive to greenwash.

### 1) Investor-induced incentives

In this regard, Lyon and Maxwell (2011) developed an economic model of greenwash in the form of selective disclosure. The model focuses on investors as the primary drivers of greenwashing, especially since stakeholder performance has become a critical aspect in determining the profitability of one investment over another.

In numerical terms, the Socially Responsible Investment movement (SRI) has grown exponentially from **$639 billion in 1995 to $6.57 trillion at the start of 2014** in the US (USSIFF 2014), and **1 trillion EUR in 2005 to 7 trillion EUR as of 2014** in Europe (Eurosif 2014).

Investor demands for information on environmental, social, and governance (ESG) issues have been answered through the creation of indices that track ESG aspects of given firms to aid and encourage responsible investors such as the Dow Jones Sustainable Index mentioned previously. In addition, investors can now turn to specialized research firms such as *KLD Research and Analytics* based in the USA, in order to access sustainability-related data which pushes firms to continue disclosing information regarding these issues.

Voluntary disclosure initiatives have also become very popular such as the Carbon Disclosure Project. In fact, the investors' base behind the project grew from 35 investors managing $4.5 trillion worth of assets in 2003, to 655 investors with assets of $78 trillion in 2012.

The demand for greater levels of transparency is one of the reasons corporate reporting has become an essential tool, pushing companies to adopt annual reports with environmental performance measures in order to show potential investors a commitment towards long-term sustainability. Taking this into account, greenwashing may become a means to an end. There is reason to believe that firms with poor environmental reputations "can reduce their unsystematic risk by making public expressions of commitment to the environment" (Lyon and Montgomery 2015). Thus, brown firms may view greenwashing as a way of making themselves more attractive for potential investors.

## 2) Consumer-induced incentives

Similar to the responsible investment movement, a new wave of environmentally friendly consumers seems to dominate the market. As a result, the so-called "green" market has done nothing but increase.

To state an example, although the market for organic products is still relatively small within the food market, its market share is roughly growing by 20% a year. While in 2002 it constituted a $23 billion market, by 2008 global organic food sales had more than doubled, reaching $52 billion.

Even in times of crisis, consumers continue to express their desire to purchase environmentally friendly products. A recent poll conducted by Time Magazine in the USA found that almost 50% of Americans valued environmental protection over economic growth, more than 60% had purchased organic products within the previous year, and nearly 40% made purchasing decisions based on the social or political values of the producing company (Gingerich and Karaatli 2015).

In Europe, as of 2013, the EU found that 26% of EU citizens were regular consumers of environmentally friendly products, 54% considered themselves "occasional" consumers of green products, while most EU citizens agreed that green products were "good value for money." Moreover, the environmental impact of a product was found to be the third most determining factor for EU consumers after quality and price (EC 2013).

Nevertheless, while those in a position to provide such goods have declared that sustainable investments are indeed driven by consumer expectations, many CEOs have also expressed the difficulties they face trying to satisfy consumer preferences.

In 2012, Accenture released a report showing that out of the 250 business executives included in their study, a third had said they could not keep up with consumer demand for sustainable products and services, a fact that suggests many could turn to greenwashing as an alternative.

Thus, from a theoretical point of view, we can safely assume that as investor and consumer pressure increases, so do the incentives to greenwash. Studies researching product environmental claims all point towards consumers as the first and most visible driver of corporate greening (Futerra 2008; TerraChoice 2009; TerraChoice 2010) with investors close behind.

### 3) Competitor-induced incentives

Last but not least, in a highly competitive global landscape, companies are constantly pushed towards maintaining their competitive edge. Competitor's actions are closely monitored and efforts are invested in keeping up with industry trends. Of course, green policies are no exception.

Throughout the years we have witnessed the way in which isolated initiatives have rapidly become standard business practice in the race to sustainability. Such has been the case of environmental reporting, which has gradually become a critical tool for assessing environmental performance. Even if the effectiveness and credibility of such reports is still in question, failing to deliver some sort of corporate disclosure is not an option.

Advertising campaigns featuring environmental commitments, policies and successes are on the rise, as companies seek to outperform one another, while the number of "green" trademarks and eco-labels visible in the market have reached unprecedented levels. As of 2014, the U.S. Patent and Trademark Office recorded more than 10,000 active applications and registrations for "green" trademarks, which often included words such as "green," "organic," and "natural."

> " When it comes to CSR practices, many companies benchmark competitors, and believe what is done is right simply because they lack in-depth knowledge on sustainability issues. Hence, out of ignorance many managing directors may fall for the 'industrial greenwashing trap. "
>
> *Luis Piacenza*
> *CROWE HORWATH*

It's no secret that business organizations seek to imitate industry leaders perceived to be more legitimate and successful. Companies within an industry or field often converge towards adopting similar corporate practices, either because they have proven to be successful in the past or because they have become common practice among direct competitors. The mentality "If it works for them, it should work for the rest" is not uncommon in the corporate world.

Even if catching up with dominant market players is virtually impossible, a firm will at least focus on maintaining its current level of legitimacy and competitiveness in relation to its direct competitors, which often involves adopting similar policies.

Research on the subject has found this is also applicable to environmental policies. To state an example, Delmas and Toffel (2008) found that facilities of heavily producing industrial sectors were more inclined to adopt visible environmental management practices when susceptible to market pressure. As the receptivity to market pressure increased so did the likelihood of adopting the ISO 14001 standard that sets out criteria for an Environmental Management System.

There are currently more than 300,000 facilities around the world with the ISO 14001 certification, many of whom have obtained it in response to the pressure exerted by their customers. It is not uncommon for large multinationals to encourage, or even require suppliers to adopt the standard. Likewise, if a company perceives that a large number of competitors have received ISO 14001 certifications, they will probably seek to certify their own facilities. As Delmas and Toffel point out, firms are often motivated to imitate the behavior of organizations tied to them through networks because they are vulnerable to mimetic pressure. (Delmas and Toffel 2008).

So it seems logical to assume that the same occurs when firms choose to actively communicate about their environmental performance and degree of commitment towards the planet. As soon as a company within a given industry begins to introduce environmentally friendly products or launch green campaigns, the rest are expected to follow. And since touting environmental accomplishments has become the common norm, those who do not may feel they are falling behind rivaling companies. Thus, fear of "losing face" can drive a brown firm to give in to the temptation to greenwash.

Moreover, in an ever changing and dynamic market, time is of the essence which makes symbolic actions all the more appealing. It's easier and quicker to launch a marketing campaign boosting a firm's environmental performance than it is to develop, implement and wait for an environmental strategy to be successful. Therefore, greenwashing can become an instant solution, preserving a company's current status which may even increase short-term benefits.

Taking into account the market pressure corporations are subject to, we can conclude that any amount of environmentally-oriented measures are generally adopted for one of five reasons:

1. Obtaining social compliance by placating external pressures;

2. Obtaining a competitive advantage;

3. Improving corporate image;

4. Seeking new markets and opportunities;

5. Enhancing product value.

Achieving any of the above will most likely increase an organization's market share and access to investors, both of which are incentive enough to consider less ethical approaches. In fact, if a brown firm believes greenwashing can guarantee these outcomes they may be tempted to choose one of two options. The first can be to greenwash while the level of environmental performance is improved gradually, in order to benefit from short-term rewards instead of waiting to communicate positively once goals are actually met. The second can be to do so without the intention of making any changes in the future whatsoever.

Once again, brown firms can be further incentivized to make false or misleading claims if they perceive that the probability of being punished is relatively small and the expected benefits seem worthwhile.

In short, institutional pressures play a critical role as they determine the extent to which a company may find greenwashing both an attractive and viable option. Nevertheless, these drivers alone do not explain the varying degrees of response amongst firms, which is why the relationship and interactions between external factors and organizational-level drivers have garnered the attention of recent studies.

> **"** The main objective is to get more; more market share, more customers, more profits…but based on something that is untrue/unethical. **"**
>
> *Antonio Fuertes Zurita*
> *GAS NATURAL FENOSA*

At the end of the day, the way a company chooses to interact with its environment depends heavily on specific organizational aspects, such as size, industry and/or ownership.

## 5.2 Organizational-Level Drivers

Naturally, corporate policies are developed and improved to address external factors accordingly. Yet while the environment has definitely become a pressing matter for stakeholders in general, corporate responses vary significantly. Why is that?

When under the same pressure, what influences a firm's decision to "talk" or "walk"? Basically no two organizations are the same. They differ in size, industry, ownership and the list goes on. Thus, the differences that exist between firms at the organizational level largely indicate why companies respond in different ways.

In particular, firm characteristics, intra-firm communication, incentive structure, ethical climate and organizational inertia have all been identified as critical factors to consider when exploring why some firms engage in both accidental and intentional greenwashing.

Figure 5. 3  Organizational-Level drivers

*Source:* Own, adapted from The Drivers of Greenwashing. Copyright 2011 by Delmas & Burbano.

> ❝ It takes a lot of stamina and resilience to embrace required
> changes, especially when it comes to reconsidering business
> models and applying deeply engrained sustainability behaviors
> within a company. In the process of this transformation,
> greenwashing can become a tempting marketing vehicle. ❞
>
> *Philippine de TSerclaes*
> *SCHNEIDER-ELECTRIC*

## 1) Firm characteristics

Firm-level characteristics usually determine the strategies available to a given firm, the costs and benefits associated with corporate actions, and the extent to which a company may be susceptible to the external drivers as described in Section 5.1. Therefore, firm characteristics will ultimately determine the expected costs and benefits of appearing to be environmentally friendly.

As included in the previous section, gaining market share and attracting potential investors are the main benefits of going green. However, at the same time, the need to *seem* green differs greatly between industries. In fact, the industry a company operates in is heavily related to the amount of public scrutiny it falls subject to. Generally speaking, firms producing manufactured goods usually experience greater regulatory pressure than those belonging to the service industry.

Companies providing consumer goods also experience higher levels of consumer pressure to adopt environmentally friendly practices than those operating in non-consumer product industries. Basically, it becomes easier for consumers and regulators alike to demand higher levels of commitment from the manufacturing industry as the end results are tangible and measurable. Therefore, we can assume manufacturing companies are further incentivized to become eco-friendly to be able to compete in the green market, as environmental attributes have become a critical component of product value. And if *becoming* eco-friendly is not a viable option, *appearing* to be eco-friendly certainly is. How else can we explain the existence of more than 400 eco-labels?

Many corporations have indeed turned to plastering their products with self-declared labels or unsubstantiated environmental claims in order to manipulate purchasing decisions and attract consumers. As mentioned in previous chapters, studies from TerraChoice, for instance, show greenwashing is definitely present among consumer goods.

Service industries on the other hand, may not expect to benefit as much from corporate greening. Nevertheless, Ramus and Montiel found that when implementing environmental policies, service firms were more likely to adopt symbolic actions than manufacturing firms (Ramus and Montiel 2005). Since they do not experience the same external pressures as manufacturing firms, they may be tempted to greenwash just because the chances of being punished are extremely low. This might be so because consumer products are tangible and thus environmental benefits and impacts are easier to identify by both consumers and regulators.

Not surprisingly, as we have mentioned repeatedly throughout previous chapters, more focus has been placed on developing product-level regulation addressing misleading environmental claims, while other aspects of corporate activity have been ignored. Ultimately, consumer firms are more visible, attracting greater attention from stakeholders which also increases the likelihood of becoming easy targets of activist led campaigns "seeking to garner public outrage due to greenwashing."

A company's size may also influence a firm's inclination to greenwash. Because of their visibility, large, publically traded companies can face additional pressure on behalf of investors and the Socially Responsible Investment community who expect high levels of environmental commitment. In order to satisfy such demands, corporations may be tempted to enhance environmental achievements and downplay failures; in other words, engage in selective disclosure.

On the other hand, smaller or privately owned firms may find it difficult to keep up with large firms with greater resource capacity and thus decide to adopt symbolic actions as opposed to costly substantive changes.

Thus, the visibility of a company, alongside its size and specific industry, are decisive drivers of corporate greening. In this regard, Marquis and Toffel explored the way organizational visibility affects compliance with institutional pressures, particularly through selective disclosure. They make a clear distinction between *domain-specific visibility* and *generic visibility*.

Domain-specific visibility refers to an organization's specific characteristics which inherently lead a given firm to stand out in a particular domain, and as such receive greater attention and exposure to institutional pressures. For instance, companies operating in the oil and gas industry have a greater environmental impact than those operating in the financial industry, exposing the former to higher levels of scrutiny from environmental groups. Oil companies with particularly strong or weak CSR ratings have been found to attract more media coverage in the event of an oil spill, than those found along the middle, just because they were more visible to begin with.

Hence, firms with high domain-specific visibility are particularly aware of the potential stakeholder scrutiny they may be subject to, suggesting they will be less inclined to engage in greenwashing.

On a broader level, generic visibility includes the given reputation, status and prominence of a company in a particular society. In this case, one might expect that prominent companies are more likely to comply with institutional pressures because their visibility means they are constantly in the spotlight. Nevertheless, an organization's visibility may also be a source of power, awarding a company the possibility of ignoring external pressures more easily.

In addition, generic visibility attracts stakeholder attention towards the company's performance in general as opposed to a specific area or domain, making it difficult for management to address all issues with equal dedication and focus. Therefore, large, well known firms may decide to invest resources in addressing issues in domains where they are more visible, while making half-hearted efforts in other areas. If environmental commitment is not a top priority for stakeholders, companies may opt to greenwash to comply with minimum social expectations.

On the other hand, if a company is under pressure to perform in an environmentally responsible way due to high domain-specific visibility, it may find it difficult to satisfy external expectations purely through tangible actions and thus decide to further boost its corporate image by greenwashing. A common example would be companies belonging to traditionally polluting industries, basically because they garner more attention than those perceived as less environmentally harmful.

Based on their findings, Marquis and Toffel concluded that all things considered, domain-specific visibility acts as a greater deterrent than generic visibility in regards to selective disclosure (Marquis and Toffel 2011; Marquis and Toffel 2014). Firms will be more inclined to provide accurate and transparent information in the domains where they are most visible, anticipate public scrutiny, and expect dire consequences in the event of exposure for not doing so.

On the other hand, companies with greater generic visibility were found to respond more proactively to institutional demands when headquartered in countries that afford greater civil society scrutiny. Thus, firms can resist institutional demands due to their perceived prominence and power only where the presence of public pressure is limited or non-existent. This would be the case in societies that are not exposed to global norms of transparency, or where the ability to mobilize and express ideas within society is limited.

Similarly, Lyon and Maxwell also focused on how a company's reputation might affect environmental corporate responses. To this end, they found that, all else being equal, firms with strong green reputations prefer to exploit their existing position, communicating as little as possible, while brown firms prefer to fully disclose information regarding environmental performance. The real risk comes from companies with "middling" reputations that perceive they have something to gain from both enhancing their environmental performance and downplaying negative impacts.

Lastly, the profitability and lifecycle of a given organization can also condition the probability of greenwashing. Again, well-established firms may resist external pressures better and therefore believe they can achieve social compliance without having to do as much as newer firms. Hence, greenwashing could help them satisfy external expectations without actually having to restructure or improve existing processes.

Growing firms, on the other hand, are on the complete opposite side of the spectrum. As expectations and requests for CSR increase, new firms become especially vulnerable to stakeholder pressures. They are expected to use advanced green technology regardless of the costs, and guarantee production and operation processes are as environmentally friendly as possible. Their response to pressures could include decoupling in order to maintain their "license to operate." In other words, growing firms experience a particularly strong tension between external pressures for social conformity and internal needs for operational efficiency which increases their incentives to greenwash (Kim and Lyon 2014).

## 2) Organizational inertia

In addition to the above mentioned firm characteristics, organizational inertia has been recognized as an influential factor that shapes firm behavior. Defined as "the strong persistence of existing form and function that underlies and hampers strategic change" organizational inertia is more likely to predominate in larger, well-established firms than in smaller, newer start-ups.

Bringing organizational inertia into the picture is important since it helps explain the time lag that can occur between public declarations of commitment, and the actual implementation of green policies, since altering existing corporate structures to attempt true greening, is both time and labor intensive. Thus, we could argue that to some extent larger older firms may engage in unintentional greenwashing by seeking to mitigate immediate outside demands for commitment, yet failing to anticipate the time and resources necessary to undergo structural changes. CEOs might publically announce future goals with the best of intentions and fail to meet them further along the line, or they might encounter internal resistance to change that can slow down the intended transformational process.

## 3) Incentive structure and ethical climate

Aside from basic firm-level characteristics, the particular structure and work environment of an organization can also influence the **ethical** nature of corporate decisions.

The theoretical framework proposed by Delmas and Burbano recognizes that ethical climate and incentive structure can be closely related to a firm's inclination to engage in unethical behavior. If we define unethical behavior as "behavior that has a harmful effect on others and is either illegal or morally unacceptable in the larger community," we can conclude that greenwashing is in fact an example of unethical corporate behavior. Consequently, both incentives and ethical climate become internal drivers insofar as they determine the likelihood of corporate greenwashing taking place within a given company.

Prior research has already demonstrated that unethical behavior can be triggered by linking incentives to arbitrary financial goals, or rewarding on-time performance while punishing late-performance. By applying these findings to environmental management, Delmas and Burbano posited that incentives that reward "brown firm" managers for fulfilling image-enhancing marketing goals or PR quotas increase the likelihood of greenwashing. These incentives can drive managers to take "short-cuts" or "look the other way" instead of properly validating environmental claims. In other words, greenwashing becomes tempting as a means of obtaining short-term rewards. However, properly designed pay schemes (i.e., those that incorporate actual environmental outputs) can improve the environmental performance of a firm, particularly in environmentally sensitive industries (Berrone and Gomez-Mejia 2009).

Moreover, the incentive structure established within a firm can also be an indication of the type of ethical climate encouraged by supervisors higher up. The ethical climate of an organization can be defined as the moral atmosphere of the work environment and the level of ethics practiced within. In other words, the norms of behavior and ethical reasoning employees perceive they are expected to follow when making decisions as part of the firm (Cullen, Parboteeah et al. 2003). Naturally, this is influenced by the organizational values and priorities the firm promotes and the extent to which they are actually incorporated into management and operational processes.

In theory, the ethical climate of an organization usually belongs to one of three basic categories (Cullen, Parboteeah et al. 2003):

1. An egoistic climate: company norms encourage satisfying self-interests;

2. A benevolent climate: Company norms support the maximization of overall well-being;

3. A principled climate: Company norms support following abstract principles independent of situational outcomes such as internal codes of ethics.

Not surprisingly, unethical behavior has been shown to occur more often in organizations predominated by an egoistic ethical climate. On the other hand, studies have also shown how the adoption of certain measures, such as the establishment of ethical codes and standards, can help discourage unethical behavior. Explicitly recognizing principles and values within internal regulations can guide employee performance towards acceptable practices, especially when reinforced with penalties that punish non-compliance.

> " When these principles are not embedded into the company's corporate culture and backed up by management, short term orientation and an 'anything goes' culture emerges, leading companies to adopt questionable risky practices such as greenwashing. "
>
> *Antoni Ballabriga Terreguitart*
> *BBVA*

Consequently, we can assume that companies with self-imposed ethical codes of conduct, will be less inclined to greenwash than those where values and principles have not been clearly defined. A lack of appropriate guidance can leave employees to prioritize goals and make decisions without taking ethical implications into consideration. For example, if the marketing department perceives that the priority is to enhance a company's image as quickly and cheaply as possible, in the absence of an appropriate ethical climate, greenwashing will most likely become a regular practice. Needless to say, the extent to which a firm's standards and codes are successfully followed depends greatly on the level of interest and commitment shown by those in charge.

## 4: Intra-firm communication

The effectiveness of intra-firm communication is another internal characteristic that can help explain firm behavior, since it is often difficult to effectively transfer knowledge among different operational departments or organizational levels. For example, suboptimal transfers of knowledge within an organization may result in less innovation. Similarly, internal miscommunication can be one of the reasons that brown firms engage in inadvertent greenwashing.

Some of the factors that inhibit knowledge sharing include the absence of direct relationships and communication between people from different subunits. Thus, if internal departments and operational divisions do not interact, collaborate and coordinate their actions, the likelihood of accidental greenwashing increases significantly.

All else being equal, ineffective communication between marketing or PR departments, and product development, production or packaging departments increases the likelihood of greenwashing, as marketing campaigns can exaggerate or overstate basic product attributes due to misinterpretation. Hence a product can be unintentionally promoted as "greener" than it actually is.

The extent to which a firm is concerned with the establishment of appropriate communication channels and close participation between departments, depends greatly on its regulatory context and stakeholder pressure. Once again, a company will be discouraged from setting processes and structures that ensure interdepartmental coordination and collaboration when there are a lack of incentives to minimize greenwashing.

## 5.3 Individual-Level Psychological Drivers

The third and last category of drivers involves the role that leaders and other individuals play within an organization's decision making process. Decisions are influenced by the context individuals find themselves in. There is a long list of factors at the individual level that explain how managers' decisions affect the environment.

For instance, my colleague Judith Walls and I found evidence that CEOs with formal and informal power and grounded in environmental expertise reduce corporate environmental impact (Walls and

Berrone 2015). Others have looked at personal values as a catalyst for corporate social action (Agle, Mitchell et al. 1999). However, to keep things simple, we will only focus on three key psychological aspects (see Figure 5.4).

Individual decision making can be heavily affected by conditions of uncertainty or imperfect information, also known in economics as bounded rationality. In turn, bounded rationality increases the predisposition towards certain tendencies such as narrow decision framing, optimistic bias and hyperbolic intertemporal discounting.

The fact that regulation is limited, enforcement is weak and global standards have not yet been defined creates confusion and uncertainty that contributes to the conditions of bounded rationality. Moreover, the limited tools and lack of criteria available to managers, directors and employees in general makes it difficult to evaluate options and make well informed decisions that might prevent involvement in greenwashing activities.

To state an example, frequently used green words are yet to be properly defined and regulated, which has posed problems in the promotion of environmental attributes. Firms have often been accused of launching misleading campaigns with unclear terms such as "sustainable" or "eco-friendly" to enhance their environmental position without being able to predict the possible consequences of their actions.

Thus, the higher the level of uncertainty and imperfect information, the higher the probability of managers and other individuals exhibiting such psychological tendencies. Consequently, Delmas and Burbano identified regulatory context as an indirect driver to the extent to which it aggravates the individual-level drivers described below.

> **❝** Amongst all the tools available, the temptation to use the shortest and quickest route can make you go for a communication strategy based on unsubstantiated claims, which at best only profits you in the short term. This is why companies make the mistake of falling for greenwashing. **❞**

*Antoni Ballabriga Terreguitart*
*BBVA*

**Figure 5.4** Individual Level Drivers

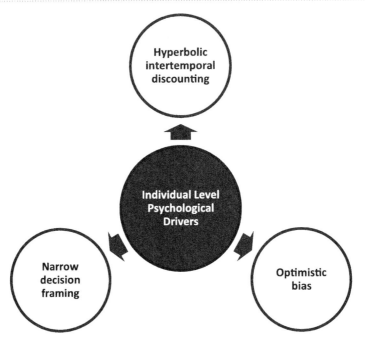

*Source:* Own, adapted from The Drivers of Greenwashing. Copyright 2011 by Delmas & Burbano.

## 1) Narrow decision framing

Narrow decision framing refers to making decisions in isolation, while ignoring the future implications. With regards to greenwashing, a manager might decide to make public commitments towards preserving the environment or announce the development of a green product without adequately considering a long-term strategy. The failure to fulfill promises further along due to poor planning and projections can unintentionally result in greenwashing.

On the other hand, empty promises may be made knowingly, due to short sighted managers focusing solely on short-term gains. Incentive structures that award longer term performance as opposed to short-term gains can help mitigate this tendency. Thus in the absence of long-term incentives, the likelihood of greenwashing due to short-sightedness increases.

### 2) Hyperbolic intertemporal discounting

In addition to isolated decision making, hyperbolic intertemporal discounting can also lead to greenwashing. Hyperbolic discounting basically generates dynamic inconsistency or preference reversals which explains why some individual's short-term choices differ significantly from their long-term goals. This dynamic inconsistency happens because the value of future rewards is much lower under hyperbolic discounting than under exponential discounting, making short-term choices that offer instant gratification much more appealing.

The most commonly cited example of this behavior involves consumers who sacrifice long-term savings because the desire to obtain instantaneous rewards in the short term is stronger than the desire to patiently implement a savings plan in the long term. Thus, individuals using hyperbolic discounting reveal a strong tendency to make choices that are inconsistent over time, making choices today that their future self would prefer not to have made.

This psychological tendency has also been used to explain a manager's predisposition to greenwash when deciding whether or not to communicate positively about environmental performance. A manager may decide to project an image associated with higher levels of environmental performance today with the intention of implementing environmental policies in the future, believing that the rewards obtained now by doing so, will be higher than those obtained in the future. However, when faced with the same choice in the future, to fulfill past promises in the present, or postpone implementation even further, the decision to greenwash is all too easily made yet again.

Impatience will always push individuals towards making decisions that provide instant results (short-term rewards) as opposed to waiting for long-term plans to bear fruit. Even when the expected outcome is better, the longer the wait, the less appealing that option becomes.

### 3) Optimistic bias

Finally optimistic bias, or the tendency to over-estimate the likelihood of positive results while under-estimating the probability of negative ones, can also cause individuals to favor the adoption of greenwashing strategies. Scholars have made a point of highlighting the fact that optimistic biases arise because future outcomes are usually based on successful hypothetical scenarios rather than on actual past results. Thus, when forecasts are biased, the expected benefits of any given strategy can greatly outweigh the potential costs of its implementation.

In the context of greenwashing, we can assume decision makers will be inclined to engage in greenwashing strategies because the associated benefits of doing so are overestimated while the likelihood of negative results are underestimated. In other words, the probability of greenwashing leading to greater levels of market share and investor interest is higher than the probability of being punished.

> " As much as it can be difficult for each one of us to fully align our behaviors to our broader aspirations (for instance 'limiting air travel' for a committed 'green citizen'), companies also struggle to fully translate their broader strategic ambitions into each and every one of their practices. "

*Xavier Houot*
*SCHNEIDER-ELECTRIC*

Finally, the influence of both external and internal drivers previously discussed, can lead decision makers to exhibit certain psychological tendencies on an individual level. As stated before, under conditions of uncertainty and imperfect information, individuals are more predisposed to narrow decision framing, hyperbolic intertemporal discounting and optimistic bias. Thus, managers belonging to a brown firm might be tempted to greenwash as a result of short-sightedness, impatience and/or biased forecasting.

Figure 5. 5  Cognitive Factors That Influence Greenwashing

*Source:* Own.

## 5.4 Greenwashing: Multiple Forces at Play

After exploring the forces that drive greenwashing strategies at multiple levels, we can conclude that no one of the three categories proposed by Delmas and Burbano is more important than the rest. The only valid way of explaining corporate inclinations towards greenwashing is to consider the intrinsic relationship that exists amongst external, internal and individual drivers, as decisions are heavily influenced by all three.

As we have mentioned repeatedly throughout the chapter, the current regulatory environment plays a large role as both a direct and indirect driver of corporate greening, but the extent to which it may influence a final decision depends greatly on a firm's specific characteristics, as well as the context in which individual decision makers adopt corporate actions and strategies.

> **"** Companies are expected to react in a short period due to the fast flow of information, driving [some] to issue responses to matters even when unprepared to do so, leading to public commitments that you may not be able to keep. **"**

*Gael Gonzalez*
*SUSTAINABILITY EXPERT, LUXURY SECTOR*

Figure 5. 7.  Greenwashing is Appealing Because...

Whether it is adopted as a short-term solution or long-term strategy, greenwashing becomes particularly appealing to brown firms as a means of:

1. preventing the establishment of stricter regulatory requirements,

2. deflecting the attention of formal and informal monitoring bodies,

3. obtaining social compliance,

4. obtaining a competitive advantage,

5. improving corporate image,

6. exploiting new market opportunities, and

7. enhancing product value.

Thus, greenwashing becomes a defensive mechanism used to maintain current levels of social and regulatory control or a proactive mechanism to reap the benefits of being green without the necessary investment. On the whole, greenwashing is believed to provide certain benefits that discourage firms from making significant changes that might disrupt their day to day operations. If symbolic actions that have minimal impact within an organization can ensure these rewards, the value of long-term strategies are likely to diminish.

> **"** Once you decide to actively communicate about environmental practices, you have to be prepared to be as transparent as possible and give access to information regarding the company accordingly. If you are only interested in disclosing a small part of your operations, or do not want to give detailed information, the initiative will most likely backfire. **"**
>
> *Gael Gonzalez*
> *SUSTAINABILITY EXPERT, LUXURY SECTOR*

CHAPTER

*6*

# Implications and Consequences of Greenwashing

> ❝ It takes 20 years to build a reputation and five minutes to ruin it. If you think about that, you'll do things differently. ❞
>
> *– Warren Buffett*

Is greenwashing really as bad a problem as some are making it out to be? Leaving all ethical considerations to the side, from a strategic point of view, it might not seem like such a bad idea.

There seems to be widespread uncertainty on the risks of greenwashing. If firms continue to ignore the potential consequences out of confusion or ignorance, the incentives to greenwash might appear to outweigh the costs of being caught. But do they really?

Many have already argued the detrimental effect greenwashing has had on *consumer* trust, and how it has led to widespread skepticism regarding all environmental claims, but now we will place attention on how this affects a firm from *their* point of view. In terms of legitimacy, reputation and market value, is greenwashing as good in practice as it is on paper?

The time has come to go into greater detail on this matter, but before we move on, a fair warning. We have finally arrived at the "nerdy" chapter, so expect to see a few more numbers, models, and samples. And while many of you will thoroughly enjoy this, for those less passionate about science do not despair! Please feel free to fast forward and focus on the neat summary boxes and bolded segments provided throughout each section.

> **"** Greenwashing may destroy the trust of customers and investors, which is probably the most difficult thing to recover, amongst other consequences such as fines, loss of the license to operate, loss of valuable business partners and ventures and so forth. In short, it's lying and the impact of lying is immense. **"**
>
> *Xavier Houot*
> *SCHNEIDER-ELECTRIC*

## 6.1 Greenwashing and Symbolism

The previous chapter pretty much summed up the main rewards associated with green firms. Not surprisingly, companies are eager to associate themselves positively with the environment to benefit from the advantages of social compliance. It is in this context that some companies adopt greenwashing policies in order to create the *illusion* of compliance, rather than embarking upon more substantial environmental endeavors. If the end results are the same, why not take a short cut?

If we **define an organization's environmental performance as the outcome of the strategic activities adopted to manage (or not) its** impact on the natural environment (Walls, Berrone et al. 2011), then we can assume that **greenwashing is expected to influence positively the perception stakeholders have about the company's level of environmental performance**. After all, a company will only benefit from corporate greening once stakeholders believe a certain level of environmental performance is met.

Hence, in practice, greenwashing will only be successful to the extent to which it positively affects a **company's perceived level of environmental performance**, which **can be measured in terms of legitimacy, reputation, and overall market capitalization** (Figure 6.1). This makes sense since the specific advantages associated with greenwashing usually derive from improving a company's position in one of three dimensions.

As we already know, when responding to environmental pressures, firms are faced with the choice of adopting symbolic and/or substantive environmental practices. **Symbolic environmental actions refer** to those that reflect policies at a broader level, as well as the reporting activities which are unlinked to the core of the business. Ultimately they serve symbolic purposes that even when applied, may not have an observable impact on the firm's environmental performance. Therefore, for the purpose of this chapter, from here on, greenwashing will be referred to as symbolic practices.

Figure 6. 1. Greenwashing and Three Corporate Dimensions

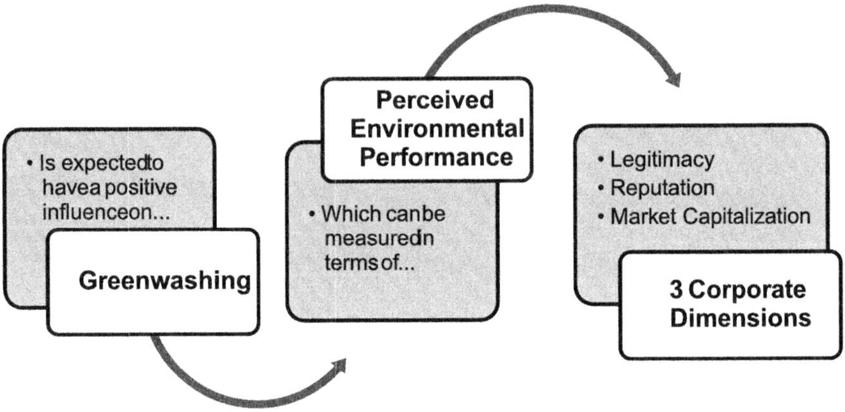

*Source:* Own

In contrast, **substantive environmental actions** tangibly improve a firm's environmental performance, but often require organizational and technological changes that cost money and time. Hence, much of the perceived value of greenwashing stems from the idea that symbolic actions alone represent a strategy by which firms can obtain certain rewards without having to undergo costly organizational changes (i.e., substantive actions).

Accordingly, to find out whether greenwashing is worth the time and effort, the question that desperately needs answering is the following; **do all environmental actions really offer the same rewards from a firm's point of view?** This question sums up the recurring theme of the chapter, which we will attempt to respond to with a more scientific approach.

For starters, we have repeatedly mentioned examples of symbolic practices throughout the book, in many cases naming companies found guilty of engaging in such practices. However, many companies have actually decided to go down a different road, investing in policies and corporate actions that pave the way for real organizational changes. Since both symbolic and substantive strategies are adopted to enhance a company's environmental position, it seems only fair **to test the overall effect of both before we can conclude the success of one over the other**.

In light of the above, the **overall structure of the chapter will consist of three basic sections** according to each of the corporate dimensions used to measure a company's environmental performance. Thus, we will explore the relationship between symbolic actions and corporate legitimacy, reputation and market value. We'll tackle each individually by testing a series of hypotheses which will help us conclude the extent to which the strategy proves to be beneficial to firms. Furthermore, in each of the corresponding models, the effects of substantive actions will be tested, allowing us to compare the results of both over the long term.

What it all comes down to is simple: **In the bigger picture, is greenwashing as successful as one might assume?** Read on and find out.

## 6.2 Alleviating External and Internal Pressures: Theoretical Framework

As illustrated in Chapter 5, greenwashing arises from the belief that symbolic policies decoupled from actual implementation represent a strategy that allows firms to alter the public perception of their image and enhance their legitimacy, reputation and market capitalization.

Regardless of the above, some institutional authors have argued that both external and internal stakeholders, actually expect more substantive corporate responses. Naturally, in terms of the environment, substantive actions often require significant changes in core practices and entail certain risks. Consequently, many companies show reluctance towards implementing policies that could threaten or disrupt the current state of their organization, and turn to symbolic procedures as an alternative. Nevertheless, where willingly adopted, substantive actions should culminate in real improvements in the firm's environmental performance, which brings companies a little bit closer towards becoming truly green.

Thus, following an institutional logic, we argue that environmental actions can convey a firm's environmental stance, and to the extent that those actions conform to the general public's expectations, they should boost the firm's environmental image.

However, stakeholders often lack sufficient information to evaluate the environmental footprints of different firms (Busch and Hoffman 2009; Lyon and Maxwell 2011) which pushes them to seek more information on the firm's current and future commitments to the natural environment. That is, even though stakeholders are increasingly concerned about environmental matters and we live in an era where information is easily accessed, substantial information asymmetry persists when it comes to evaluating a firm's environmental quality.

As a result, the combination of environmental pressures and information asymmetry creates strong incentives for firms to adopt policies and programs that might improve their environmental performance (Borial 2007), while releasing signals that create a suitable green image at the same time.

However, expounding on our original question, **which environmental actions and in what conditions, are likely to deliver** the greatest rewards in terms of legitimacy, reputation, and market capitalization?

Our theoretical framework blends elements of institutional theory (Scott 1995) and signaling theory (Connelly, Certo et al. 2011). The former provides a means to analyze companies' strategic choices and actions in their efforts to match their corporate values with societal values, while the latter investigates how agents use different signals to overcome problems and inefficiencies associated with information asymmetry.

Using institutional theory alone (Meyer and Rowan 1977; DiMaggio and Powell 1983; Scott 1995) does not capture the varying degrees of success of corporate environmentalism, but by introducing signaling theory we add a new layer that distinguishes environmental actions according to the quality of the signal they convey. Along these lines we investigate which environmental actions work better as signals to improve a firm's corporate image, and when (Berrone and Gomez-Mejia 2009; Berrone, Fosfuri et al. 2013).

Certain corporate actions and policies might reduce information asymmetry, so in order to simplify the basis of our investigations, we refer to signals that are highly visible and costly to imitate as *strong signals* (Certo 2003) or *substantive actions*, and differentiate them from *weak signals* or *symbolic actions*. With this logic we posit that while all environmental actions might help a firm conform to societal expectations, some actions work better than others to signal underlying environmental quality and behavioral intentions.

Finally, social and environmental claims usually come from both external and internal constituencies (Weaver, Treviño et al. 1999). In particular, prior research (Henriques and Sadorsky 1996; Henriques and Sadorsky 1999; Alvarez-Gil, Berrone et al. 2007) has identified five general groups that demand that firms protect the natural environment:

1. Government

2. Communities

3. Shareholders

4. Customers

5. Employees

Therefore, we must consider how symbolic and substantive environmental actions towards these groups can influence public opinion according to the measures corporations typically resort to in each case, some of which have already been included in Chapters 4 and 5.

## 6.3 Choosing Symbolic Actions to Obtain Legitimacy

The first corporate dimension we are going to focus on is environmental legitimacy. Broadly speaking, legitimacy refers to the degree to which actions by organizations are accepted as appropriate and useful by society (Scott 1995; Schuman 1995), that in turn rewards firms by granting them a **"license to operate."**

When companies adopt strategies that conform to institutional demands, they reflect an alignment of corporate and societal values which allows them to obtain external validation commonly referred to as **legitimacy** (Scott 1995). From a strategic point of view (Scott 1995; Deephouse 1999), legitimacy is of vital importance as it sustains organizational operability and enables the firm to compete more effectively by allowing better access to resources, attracting better employees, and improving exchange conditions with partners (Pfeffer and Salancik 1978; DiMaggio and Powell 1983; Oliver 1991; Aldrich and Fiol 1994; Turban and Greening 1997). Consistent with the above, a key premise of stakeholder management is that satisfied stakeholders grant a firm the social legitimacy (Wood 1991) needed to secure survival and success in the long term (Freeman 1984; Freeman and McVea 2001; Hillman and Keim 2001).

Thus, environmental legitimacy is awarded whenever firms are perceived to successfully respond to the pressure exerted by different actors that establish social norms and common beliefs (Hoffman 1999; Wade-Benzoni, Hoffman et al. 2002). When firms manage to fulfill stakeholder's environmental expectations, these in return grant legitimacy to the firms who benefit by gaining reputational capital.

On the flip side, poor environmental performance endangers social legitimacy and threatens a firm's overall survival (Hart 1995; Fombrun 1996; Bansal and Clelland 2004; Godfrey 2005). As Wood 1991: 697) argues, when **"stakeholders lose confidence in the firm's performance, legitimacy can be withdrawn as the stakeholders refuse to provide their share of reciprocal benefits. Customers stop buying products, shareholders sell their stock, employees withhold loyalty and best efforts, government halts subsidies or imposes fines or regulates, environmental advocates sue. If the firm cannot compensate for lost stakeholder benefits, it becomes illegal and dies."**

But to what extent do symbolic procedures/weak signals enhance legitimacy?

### 6.3.1 Testing the impact of symbolic and substantive actions

To test the effectiveness of symbolic and substantive actions on legitimacy, we collected data about 167 publicly traded US firms in environmentally sensitive organizational fields. In line with previous research (Russo and Harrison 2005; Berrone and Gomez-Mejia 2009), we focused on firms operating in the 20 most polluting sectors according to the Toxic Release Inventory (TRI) program of the US EPA, which requires facilities exceeding a certain threshold to report their emissions. Since these firms are subject to the same regulatory framework, we can assume they face similar media attention, scrutiny from activists, community concerns, and changes in consumer preferences (Berrone and Gomez-Mejia 2009). The final sample after dropping firms with missing values was an unbalanced panel of 167 firms that were in operation between 1997 and 2002.

Next, we drew on media accounts (Hamilton 1995; Konar and Cohen 1997; Bansal and Clelland 2004) to assess environmental legitimacy (the dependent variable), choosing to use the Wall Street Journal as the media source, given its national coverage and its importance as a communication medium (the largest circulation in the US in 2011). By focusing on a single source, duplication of news would be avoided since our measure of environmental legitimacy is sensitive to the number of articles taken into consideration. Using this media source, we then followed Bansal and Clelland (2004) to construct our measure.

### 6.3.2 Independent variables: Symbolic and substantive actions

Having established the measure of the dependent variables we considered five symbolic actions and two substantive actions, which vary in their visibility and implementation costs and therefore in their potential effectiveness for signaling environmental quality.

### a. Symbolic actions

■ *Voluntary government programs:*

You may recall that firms frequently respond to regulatory pressures by participating in **voluntary programs** established by the government. These environmental programs sponsored by agencies such as the EPA, seek corporate commitment to actions that improve the natural environment. Presumably, membership in environmental programs will benefit the firm in terms of **governmental acceptance** and thus increase the firm's legitimacy.

*Hypothesis 1a: Participation in voluntary environmental programs sponsored by governmental agencies has a positive effect on environmental legitimacy.*[12]

■ *Community communication:*

To alleviate social monitoring and public scrutiny, companies usually invest efforts in environmental communication that projects an image of a "good corporate neighbor." Through **formal communications**, such as **annual reports**, firms publicize that they are transparent and socially responsible in order to manage public opinion, respond to public pressure, and react to perceived public perception about their legitimacy (Patten 1992; Hooghiemstra 2000). While these communications may be largely decoupled from the actual implementation of policies (Weaver, Treviño et al. 1999; Stevens, Steensma et al. 2005) the community is expected to give these firms the "benefit of the doubt" regarding their environmental behavior.

---

[12] Following Delmas and Keller (2005), we use the EPA's Waste Wise program in order to estimate the effect of participation in these types of initiatives on environmental legitimacy.

Thus we expect that formal mechanisms of corporate disclosure help firms **obtain social compliance.**[13]

*Hypothesis 1b: Formal reporting procedures have a positive effect on environmental legitimacy.*

- *Environmental-dedicated board committee:*

To respond to socially conscious investors demanding better representation of their social interests within firms (David, Bloom et al. 2007), many companies explicitly and formally delegate environmental issues to board committees who assume oversight responsibilities. Presumably, the presence of environmental committees place the board in a better position to assess the firm's environmental performance by drawing on the expertise of directors. Nevertheless, many scholars have argued that these environmental committees are merely symbolic (Berrone and Gomez-Mejia 2009), used to signal that the environment is a corporate priority (Walls, Berrone et al. 2011), which might be enough for investors to assume that the firm is on the right path (Berrone, Surroca et al. 2007).[14]

*Hypothesis 1c: The presence of a dedicated environmental board committee has a positive effect on environmental legitimacy.*

- *Environmental trademarks:*

Consumers have becomes increasingly concerned about the environmental footprint of the products they consume (Vandermerwe and Oliff 1990; Polonsky 1995; Bonini and Oppenheim 2008) and even though there is reason to believe that green brands might not

---

[13] We drew on the KLD database (Graves & Waddock, 1994; Johnson & Greening, 1999; McWilliams & Siegel, 2000; Neubaum & Zahra, 2006; Waddock & Graves, 1997).

[14] We used a measure constructed by Berrone and Gomez-Mejia (2009) to identify those firms that had an environmentally-dedicated committee on the board.

necessarily mean green companies (TerraChoice 2009; EnviroMedia 2015), firms responses are based on the notion that **consumers may prefer to buy products from companies that claim to offer environmentally friendly products** as they are seen as trustable and valuable (Thogersen 1999).[15]

*Hypothesis 1d: Green Trademarks have a positive effect on environmental legitimacy.*

■ *Environmental pay policies:*

Pressure for good environmental performance may also come from groups inside the firm (Polonsky 1995), as more and more employees prefer to work for companies that are socially responsible. One way companies show their employees that they are committed to environmental issues is by formulating related policies (Russo and Harrison 2005; Berrone and Gomez-Mejia 2009). Such policies might include:

▶ Environmental criteria as a measure of employees' efforts

▶ Recognizing the value of good environmental performance

▶ Rewarding staff commitments to environmental targets

A formal tie between environmental performance and employees' pay may help focus employee efforts on environment-related activities (Lothe, Myrtveit et al. 1999). And even though recent research (Russo and Harrison 2005; Berrone and Gomez-Mejia 2009) suggests performance is not necessarily enhanced, this practice allows firms to send a positive signal to employees regarding the relatively-higher importance given to environmental issues than in firms that adopt a

---

[15] We obtained total environmental trademarks registered at the US Patents and Trademarks Office for each of the firms in the sample, extracting those that included at least one of the keywords identified.

less formal stance. Consequently, employees will value a company's efforts and reward it accordingly (Turban and Greening 1997).[16]

*Hypothesis 1e: The adoption of environmental pay policies has a positive effect on environmental legitimacy.*

### b. Substantive actions

■ *Pollution prevention:*

Pollution prevention (PP) strategies are intended to minimize or eliminate the creation of toxic chemical agents during the various stages of production, and have shown to provide organizations with unique advantages (Hart 1995; Russo and Fouts 1997; Klassen and Whybark 1999; Christmann 2000; Sarkis and Cordeiro 2001).

In addition to requiring structural investments in cleaner technologies, PP strategies are complex and risky (Russo and Fouts 1997; Aragon-Correa 1998; Klassen and Whybark 1999; Aragon-Correa and Sharma 2003). Yet given that PP strategies reduce and eliminate waste generation, they can potentially satisfy the demands of stakeholders who can in turn grant environmental legitimacy.[17]

*Hypothesis 2a: Evidence of pollution prevention strategies has a positive effect on environmental legitimacy.*

■ *Environmental innovation:*

Pressures for the conservation of the environment can also generate opportunities for innovation, providing organizations with a means of

---

[16] We used a measure constructed by Berrone and Gomez-Mejia (2009) to identify those firms with an explicit environmental pay-policy

[17] Following previous environmental literature (King & Lennox, 2000; King & Lennox, 2002), we measured PP strategies as the difference between a predicted value and dome actual pollution level using a measure computed by Berrone & Gomez-Mejia (2009).

becoming unique or at least sufficiently different to avoid competitors' imitations (Peteraf 1993; Barney, Wright et al. 2001). Yet, by definition innovative activities are inherently risky, as possible outcomes are as varied as they are unknown, and the probability of failure is greater (Baysinger, Kosnik et al. 1991). Moreover, innovative endeavors require long-term investments (Hoskisson, Hitt et al. 1993), which involve significant commitments in terms of resources and time.

> **"** Innovations are triggered by a fair understanding of where future markets will be tomorrow. What are my customers keen to get to? Are they willing to become less resource intense, spend less, and enjoy their lives better? There are massive needs for new business models, such as towards use versus buy, towards longer lasting and reparable products. **"**
>
> *Xavier Houot*
> *SCHNEIDER-ELECTRIC*

At the same time, environmental related innovations are intended to reduce the toxic burden of production processes and therefore respond to stakeholder claims appropriately. For that reason, by engaging in environmental innovations, firms can successfully conform to social demands while searching for competitive advantage (Berrone, Gelabert et al. 2008).[18]

*Hypothesis 2b: Environmental related patents have a positive effect on environmental legitimacy.*

---

[18] We used patent data from the CHI's Patent Citation Indicators database to measure environmental innovation, representing more than 60% of all US patents granted since 1992 and more than 70% of those patents that are not held by private individuals. We gathered information provided by Nameroff et al. (2004) about company-assignees of over 3,200 environmental-related patents during 1983-2001 and the number of forward citations for each of these patents (see Nameroff et. Al. (2004) for a more comprehensive description of the CHI Research Inc database).

### 6.3.3 The win-win of combining symbolic and substantive actions

In the previous paragraphs we hypothesize that both environmental symbolic and substantive actions may have a positive impact on environmental legitimacy. Therefore why settle for one? Symbolic actions have been traditionally analyzed as decoupled from substantive actions, treated as "either/or" type options. However, it is reasonable to expect that when both kinds of actions are combined the result will be greater legitimacy. Consequently when symbolic actions are accompanied with consistent substantive initiatives, the effect on legitimacy should be higher (King and Lennox 2000; Berrone and Gomez-Mejia 2009).

*Hypothesis 3: Symbolic environmental actions will have greater impact on environmental legitimacy if coupled with substantive environmental actions.*

> ❝ Provided the claims are substantiated, we are entitled to make them because it is part of why we invest billions in R&D, to win the confidence of our customers, then for our customers themselves to succeed in their respective businesses. It's not PR, it's about making people aware of what we do and delivering our successes as much as, sometimes, our shortcomings. ❞
>
> *Xavier Houot*
> *SCHNEIDER-ELECTRIC*

### 6.3.4 Short-term solutions vs. long-term achievements

Above all, the decision to adopt symbolic procedures is based on the notion that practices like messages and signals represent sufficient corporate commitment to obtain legitimacy from stakeholders. That is, stakeholders do not actually verify any of the firm's claims, because they naïvely believe what companies tell them to believe.

While this might be true in the short term, it might not be the case in the long run. As time passes, there are more chances for stakeholders to realize the dissonance between organizational actions and societal requirements (Milstein, Hart et al. 2002). Moreover, symbolic actions are generally more visual, cheaper, and easier to implement than substantive actions, which also means they are more easily copied. Hence, we argue that symbolic actions will have a limited impact on legitimacy. On the other hand, substantive environmental actions have the potential to become organizational capabilities and as such are more difficult to imitate. As a result we propose they have a more enduring effect on legitimacy.

To explore the long-term effect of symbolic versus substantive actions we included a one year lag of each of the above mentioned actions.

*Hypothesis 4a: Symbolic environmental actions will only have a positive impact on environmental legitimacy in the short term*

*Hypothesis 4b: Substantive environmental actions will have a positive impact on environmental legitimacy both in the short and long term*

### 6.3.5 Controls

Finally following Deephouse (1996), we further controlled for other potential determinants of environmental legitimacy such as company size, age and financial performance. We measured size by the logarithm of the total number of employees, obtained the foundation year to compute the firm age and proxied financial performance using

## SUMMARY BOX 1: Methods

### 1. Sample and data collection

- Identified firms belonging to the 20 most polluting sectors according to the EPA's TRI program
- Cross referenced initial sample with the KLD and Compustat database and searched for data from other sources
- Final sample was an unbalanced panel of 167 firms between 1997 and 2002

### 2. Measures

*Dependent variable – environmental legitimacy*

- Assessed using articles published in the Wall Street Journal that mentioned both the company name and at least one of the keywords used by Bansal and Clelland (2004).

*Independent variables and controls*

*a. Symbolic actions*

- Voluntary government programs
- Community communication
- Environmental-dedicated board committee
- Environmental trademarks
- Environmental pay policies

*b. Substantive actions*

- Pollution prevention
- Environmental Innovation

*c. Controls*

- Size
- Age
- Financial performance

### 3. Empirical analysis
- Tobit model with random effects and a linear model with random and fixed effects

the annual return on assets (ROA).[19] Ceteris paribus, firms with higher emissions are expected to have lower environmental legitimacy. All the specifications include sector dummies at the two-digit SIC code and annual dummies.

## 6.3.6 Results

The results obtained from both models, indicate that **community communication** is the only symbolic measure that *has a significant positive effect.* In contrast, the presence of an **environmental committee** has a *significant negative effect* on environmental legitimacy. **Substantive actions** on the other hand, have a *positive and significant effect* across all the specifications, providing **strong support for hypotheses H2a and H2b**.

Regarding the combined effect of both symbolic and substantive actions, results suggest that symbolic actions have a significant positive effect only when accompanied by substantive actions. In other words, when substantive actions are not implemented, the effect of symbolic actions is not nearly as significant.

This is confirmed when analyzing the long-term effects of symbolic and substantive actions, which were tested including a one year lag of each of the actions considered. Not surprisingly, symbolic actions that were found to be significant only had short-term effects on environmental legitimacy, while once again, substantive actions were found to have a positive effect both in the short and long term.

As for the control variables, size was not found to be significant, probably due to little variation in the number of employees within firms for the period under analysis. The same applies to company age

---

[19] All three measure were obtained from Compustat database.

and performance. Lastly, as expected, a marginal increase in the level of firm emissions with respect to total sales (in dollars) reduces the firm's level of environmental legitimacy.[20]

### 6.3.7 Lesson 1: Symbolism can only get you so far

Ultimately, managers might be tempted to engage in symbolic procedures, believing that minimum compliance with stakeholder requirements is the best way to obtain legitimacy. This would allow firms to respond to external pressures while maintaining internal flexibility and control (Meyer and Rowan 1977; Schuman 1995). However, our results debunk this assumption since just one of our symbolic measures (community communication) appeared to have a positive and significant effect. As a result, there is evidence to believe that within strong polluting industries, it is extremely difficult to achieve legitimacy only through symbolic actions (Berrone and Gomez-Mejia 2009).

This is consistent with environmental management literature that suggests that the true value of environmental strategies lies in those that can effectively minimize or eliminate the creation of toxic chemical agents rather than those oriented towards compliance only. In fact, symbolic actions could even be considered high risk, since in some cases a company's overall legitimacy might actually be threatened. Indeed, this is clearly illustrated in the case of environmental-dedicated committees. Contrary to what was expected, and far from enhancing corporate legitimacy, this measure was found to have negative effects on social acceptance.

---

[20] Robustness checks: We ran other models to verify the robustness of results and to allow for the possibility that the Wall Street Journal has a certain bias in the type of firms they cover. In order to check that the results were not driven by the behavior of firms with no environmentally related articles, we re-estimated all the models including only those firms that had at least one environmentally related article.

There are several possible reasons for this. First of all, stakeholders tend to be hypercritical and scrutinize firms very carefully, thus signals are likely to be insufficient, as firms are expected to provide the public with facts and measurable outputs. Secondly, symbolic actions will most likely be effective when performance is difficult to measure. When facts do not match environmental symbolism, firms can be accused of telling "green" lies and making misleading claims, resulting in less legitimacy and not more. Finally, precisely because symbolic actions are typically more visible than substantive actions, stakeholders tend to dismiss these as "cosmetic" or "opportunistic" (King and Lennox 2000). Consequently, if companies rely exclusively on symbolic actions they may eventually be seen as untruthful, unreliable, calculating and manipulative. Thus, measures like adopting an environmental committee may be interpreted as being "too obvious" and merely a green artifice, resulting in reduced legitimacy.

On the other hand, while the remaining symbolic actions might not be detrimental per se, they have been shown to have little to no impact. This brings us to our next point: at best, symbolic actions only work in the short term.

For instance, companies that participate in voluntary government programs believe that by sending a "signal" that they are proactive in their environmental management, governments will consider them greener and cleaner than non-participants. However, although initially this may be a good first step, extant research has shown that poorly-performing firms are likely to be engaged in voluntary programs (Klassen and Whybark 1999; King and Lennox 2000). Thus, in the long term the initiative lacks value if companies fail to follow through on their commitments. The only way to preserve legitimacy over time is through definitive responses such as environmental innovation or pollution prevention strategies.

Nevertheless, while our results suggest that symbolic actions may not be sufficient to achieve legitimacy, they do not indicate that they are not important. In fact, symbolic and substantive actions are actually complementary instead of supplementary to each other, and when combined, they have a greater impact on legitimacy. In particular, our results suggest that community communications may be important in gaining legitimacy at least in the short term. Therefore, companies may want to dedicate some efforts to conveying a green message to society, but without forgetting that the effect is short term.

Overall, approaches that suggest decoupling as an effective strategy are here called into question. Investing greater efforts in signaling being green, rather than spending resources on environmentally sound practices, may jeopardize a company's legitimacy in the long run as it may be perceived as deceitful. Hence, while certain symbolic actions may mollify stakeholders temporarily, sustainable satisfaction is only achieved through substantive actions.

> " If a company uses symbols, it is both appropriate and necessary for these to be backed up by real and concrete evidence. Just like Thomas Friedman says, 'In a flat, hyper connected world, you better be good. "
>
> Ernesto Lluch Moreno
> G-ADVISORY

Furthermore, because symbolic actions are easily copied by rivals, they have little potential to become a differential element. For example, although transparency in communication has been shown to have an impact on legitimacy, disclosure on sustainability performance has become a standard business practice partly because it is easily mimicked. Consequently, environmental substantive actions are the only way of effectively gaining legitimacy that will endure over time, and therefore constitute a base for competitive advantage.

Our findings do not suggest that symbolic actions are entirely worthless. On the contrary, when properly balanced with more definitive environmental responses, they become the perfect complement for substantive endeavors, and boost legitimacy.

## 6.4 Choosing Symbolic Actions to Boost Reputation

While gaining legitimacy is indeed one of the main outcomes of environmental conformity, corporate actions also impact other intangible assets such as organizational reputation.

Corporate reputation can be defined as stakeholders' overall perception of a firm's appeal and relative standing (Fombrun 1996). And unlike legitimacy, it constitutes a strategic intangible asset that creates value and makes replication more difficult, enhancing the firm's ability to deliver value superior to that of its competitors (Roberts and Dowling 2002; Rindova, Williamson et al. 2005). In other words, focusing on reputation is important precisely because it provides a significant competitive edge, which contributes to firm performance and survival (Fombrun 1996; Deephouse 2000). Moreover, because corporate environmentalism holds a strong likelihood of opportunism and high economic stakes (Delmas and Burbano 2011; Lyon and Maxwell 2011), stakeholders are willing to invest more time and effort into obtaining information about a firm's practices to reduce the risk of adverse selection and avoid the losses this entails.

Several reasons support the view that reputation becomes particularly relevant as a valuable measure of outcome. First, the lack of universal and cross-national regulations and norms to incentivize responsible environmental behavior and sanction misconduct has left much room for opportunistic behaviors such as greenwashing and window dressing (Delmas and Burbano 2011; Lyon and Maxwell 2011). Moreover, in the event of wrongdoing, the economic losses can be substantial for both firm and stakeholders, as evidenced by the recent Volkswagen scandal.

In this context, external constituencies will tend to resort to reputation rather than legitimacy, when evaluating a firm's environmental performance (Bitektine 2011). As we have already seen, legitimacy is related to the social acceptance of an organization depending on whether it conforms to prevailing social norms (Dowling and Pfeffer 1975; Aldrich and Fiol 1994; Washington and Zajac 2005). Consequently, since this applies to all organizations alike, the road to legitimacy is naturally associated with organizational isomorphism.[21] In contrast, the emphasis of reputation is on comparing organizations according to their differences (Whetten and Mackey 2002; Deephouse and Carter 2005), which enables stakeholders to predict the future behavior of an organization based on past actions. This extends beyond the notion of social acceptance, so reputation is actually a stronger indicator of firm performance heterogeneity (Weigelt and Camerer 1988; Jensen and Roy 2008; Podolny 2010). In other words, when stakeholders observe strategic choices and behaviors to draw conclusions regarding a firm's capabilities and future behavior they are forming a judgment about its reputation (Basdeo, Smith et al. 2006).

---

[21] **Mimetic isomorphism** in organization theory refers to the tendency of an organization to imitate another organization's structure because of the belief that the structure of the latter organization is beneficial. In this case, mimicking another organization perceived as legitimate becomes a "safe" way to proceed.

**But do symbolic actions really have a positive impact on firm reputation?**

### 6.4.1 Testing the impact of symbolic and substantive actions

As before, in order to test the impact of symbolic and substantive actions, we collected data on companies facing similar institutional pressures. Following the approach of previous studies, we used *Fortune Magazine's* ranking of the "World's Most Admired Companies," identifying 212 firms from 23 industries that were rated consistently from 2006 to 2012 (Fombrun and Shanley 1990; Roberts and Dowling 2002; Basdeo, Smith et al. 2006; Love and Kraatz 2009).

To measure reputation (the dependent variable) we used the overall raw scores attributed to the firms figuring in Fortune's ranking, which are obtained through a large-scale survey of companies listed in the Fortune 1000, Global 500, and other top foreign companies operating in the US.[22] This method of measuring reputation makes information asymmetry less severe, as the rating executives are part of the observing community of the rated firms, and through it we can presume that all the firms included in the reputation ranking are likely to be equally visible and under high surveillance by their counterparts.

### 6.4.2 Reliable vs. unreliable signals

The perceptual nature of reputation implies that it can be heavily influenced by company actions and communication efforts, making it particularly sensitive to a firm's signaling strategy. Therefore, taking a slightly different approach than with legitimacy, we focus on reputation

---

[22] 15 000 executives and directors rated approximately 600-700 (depending on the year) from 32 countries, covering 58 industries, on nine attributes: 1) ability to attract and retain talented people, 2) quality of management, 3) social responsibility to the community and the environment, 4) innovativeness, 5) quality of products and services, 6) wise use of corporate assets, 7) financial soundness, 8) long-term investment value, and 9) effectiveness in doing business globally.

particularly within the context of signaling theory (Spence 1973; Porter 1980), where corporate environmental actions are adopted as signals that convey the intentions and abilities of a given firm to protect the environment. These in turn target stakeholders, who by interpreting a firm's signals, draw conclusions about the firm's future behavior and build reputational beliefs (Prabhu and Stewart 2001; Basdeo, Smith et al. 2006).

However interpreting green messages is confusing for most, precisely because, more often than not, greening is not clear cut. In this regard, signaling theory addresses a relevant concept which relates to this particular issue: signal reliability. Signal reliability is based on the idea that information asymmetry lessens when signals are reliable, but increases if the signals are unreliable. Logically, a signal is reliable when observers (in our case stakeholders) believe it is honest, acting as an accurate indicator of quality (Arthurs, Busenitz et al. 2009). In contrast, an unreliable signal is sometimes honest and sometimes dishonest. In fact, firms are tempted to engage in opportunistic behavior when the cost of a dishonest signal is lower than the benefits to be gained (Kirmani and Rao 2000), bringing us to the practice in question.

For example, the lack of legal regulation and vague norms regarding the term "green" has led to greenwashing among firms that tend to label products as green even in the absence of environmental benefits (TerraChoice 2010; Delmas and Burbano 2011). As a result, a green label constitutes an unreliable signal since consumers are unable to distinguish the actual "green" products from those with false or misleading claims. At the same time, low-quality firms benefit from greater information asymmetry, as the cost of using "green" as a signal is far lower than the potential adverse selection it generates.

Another example of unreliable signals is corporate environmental policies. Firms may have incentives to publish environmental policy statements because it is inexpensive and can influence public opinion (Ramus and Montiel 2005). Not surprisingly, a large number of firms have adopted environmental policy statements to demonstrate conformity, and while the level of subsequent implementation tends to vary across industries, it is generally low. Thus, the likelihood of using these announcements as a symbolic response to stakeholder pressure is exceptionally high, therefore stakeholders are unable to rely on corporate environmental policies to evaluate a firm's level of environmental commitment.

In light of the above, we posit that symbolic environmental actions are actually unreliable signals of a firm's future behaviors for two interrelated reasons. First, because corporate environmentalism is prone to opportunistic behaviors, stakeholders tend to view firms' actions in this area with skepticism. In this context, symbolic actions are likely to be viewed as opportunism. Thus in the absence of reliable information to distinguish responsible from irresponsible firms, symbolic procedures can seriously damage stakeholders' impressions of a firm's environmental commitment (Skowronski and Carlston 1989; Mishina, Block et al. 2012). Secondly, because symbolic actions are inherently unreliable they generate greater information asymmetry, which conflicts with stakeholders' objective of avoiding adverse selection. Since stakeholders have limited access to information they will probably punish the use of symbolic actions because they increase both the risk of adverse selection and the cost of information.

Therefore, we propose that the use of symbolic environmental actions as signals of environmental commitment will lead to reputation loss. The exact opposite of what firms expect when choosing to engage in greenwashing.

*Hypothesis 1: Symbolic environmental actions have a negative effect on reputation.*

If symbolic actions are unreliable at predicting a firm's future environmental behaviors, then what type of actions can we consider to be reliable signals? Well, the main mechanism by which firms can reduce information asymmetry is to increase the cost of signaling (Sorescu, Shankar et al. 2007). Endeavors that are observable and costly to imitate are likely to discourage replication by low-quality competitors (Arthurs, Busenitz et al. 2009). For instance, a firm with superior environmental performance can report low emissions more easily than one with inferior performance, simply because the former possesses the actual quality whereas the latter needs to invest resources to appear similar. As a result, given the high cost of reproducing the same signal, firms with inferior environmental performance will have less incentive to imitate superior competitors.

Along these lines, substantive actions such as waste management or recycling practices can be considered costly signals because they result from a long-term investment plan that over time leads to more effective pollution prevention activities (Delmas and Montes-Sancho 2010). Whereas symbolic actions represent formal responses to external pressures without correlation to actual performance, substantive actions aim directly at minimizing the firm's environmental impact (Berrone and Gomez-Mejia 2009; Delmas and Burbano 2011). Therefore, this type of action is far more reliable than symbolic actions at signaling environmental conformity and stewardship. Given the clearer link between substantive actions and performance outcomes, stakeholders will most likely resort to these actions when evaluating a firm's environmental performance and future behavior, rewarding the firm with reputational gain whenever these actions are observed.

*Hypothesis 2: Substantive environmental actions have a positive effect on reputation.*

### 6.4.3 Independent variables: Symbolic and substantive actions

To test these hypothesis, we retrieved data related to environmental actions from MSCI's[23] Intangible Value Assessment (IVA) database to derive a set of symbolic and substantive actions. The IVA provides ratings for approximately 5, 000 global firms on 32 environmental and social attributes. Because the IVA[24] consolidates the KLD and Innovest Sustainability Indices, it can be considered a relatively strong measure of corporate environmental and social performance. The IVA rates each company on 15 attributes, so we used the conceptual definition of each type of action to classify the attributes.

Since, actual implementation of a particular policy is often difficult for external observers to verify due to information asymmetry (Christmann and Taylor 2006), and is not necessarily correlated with performance (Bromley and Powell 2012), we decided to distinguish symbolic from substantive actions based upon how each attribute links with environmental outcomes and contributes to a firm's overall environmental performance as opposed to the degree of implementation (Westphal and Zajac, 1993, 1998, 2001).

---

[23] Morgan Stanley Capital International.

[24] The IVA rates each company on 15 attributes: 1) historic liabilities, 2) operating risk, 3) leading/sustainability, 4) industry-specific risk, 5) environmental strategy, 6) corporate governance, 7) environmental management systems, 8) audit, 9) environmental accounting/reporting, 10) environmental training and development, 11) certification, 12) products and materials, 13) strategic competence, 14) environmental opportunity, and 15) performance. Each attribute is a summary of several sub-attributes, rated on a scale from 1-10. We analyzed the descriptions of the 15 attributes to classify them into either symbolic or substantive actions.

Symbolic actions are mainly based on a guidance or policy principles without standardized performance indicators that measure actual implementation. On the other hand, we classify an action as substantive when the company reports a set of standardized indicators to show evidence of superior environmental performance.

### a. *Symbolic actions*

■ *Environmental strategy:*

The quality of the company's policies in terms of integrating environmental considerations in its operations, along with its compliance with regulations and its response to past environmental controversies.

■ *Corporate governance:*

The governance structure regarding environmental issues and how well these issues are considered by the board of directors.

■ *Environmental management system:*

Establishment and monitoring of environmental performance targets, presence of environmental training, and stakeholder engagement.

### b. *Substantive actions*

■ *Sustainability risk indicators:*

Carbon emissions, product carbon footprint, mitigation of climate change risk, and energy efficiency, provided as absolute and normalized emission output.

■ *Certification:*

Certification by ISO or other industry and country-specific third-party auditors.

- *Audit:*

External independent audits of environmental performance.

- *Products/materials:*

"End-of-life" product management, controversies related to environmental impact of products and services.

- *Performance:*

Percentage of revenue represented by identified beneficial products and services.

### 6.4.4 The moderating effect of reporting practices

In signaling theory, improving both the frequency of signals and the quality of the signaling process effectively reduces information asymmetry (Prabhu and Stewart 2001; Connelly, Certo et al. 2011). External observers do not necessarily understand the meaning of a particular signal right away, thus when signals are repeated over time, they convey transparency and enable observers to form their own interpretation which helps to reduce information asymmetry.

The quality of the signaling process can also have similar effects. For instance, a study of corporate environmental disclosures found that high procedural commitment increases the perceived credibility of a firm's environmental claims which eventually leads to improved reputation. Nevertheless, the question remains as to whether the moderating effect of reporting practices (frequency and quality) would be similar for both types of actions.

Although symbolic actions may not be reliable, it seems probable that improving the quality of the signaling process through more frequent and more comprehensible reporting practices will facilitate stakeholders' interpretation of this type of action. Thus, drawing on the findings above, we propose that reporting practices may actually influence stakeholders' perception of the quality of the signal.

In this case, quality reporting practices would mitigate the skepticism surrounding symbolic procedures as stakeholders interpret increased frequency and improved quality as a sign that the firm's intentions are trustworthy. Even though better reporting practices may not fully offset the negative perceptions of symbolic actions, they may attenuate skepticism and suspicion.

Similarly, we expect quality reporting to enhance the positive effect of substantive actions. Hence, in both cases, the perceived transparency of reporting firms should lead to a more favorable reputation when compared to less transparent counterparts.

*Hypothesis 3a: The negative effect of symbolic actions on reputation is weaker for firms with higher signaling process quality (reporting practices)*

*Hypothesis 3b: The positive effect of substantive actions on reputation is stronger for firms with higher signaling process quality (reporting practices)*

With this in mind we calculated a moderating variable taking into account the frequency and format of the reports issued by each of the firms under analysis.

## SUMMARY BOX 2: Methods

### 1. Sample and data collection

- Identified 212 firms from 23 industries belonging to Fortune Magazine's ranking of "World's Most Admired Companies" that were rated from 2006 to 2012

### 2. Measures

*Dependent variable – corporate reputation*

- Measured using the overall raw scores the firms received for each of the attributes on which they were rated to figure in Fortune's ranking.

*Independent variables and controls*

*a. Symbolic actions*

- Environmental strategy
- Corporate governance
- Environmental management system

*b. Substantive actions*

- Sustainability risk indicators
- Certification
- Audit
- Products/materials
- Performance

*c. Controls*

- Age
- Size
- Financial performance

### 3. Empirical analysis
- Standard econometric model with fixed effects

### 6.4.5 Controls

We controlled for inter-year variability but not for industry sensitivity as we use fixed-effect models. Again, we controlled for company age and size using COMPUSTAT, since those factors also influence an organization's perceived prestige (Fombrun 1996).[25]

### 6.4.6 Results

As expected, results on control variables is consistent with literature on reputation. Firm size and age has a positive effect on reputation in all models, which supports past research.

As for symbolic procedures, results show symbolic actions have a negative effect on reputation in all models, confirming our first hypothesis, H1. On the other hand, our full model shows that substantive actions have a positive effect on reputation, strongly supporting our second hypothesis, H2. In other words, we can conclude that only substantive environmental actions enhance a firm's reputation, while symbolic efforts have the opposite effect; they damage a firm's reputation.

Finally, results show reporting practices indeed act as a positive moderator, mitigating the negative relationship between symbolic actions and reputation, thus confirming H3a. However, an analysis of the firms and industries showed that the interactive effect of reporting practices and substantive actions can in fact sometimes be negative, which contradicts H3b. We expound on this in the next section.

---

[25] To control for the financial performance in the robustness check model, we calculated a two-year averaged return on assets (Deephouse, 2000; Deephouse & Carter, 2005; Philippe & Durand, 2011).

### 6.4.7 Lesson 2: Symbolism puts your reputation at risk

While symbolic actions might be sufficient for building a façade of legitimacy (at least for a little while) they are most definitely counterproductive where reputation is concerned. A firm's reputation wanes when firms use symbolic actions as a way of demonstrating environmental commitment. Why? For starters, the logic linking symbolism to legitimacy works in a context where economic stakes are low, meaning stakeholders are unwilling to invest time and effort in acquiring additional information. Rather, stakeholders will willingly rely on symbolic commitments as evidence of the organization's conformance to social expectations, granting legitimacy which will ultimately affect the firm's survival.

> **“** The main risk associated with greenwashing is the potential reputational damage associated with being caught. It becomes counterproductive; if you don't do anything no one criticizes, but if you do and then get caught the public backlash is far worse than doing nothing. **”**
>
> *Antonio Fuertes Zurita*
> *GAS NATURAL FENOSA*

However, when larger economic stakes are in play and the probability of opportunistic behaviors is high, stakeholders will likely resort to reputation when making decisions. In this case, as reputation requires stakeholders to allocate considerably more time and effort in order to effectively predict an organization's future behavior, they will also be less inclined to buy into symbolic gestures. This happens for two reasons: 1) it is precisely the type of action that can be associated with opportunistic behaviors, and 2) it increases information asymmetry.

Accordingly, using symbolic actions as signals of environmental commitment may be punished by stakeholders, leading to reputational loss.

Conversely, just as we anticipated, substantive actions have quite the opposite effect. Since the cost of signaling is inversely related to firm quality, the higher cost of substantive actions prevents replication by lower-quality firms that would have to invest a considerable amount of resources to mimic costly signals. Furthermore, costly signals are not only more reliable, but better at reducing information asymmetry between firms and stakeholders. As a result, if stakeholders believe they can rely on these signals to evaluate a firm, such behavior will be rewarded with a favorable judgment that will ultimately improve a firm's overall reputation.

> **66** (…) The main one (risk) being the loss of credibility which ultimately leads to broken trust and damaged reputation, the two most important assets of a company today. **99**
>
> *Antoni Ballabriga Terreguitart*
> *BBVA*

Nonetheless, we also found that a firm can mitigate the negative impact of symbolic actions on reputation with frequent, high-quality reporting practices. By doing so, a firm can ensure that the message sent is at least clear which facilitates stakeholders' interpretation. This in turn can create a more favorable starting point on which to base judgment.

However, while this may be true for symbolic actions, the opposite seems to apply when we consider substantive actions. Funnily enough, improved reporting practices negatively moderates the impact of substantive actions on reputation. While this unexpected result is somewhat challenging to interpret, this may be explained within the current context of corporate environmentalism that favors stakeholder skepticism. As a matter of fact, given the nature of substantive actions, one could argue that these alone should be enough to create a positive perception. Thus if signals speak for themselves, repetition can actually undermine the initial positive evaluation which tends to decrease as exposure increases.

In other words, if people already think you are green, repeating a positive cue may actually put your image at risk, as overselling may be viewed with suspicion by stakeholders. If the action itself is good, why the need to continuously remind external observers? Does it mean the firm is using one action to cover up other events? Is this a diversion tactic? All these questions could arise, especially in a context where skepticism and suspicion is constantly present. Not surprisingly when Lyon and Maxwell focused on how a company's reputation might affect environmental corporate responses they found that firms with strong green reputations prefer to exploit their existing position with minimal additional communication.

> **"** Marketing practices that are seen negatively, deemed either as false or as exaggerations, can damage the brand image and reputation of a company, in spite of having high quality products. **"**
>
> *Pablo Bascones Ilundain*
> *PwC*

Overall, in analyzing reputation as an outcome of environmental actions, we challenge the view that all firms must respond to institutional pressures with increased symbolic actions. The reputation analysis helps clarify some of the reasons organizations over-conform and decide to adopt a proactive environmental stance. Our findings show that greenwashing is not only *not* beneficial, but actually *threatens* a corporation's reputation. Clearly, well-established firms have more to lose from engaging in symbolic actions than what they stand to gain. Years of hard work and efforts invested in building a reputation can be just as easily undermined when managers decide to take the easy way out.

## 6.5 Choosing Symbolic Actions to Boost Market Capitalization

Finally, should environmental policies serve their purpose, legitimacy and reputation are not the only gains firms expect to receive.

By adopting environmental actions, companies seek to benefit from the advantages of being green, which will ultimately affect the organization's overall value; or what is referred to as market capitalization. Market capitalization or market cap, is the total money market value of the shares outstanding of a publicly traded company, which is equal to the share price times the number of shares outstanding.

Since outstanding stock is bought and sold in public markets, capitalization is often used as a proxy for the public opinion of a company's net worth and is a determining factor in some forms of stock valuation. In fact, the investment community uses this figure to determine a company's size, as opposed to sales or total asset figures. For instance, companies with tremendous growth potential but relatively small sales numbers may have high market caps as investors bid up the stock price. Thus, market cap measures not only what a company is worth on the open market, but also the market's perception of its future prospects because it reflects what investors are willing to pay for its stock.

Hence, while legitimacy and reputation can be considered intangible assets, market capitalization provides a means with which to evaluate a company's worth in numerical terms. It is the most important determinant of a company's size because it reflects market value, and therefore, expectations about a company's future which ultimately determines the company's future survival.

In this context, similar to reputation, we expect stakeholders to resort to market capitalization to predict the future behavior of corporations. If environmental expectations have been successfully fulfilled in the past, the market value will factor in the assumption that the firm will continue to do so in the future. However, if a company fails to satisfy these expectations, trust will be lost and market value will drop. Furthermore, unlike legitimacy, market capitalization captures the differences between companies which makes it a useful tool for comparison. How does the company compare to others of a similar size in the same industry?

However, while market capitalization is typically used by investors, the degree to which a company satisfies other stakeholder groups may also determine its market value. For instance, a company will only be competitive as long as it successfully satisfies consumer demands for greener products. If a firm fails to maintain its competitive edge, Investors will be unwilling to provide finance as the operation will be both risky and unprofitable. Ultimately, environmental actions that lead to building a positive reputation and acquiring environmental legitimacy should also be reflected in a firm's market capitalization.

**Thus, how do symbolic actions affect a firm's market capitalization?**

### 6.5.1 Testing the impact of substantive and symbolic actions

To determine the degree to which environmental policies might impact a company's market value, we analyzed 990 publicly traded companies from the EU and US during the time period between 2008 and 2013; 419 companies from Europe[26] and 571 from the USA. This ensured the sample was fairly represented, since companies trading in major stock exchanges are subject to the same amount of institutional pressure and public scrutiny. Moreover, we were able to extend our sample to include corporations belonging to the EU, giving the opportunity to compare results between two major markets.

Unlike with legitimacy and reputation, measuring market capitalization (the dependent variable) is pretty straightforward; it is calculated by multiplying a company's shares outstanding by the current market price of one share.

### 6.5.2 Independent variables: Symbolic and substantive actions

Following the theoretical framework laid down in the previous section, not all environmental actions are considered equal. As a result, we chose to use performance as a determinant factor to distinguish symbolic from substantive actions yet again. Since some signals are stronger than others based on the extent to which they generate measurable environmental outcomes, we assume that actions unlinked from core business activities will hold a weaker relationship with a firm's overall environmental performance.

---

[26] 39 from Switzerland; 56 from Germany; 22 from Spain; 67 from France; 214 from UK and 21 from Italy.

Consequently, in this case, symbolic actions refer to those that reflect policies at broad levels and aspects, such as those oriented towards the community and climate change, as well as certain reporting practices. While firms adopt these procedures as a way of demonstrating their environmental stance, the fact that these are ultimately unlinked from the business core activities leads us to believe they may be implemented for symbolic purposes and as such do not significantly affect a firm's environmental behavior.

On the other hand, consistent with the definition of substantive actions, we identified measures that had a clear and direct impact on the core functioning of the companies such as the range of environmentally friendly products brought to the market, as well as cost and resource management.

To identify the relevant symbolic and substantive actions we used CSRHub, an independent organization that provides information on social practices.

### a. Symbolic actions

- *Community development and philanthropy:*

This measure includes any corporate actions that reflect a company's community citizenship through charitable giving, donations of goods, and volunteerism of staff time to environmental organizations. While these activities can be a sign of good will, the fact that they are completely unrelated to business core activities may suggest that there is no intention of undertaking tangible changes that benefit society in the long term. Therefore this type of gesture might be used as a diversion from unacceptable corporate practices.

- *Climate change policies:*

A pressing environmental concern that has transcended into the investor community is climate change. For this reason, voluntary disclosure initiatives such as the Carbon Disclosure Project have become very popular, as the investor base behind the project has done nothing but increase. Although this is but one example of the many steps firms are taking to fight climate change, this measure does serve to indicate a company's level of commitment to climate change through a number of different policies.

- *Environmental reporting:*

Again, environmental reporting does not necessarily convey a reliable signal of commitment. Nevertheless, this measure accounts for the extent to which compliance with investor, regulatory and stakeholders' requests for transparency is achieved through reporting. This includes a company's environmental reporting performance and adherence to environmental reporting standards such as the Global Reporting Initiative.

### b. Substantive actions

- *Environmental product:*

This accounts for the company's capacity to reduce environmental costs, create new market opportunities through sustainable technologies or processes, and produce or market goods and services that enhance the health and quality of life for consumers. This is important to retain and improve the firm's market share.

- *Responsible resource management*

This covers how efficiently resources are used in manufacturing and delivering products and services, including those of a company's suppliers. It includes a company's capacity to reduce the use of

## SUMMARY BOX 3: Methods

### Sample and data collection

- Identified 990 publicly traded companies from the EU and US and collected data between 2008 and 2013

### Measures

*Dependent variable – market capitalization*

- Company's shares outstanding x current market price of one share

*Independent variables*

*a. Symbolic actions*

- Community development and philanthropy
- Climate change
- Environmental reporting

### b. Substantive actions

- Environmental product
- Responsible resource management

### c. Controls

- Size
- Financial performance
- Intangible Assets
- Ownership
- Country
- Year

### Empirical analysis
- Standard econometric model with fixed effects

materials, energy or water, and to find more efficient solutions by improving its supply chain management. This variable includes environmental performance relative to production size and is monitored by the production-related Eco Intensity Ratios (EIRs) for water and energy defined as resource consumption per produced or released unit. Resource management data includes waste and recycling performance.

### 6.5.3 Results

From our results, we found that two out of three symbolic measures had a negative and significant impact on market capitalization. More specifically, the greater the number of philanthropic actions, and the higher the frequency of environmental reporting, the lower the market capitalization. As expected, we can conclude that symbolic actions not only fail to enhance a company's market value, but in actual fact diminish its worth as weaker signals of commitment are punished. As for climate change policies, the effect was neither significantly positive nor negative, thus we can assume that policies of this type are expected and as such are neither rewarded nor punished.

These findings were found to be less significant within the European market when compared to US companies. This might be because the American market is better at detecting the symbolic actions of companies, or American firms are actually better at transforming environmental efforts into profitable products and services. However, it seems more likely that in Europe environmental efforts are less a source of differentiation, perhaps due to an overall greater "green consciousness." As a result, society expects companies to invest in green products and responsible resource management, and therefore rewards companies less for conforming to these expectations.

### 6.5.4 **Lesson 3: Symbolism isn't worth the risk**

Clearly, symbolic environmental actions are far from effective when it comes to influencing a company' market value. Since market capitalization is closely related to a firm's reputation, in the sense that both are used to predict future behavior based on past events, it follows that the results obtained in each study reflect the same trends. Hence, consistent with the conclusions drawn in the previous study, we challenge the assumption that a corporation does not need to actually undertake substantive actions in order to reap the benefits of a green image. Symbolic procedures negatively impact reputation, which in turn takes its toll in the market, damaging a firm's market capitalization.

Firms may be tempted to take visible symbolic actions that demonstrate concern for the environment and social well-being, but when these are so obviously detached from a firm's daily activities, they become counterproductive and backfire. Once more, when larger economic stakes are in play and the probability of opportunistic behaviors is high, stakeholders tend to view symbolic gestures with skepticism. In addition to being regarded as "too convenient," symbolic actions also increase information asymmetry and generate confusion which makes it even more difficult to distinguish the real thing from greenwashing. Consequently, corporate symbolism is often deemed to be unhelpful, unnecessary and outright worthless, and stakeholders punish firms accordingly.

This is also supported by the fact that, in contrast to the legitimacy point, the interaction between symbolic and substantive actions is not significant when it comes to market value. While symbolic actions that serve to complement more substantive efforts may drive stakeholders to grant legitimacy, similar symbolic actions have no effect whatsoever on market capitalization. In order to receive tangible rewards, tangible measures must be taken.

Hence, in the midst of green confusion, the only environmental actions deemed appropriate are those which provide real value, like environmentally friendly products that allow consumers to factor environmental concerns into their daily choices and overall lifestyle. Investors are also more likely to look for signs that corporate environmentalism contributes to pollution prevention in the long term, which in turn leads to more efficient production processes.

Eventually green investors avoid and boycott polluting companies that do not project an appropriate green image through reliable signals, causing share prices to fall as a result. The larger the market share controlled by green investors the more expensive it will be to be labeled a polluter.

However, companies then make the mistake of believing that the general public will automatically trust public statements of commitment to preserving the environment. From a firm's perspective there is little downside to making a vague public commitment. It generates good publicity, and since there are few specifics regarding implementation, the firm is not bound by strict standards or objectives. Essentially, there is no way of measuring the progress made and determining whether the firm is either succeeding or failing to improve environmental performance.

With society waking up to the presence of greenwashing and corporate misconduct, it has become increasingly difficult for corporations to get away with such behavior. In actual fact, as we have seen from the results obtained, stakeholders are no longer giving the benefit of the doubt. On the contrary; when in doubt, symbolic procedures are systematically punished.

## 6.6 The Dangers of Embarking on Symbolic Strategies

As more and more organizations jump on the green bandwagon, the temptation to greenwash increases significantly. However, if nothing else, our results suggest that by adopting symbolic actions, be it out of good will or because of underlying purposes, companies stand to lose much more than what they might expect to gain. The realization that some firms willingly choose to "cheat" their way into the green trend, has driven stakeholders to adopt an offensive position; when in doubt, punish. This increases the likelihood that firms will eventually be singled out for making misleading claims and exploiting society's environmental concerns.

> **"** One may argue that companies are even pushed towards greenwashing in order to save face. But in the end, unless there is some sort of [consistent progress] over time, there is little credibility. **"**
>
> *Gael Gonzalez*
> *SUSTAINABILITY EXPERT, LUXURY SECTOR*

Perhaps the most important message that should stick, is that only genuinely green credentials are effective when building a long lasting and profitable corporate image. For external stakeholders, the reality of a firm's environmental actions is hard to verify. The examples of legitimate companies found guilty of misleading behavior are in fact numerous. Therefore, it seems logical to assume that when evaluating a firm's environmental quality, observers tend to look past the symbolic façade and reward more reliable signs of commitment.

Consequently, managers should realize that an environmental stance is really very difficult to fake, especially when your company belongs to an environmentally sensitive industry. Still unconvinced? Let's take a closer look at what happens when "caught in the act." As one of the most notorious corporate scandals has recently demonstrated, the consequences of "being green while being mean" to the environment are indeed disastrous. Moreover, these situations underline the fact that many companies still fail to realize the dangers of embarking on symbolic strategies even if they do so for the right reasons.

Box 6. 1  Too Big to Fail? : The Volkswagen Scandal

Volkswagen is currently living a firm's worst fear. The world's biggest automaker is in crisis after being caught rigging diesel engine emissions tests in the US and Europe. According to the EPA, the company installed software devices in diesel engines that could detect when they were being tested, enabling them to change their performance and improve results. However, once on the road, the engines switched from test mode to normal performance, resulting in emissions of nitrogen oxide pollutants that were up to 40 times above legal requirements in the US. Diesel engines, while being more fuel efficient, have been shown to emit more pollution. Because of this, the US has attempted to drive corporate efforts into investing in solutions by limiting the level of emissions permitted. Evidently, Volkswagen was intentionally cheating in order to sell their cars without incurring in legal sanctions.

The EPA's findings cover almost 500, 000 cars in the US alone, including brands as popular as the Audi A3, the Beetle, and the Golf. However, after raising the alarm, matters have gone from bad to worse. A scandal that started in the US has spread to Europe, as well as a number of other countries, where formal investigations have been opened regarding the approximately 11 million VW diesel cars that are now under suspicion.

With the company publicly admitting their guilt, there is little that can be done. At the moment €6.5 billion has been set aside to cover costs, however the financial impact of the scandal has only just begun. For starters, the EPA has the power to fine VW with up to USD$18 billion ($37, 500 per vehicle), while Germany could also punish one of its most prominent companies by imposing heavy legal sanctions. Additionally, legal action is expected to follow from the considerable amount of angry consumers and shareholders who have been intentionally and willfully misguided. As Martin Winterkorn declared before resigning, his company has "broken the trust of our customers and the public." Volkswagen has seriously endangered its position, tarnished its reputation and image, and undermined years upon years of effort and investments.

Western Europe, the most important market for Volkswagen, is unlikely to forgive and forget. One in four new cars is manufactured by the group, however, there is no doubt that the company will face serious difficulties in regards to maintaining current sales and production levels.

Not surprisingly, company shares plunged around 30% in the first couple of days after the scandal broke, with other carmakers also suffering big falls in their stock prices. In other words, about a third of the company's market value has been wiped out, affecting powerful shareholders such as the Porsche family, Qatar and the German state of Lower Saxony.

Volkswagen has much to resolve before it can once again wave a green flag.

As we've seen, a company may pretend to be green and hope that no one will investigate their credentials too closely. But this is simply naïve these days, most especially if you belong to a high polluting industry. Clearly, environmental issues can no longer be ignored by corporations. While greenwashing their way into society's good books might seem like an attractive first option, eventually "the truth will out," threatening a firm's survival and endangering strategic intangible assets. What is more, the mere suspicion of greenwashing can be enough to affect a company. So although obvious environmental infractions such as those involving Volkswagen are bound to have catastrophic results, even just paying lip service to social and environmental concerns is a risky strategy for companies.

> " A sustainability strategy shouldn't be about solving that which went wrong, but learning how to do it right from the beginning. "
>
> *Luis Piacenza*
> *CROWE HORWATH*

While Volkswagen has only just begun to suffer the consequences of its recent car scam, BP has already experienced just how hard it can get. In the early 2000s, BP changed its logo and adopted the slogan "Beyond Petroleum," in an attempt to reposition its brand and present itself as the only green alternative in the petrochemical industry. As we covered in sections 3.7 and 4.3.2., at first, everything seemed to go smoothly. BP committed itself to investments in renewable energies, and its rebranding efforts appeared to be paying off, with many consumers switching brands from less-well-regarded rivals.

But BP's actions began to contradict its words. Record oil prices in 2008 prompted the company to refocus its strategy once again on oil extraction, including the controversial acquisition of a Canadian oil sands property. A year later, when BP made significant cutbacks to its alternative energy headquarters in London, serious doubts were raised about its true commitment to sustainability.

Then along came a series of events in 2010 that BP has still not recovered from. Besides the DeepWater Horizon offshore rig explosion, which became known as the worst oil spill in US history, it came to light that BP had released toxic emissions into the atmosphere from its Texas City refinery earlier that year. These two events alone cost BP tens of billions of dollars in damages, while also highlighting the enormous gap that existed between what was being said, and what was being done.

In the context of the Volkswagen and BP scandals, the message is loud and clear: **More environmental symbolic actions do not mean a greener company.**

# CHAPTER 7

# Proactive Alternatives to Greenwashing

> **"** Don't talk unless you can improve the silence. **"**
>
> *– Jorge Luis Borges*

As seen in the previous chapter, symbolic endeavors alone may not be in a firm's best interests for two reasons. First, symbolic actions are easily copied by rivals, having become so much the norm as to be virtually meaningless. As such, companies stand little chance of differentiating themselves from their rivals. Second and more importantly, a company that merely adopts environmental behavior in a symbolic manner without pursuing substantive actions may be perceived as deceitful. By talking the talk but not walking the walk, companies risk attracting much greater scrutiny of the real social and environmental impact of their actions.

> **"** If sustainability is not integrated into the strategy then 'sustainability' within the company is not sustainable. **"**
>
> *Pablo Bascones Ilundain*
> *PwC*

Furthermore, consumers today are far more discriminating and better equipped to measure the real impact of a company's operations. From the stakeholder perspective, if one is truly green, there is no need to over-engage in symbolism since actions speak louder than words. As many companies have learned the hard way, failure to follow through on their promises can undermine their legitimacy, damage their reputation, and cut into their bottom line. Greenwashing can only hide irresponsible behavior for so long.

## 7.1 The Long and Winding Road to Sustainability

We have come a long way, there is no doubt about it (see Figure 7.1 for a snapshot). In the early stages of sustainability, the notion that firms needed to be green (or greener) was essentially launched on moral grounds. Being green was the right thing to do and the idea was completely disconnected from the impact this might have on business output. "Green guilt" was the major mechanism to push firms to engage in sustainable practices. Eventually, governments echoed these societal concerns to promote green regulation and coerce companies to behave in an environmentally sound manner. Sustainability then was a legal obligation and thus considered a cost. Later, we moved beyond the need for legal compliance to the tempting notion that sustainability could be profitable, introducing the so-called business case.

The business case implied that sustainability was an opportunity to make money. It allowed companies to save costs, reduce risks, and control corporate issues such as absenteeism. At the same time, sustainability improved productivity, facilitated entry into new markets, enhanced company reputation by adding value to all stakeholders, and was a source of differentiation by ensuring customer loyalty. Too good to be true, right?

Figure 7. 1  The Concept of Sustainability: Evolution

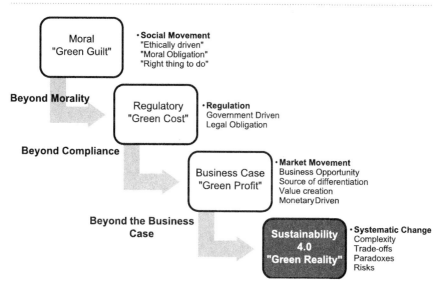

*Source:* Own.

Sure enough, during the period that the business case became the dominant paradigm, greenwashing peaked. In the end, it is just another way of attempting to reap the benefits of being green without making the necessary investments. But is sustainability really that profitable? Is it worth the effort?

## 7.2  Sustainability Pays-Off...But it is Not Easy to Be Green

Much of the problem preventing firms from moving wholeheartedly into Sustainability 4.0 (pictured in Figure 7.1) stems from the belief that managers have to choose between being socially responsible and being financially profitable. However, a number of academic research and practitioner reports show evidence that this simply isn't true, at least for some. For instance, the most recent "State of Green Business" report published annually by the GreenBiz Group, found that over half of US companies reported environmental profits or savings in 2013, a number that has increased notably since 2009. This trend is also visible on a global scale, having gone from under 10% in 2009 to 22% in 2013 (Figure 7.2) (Makower 2015).

> " A sustainable business is that which is able to ensure the long term success of a business model based on the three pillars (social, economic, and environmental) which are the equivalent to the 'moral compass' of a person. "
>
> *Valentín Casado*
> *ELMET S.L.U*

Figure 7. 2  Companies Reporting Environmental Profits or Savings

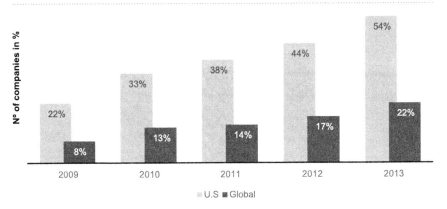

This significant increase suggests opportunities indeed exist for those willing to bet on long-term sustainability. Leading companies are driving sustainability strategies precisely because they produce real results and have been identified as having the potential for

innovation and growth. As UL (a global independent safety science company) recently highlighted in "The Sustainable Edge," those who adopt a proactive approach can indeed benefit from decreased costs, product innovations that open new markets, brand loyalty, rising stock values and risk mitigation, and can take advantage of the numerous possibilities sustainable development has to offer.

For instance, adapting business operations to improve resource efficiency can provide important cost savings across the supply chain, while offering an opportunity to demonstrate commitment and satisfy stakeholder demands.

In numerical terms, 79% of companies that have become involved in product sustainability claim to have achieved savings in their manufacturing costs, while 90% of retailers report that sustainability efforts have effectively lowered their costs (UL 2014).

To state an example, in 2012, finance industry company Bloomberg claimed to have achieved a 200% return on sustainability investments, as every $1 spent had saved the company $2 in operating costs, resulting in net savings of $25 million since 2008 (Bloomberg 2012). To this day, the company continues to benefit from sustainability efforts, as savings derived from projects that reduce environmental impacts and generate positive financial return has gone up to $68 million in only two years (Bloomberg 2014).

Additionally (and as we demonstrated in Chapter 6.5), companies engaging in environmental and social responsibility have been shown to obtain much more than operational cost savings; **they could boost their financial value too.**

> **"** Interest groups are asking for greater commitment from the business world, as the triple bottom line continues to gain importance.
>
> This is benefitting companies in several ways such as obtaining long-term customer loyalty or finding new markets. It also offers the opportunity for firms to improve operational efficiency and risk management procedures (avoiding reputational damage for example) and attracting new talent. **"**

*Antoni Ballabriga Terreguitart*
*BBVA*

A 2013 study by Harvard Business School and the London Business School, investigated the impact of corporate sustainability on organizational processes and performance to verify its profit potential. When examining the financial performance of companies that had voluntarily adopted corporate-level sustainability policies against companies that hadn't—or as they denominated "high-sustainability" versus "low-sustainability" companies—they found **that high-sustainability companies notably outperformed their counterparts**. For example, if someone had invested $1 in a portfolio of high-sustainability companies in 1993, that investment would have grown to $22.60 by 2010, while that same $1 invested in a low-sustainability portfolio would have only delivered $15.40 (Eccles, Ioannou et al. 2012; MIT and BCG 2013).

### 7.2.1 Five reasons firms still struggle with sustainability

But if profiting from sustainability is so straightforward, why don't all companies engage in such strategies?

The truth is that the path to success is not always clear, as even when companies do decide to go beyond, they often find that achieving real improvement is much easier said than done. As a matter of fact, the last CEO Study conducted by Accenture and the UNGC, found that a clear majority (67%) do not believe business is doing enough to address global sustainability challenges but at the same time are satisfied with the execution of their own sustainability strategy (76%). This disconnect suggests there is a significant gap between what is expected and what is implemented (Accenture 2010; Accenture 2013). While leading companies have adopted an approach focused on innovation, growth and new sources of value, the vast majority continue to concentrate on philanthropy, compliance, mitigation and the license to operate.

Ultimately, firms are struggling to quantify and capture the business value of sustainability (Accenture 2013), and failure to make a business case for the cause often leads to incremental advances at best, and disengagement at worst. Again, as of 2013, MIT and BCG found that roughly half of respondents found it difficult to quantify the intangible effects of sustainability, and 37% claimed sustainability oriented policies conflicted with other priorities, claiming higher operational and administrative costs connected with sustainability programs drained profits instead of improving margins.

Why do firms struggle with sustainability? Why is it so difficult for so many companies to reach the panacea of the business case? Over the years, I have been able to compile a list of five reasons, which can be described as the "uncomfortable truths" about corporate sustainability:

1. **Unclear standards:** The lack of a uniform standard, or set of standards, defining environmentally responsible companies means many a firm is at a loss of what it means to be "green";

2. **Consumer behavior:** There's a significant gap between green concern and green consumerism. *Under what conditions are consumers willing to make a greener purchase?* Consumers want green without compromise or sacrifice;

3. **Scattered approach:** Environmental challenges are vast and diverse; no company can do it by itself. Competitive dynamics require a *systemic* approach;

4. **Gaps in knowledge:** There is a big gap in our knowledge about *how* to move corporations powerfully and effectively towards sustainability;

5. **Culture and leadership:** The source of sustainability lies with fundamental change in organizations' *culture* and individuals' *leadership* style.

The above suggests a much more complex picture than what the "business case" actually portrays. It reveals the intricacy of the process of becoming green, and illustrates the unavoidable trade-offs that exist when making green choices. More importantly, it stresses the need for *change*. A change in terms of how we consume, how we do business, how we work, and how we approach innovation. In short, a change in our mindset. And change is difficult. Without a struggle, there can be no progress.

Thus, how do firms overcome these "uncomfortable truths"? *What is* the secret to success, or in this case sustainability? Let's explore a few cases to see if we can spot some clues.

## 7.3 Revealing the Gap Between Walkers and Talkers

In 2013, the MIT Sloan Management Review and The Boston Consulting Group collaborated on a research project to assess how businesses address their sustainability challenges (MIT and BCG 2013). The study focused on companies that recognized the importance of sustainability issues and thoroughly addressed them. Not surprisingly, firms that "walk the talk" or "walkers" were found to share distinct characteristics as efforts were redirected to five business fronts (see Figure 7.3).

Figure 7. 3  Five Ways That Walkers Walk

*Source:* Adapted from *"Sustainability's Next Frontier."* Copyright 2013 by MIT.

Separating the "talkers" from the "walkers," revealed the significant gap that lies between one approach and the other. A full 90% of walkers were found to have developed a sustainable strategy, in contrast to only 46% of talkers. Likewise, nearly 70% of walkers claimed to be developing sustainability business cases, compared to less than a third of talkers (20%). And so forth on all five fronts.

Organizational capabilities including, leadership, communication and measurement, and business model innovation, have been repeatedly identified as the keys to unlocking a sustainable competitive advantage. In fact, the study also found that managers profiting from sustainable endeavors claimed sustainability was the main driver of business model innovation, an approach that looks beyond product, service or technology advances (MIT and BCG 2013).

So how to evolve from a talker to a walker? Hopefully, the following success stories will help shed some light as to where 21st century companies are heading.

### 7.3.1 Walker case studies: Innovation is king

A few years ago, my colleagues and I conducted a study that showed how external pressures affected environmental innovation (Berrone, Fosfuri et al. 2013) Although our research found that managers in firms whose reputations have suffered from environmental misconduct or compliance problems might be more sensitive to pressure from regulators and institutions than managers in other companies and thus invest in environmental innovation, we also stressed that managers don't need to wait for criticism before developing environmental innovation. They can, and should take the lead on this type of activity, since it should have a positive effect on firm performance.

A good example of a firm that bet on innovation early on is 3M. With worldwide sales of $25 billion, 3M is a leader in scores of markets, from health care and highway safety to office products and optical films for LCD supplies. After facing significant lawsuits for its negative environmental impact, 3M decided to implement the pioneer program Pollution Prevention Pays (3P). Based on the belief that a preventive approach is more effective than conventional pollution controls, the program has spawned numerous environmentally friendly innovations since its launch in 1975.

Back then, the initiative challenged well-established practices by seeking to prevent pollution from the source through product reformulation, process modification, equipment redesign, and recycling and reuse of waste materials. However with products such as the Task Light, an energy efficient desk lamp that reduces reflective and veiling glare on reading materials and work surfaces, or the Safest Stripper Paint & Varnish Remover, an alternative to traditional paint and varnish removers which is non-flammable, non-toxic and biodegradable, contains no methylene chloride and cleans up with water, the firm has successfully reduced its environmental impact.

According to 3M, more than 2 million tons of air, water and waste pollution has been prevented in the last 40 years, proving the success of the company's once visionary program.

> One must think in different terms; in Einstein's words 'We can't solve problems by using the same kind of thinking we used when we created them.' Innovation is fundamental, essential, and can be achieved through a series of ways, if possible disruptively rather than incrementally.
>
> *Ernesto Lluch Moreno*
> *G-ADVISORY*

To this day, many companies continue to follow 3M's lead, looking for new ways to tackle the environmental crisis we find ourselves in. Instead of looking at the cost of sustainability, focus must be placed on how efforts can build a competitive advantage, and in view of the many successful examples of sustainability-driven innovation, the range of opportunities is significantly wide.

Incremental steps are always a good starting point, as minimal investments can significantly improve efficiency and reduce costs. Similar to Bloomberg, Sainsbury's has been able to reduce its water use by 54% since 2006 just by improving efficiency in its stores, proving once again how simple incremental measures can go a long way, reducing not only the company's operating costs, but its impact on the environment as well.

On a different note, Nestlé has successfully reduced its dependency on natural gas by giving coffee grounds a new use. Although hard to believe, the by-product of the company's manufacturing process has gone from waste to a new source of energy, after they realized that the steam generated by burning the coffee grounds could be used in their factories. To this day, spent coffee grounds represents 26.7% of the company's renewable energy mix, helping to reduce carbon emissions and achieve Nestlé's "zero-waste" goal by diverting millions of tons of waste away from landfills. When it comes to large corporations, no change goes unnoticed, as small as it may seem.

Evidently, the supply chain is a natural place for innovation. However, while extensions, enhancements, and carbon offsets will continue to play a major role in making green a little more mainstream, it's the disruptive end of the eco-innovation spectrum that's most exciting and perhaps the most promising in the long term (Figure 7.4).

Figure 7. 4  Shades of Green innovation

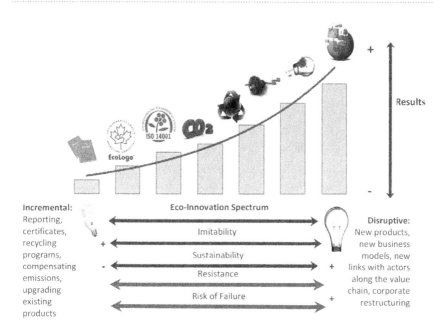

*Source:* Own

Over the next few years, organizations that are truly committed to sustainability will use their drive to "Go Green" as a platform for truly disruptive change. Size, experience, and brand name will be less important to success in the marketplace than the magnitude of innovation that some companies attain—and breakthroughs will be born across industries, presenting solutions to some of our most seemingly-intractable environmental issues.

### 7.3.2  Walker case study: Boosting your value proposition

Early last year, together with my friend and colleague Judith Walls, I published an article entitled *"The Power of One to Make a Difference: How Informal and Formal CEO Power Affects Environmental Sustainability,"* where we showed the relevance that the CEO preferences, background and values have on environmental performance (Walls and Berrone 2015).

A case in point of this is the apparel company "Patagonia." True to the principles of its founder, Yvon Chouinard, Patagonia has long since become an example to the business community, as its long standing commitment towards the environment can be traced back to its very origins. Since 1985, the high-end brand has given at least 1% of its sales to environmental charities, and in 2001, Chouinard cofounded One Percent for the Planet, an alliance of mainly small companies that pledge to do the same. With over 1000 members in 44 countries, to this day the alliance has given back more than $115 million dollars to over 3,500 NGOs (2015) that work on a variety of sustainability initiatives. [27]

However, the company is best known for an ad purchased in the New York Times in 2011, where customers were encouraged not to buy one of its products. Patagonia's "Buy Less" campaign was actively denouncing the wasteful and consumerist society we live in, blaming our habits for diminishing the world's resources, and advising that people not buy what they don't need (Gunther 2011; Penhollow 2015). The company had already launched the Common Threads Initiative earlier that year, seeking to embrace the concept of "Reduce, Repair, Reuse, Recycle, Reimagine," by encouraging a partnership between Patagonia and their customers to buy and use clothes more sustainably.

This includes making quality products that will last a long time, or offering advice on how to take care of their clothes so they will not have to be thrown away. Once purchased, Patagonia offers to repair

---

[27] For more information please access <http://onepercentfortheplanet.org/>.

products for free when it appears the company is responsible for the need, and for a "fair price" when not. Next, Patagonia encourages users who no longer want their products to donate them to a charity or sell them, offering consumers the possibility to sell their products through their Common Threads website or through eBay. However, if the product is worn out, then Patagonia will take the product and recycle it into something else; since 2005 Patagonia has turned more than 82 tons of recycled clothes into new clothes (Patagonia 2015).

Although it seems as though Patagonia wants to accomplish two conflicting goals, having a profitable company while denouncing materialism and consumerism, the firm's success challenges traditional business models. Following through their promise to *"Build the best product, do no unnecessary harm, use business to inspire and implement solutions to the environmental crisis,"* the idea of "profitable good" which is embedded into their core business model, has boosted their value proposition. Evidently, Patagonia doesn't just talk the talk, but walks the walk. They set an excellent example of how sustainability can indeed drive profits by unlocking unique competitive advantages as long as one is willing to commit.

> " With sustainability in [woven into a new company's] DNA, the likelihood of greenwashing decreases dramatically, as opposed to well established companies that require a transformational change. "
>
> *Gael Gonzalez*
> *SUSTAINABILITY EXPERT, LUXURY SECTOR*

### 7.3.3 Walker case study: Better *plus* greener products

As seen above, identifying how to boost your value proposition or improve your operating model is a successful way of making sustainability profitable. Nonetheless, the survey conducted by BCG and MIT found that the most powerful formula was when companies combined the two. That is, when two or more elements of a business model are combined and reinvented to deliver value in a new way.

Some may argue that well-established corporations face greater resistance when changing existing practices and challenging traditional assumptions, yet they are also the ones that have the biggest opportunities within reach, capable of bringing about significant results. For instance, firms focused on combining target segments with value chain innovations have found a powerful formula without having to make drastic changes to their existing business models, as was the case for Mondelez International.

An important part of the strategy followed by Mondelez addresses sustainable sourcing. As a multinational food company, ensuring continued access to reliable sources of crops such as cocoa or coffee is critical to survival, and with global food demands steadily increasing, understanding the challenges ahead and investing in sustainable farming just makes sense. Besides acting as a guarantee for future operations, providing a sustainable product has also expanded the company's customer base. Almost 70% of global coffee is currently sustainably sourced, and as consumers have shown to care about the precedence of products, obtaining well-established certifications such as the Rainforest Alliance Certified Seal helps to boost sales.

Nonetheless, a less obvious supply chain innovation proved to be as effective (if not more) when building business in target segments. When Mondelez revisited production processes, the company identified an opportunity to reduce packaging costs for its YES Pack commercial salad dressings through a new, "more sustainable" plastic container that used 28% less raw materials and 50% less energy to produce. The new packaging became an instant success, but not for the same reasons one would believe. Of course the product was "greener," but the added value for customers and the popularity of the product came with the new design of the package which was bigger and easier to use.

> **"** Consumers aren't ready to sacrifice quality for the environment yet…but buying a product of excellent quality that is also eco-friendly is a different story. **"**
>
> *Gael Gonzalez*
> *SUSTAINABILITY EXPERT, LUXURY SECTOR*

The moral of the story? Service must promise additional benefits beyond its superior environmental attributes. It must be cheaper, faster, whiter, brighter, easier to use, more effective, or simply cooler. In other words: Products and services need to be more than merely greener. They need to be better.

## 7.4 Generating a Competitive Advantage Over Rivals

Having seen examples that range from "doing things differently to doing different things"(MIT and BCG 2013) what is pushing these companies towards embracing sustainability? Is it external pressure in the form of international protocols from Kyoto to the COP 21, investors discounting prices of companies poorly positioned to compete in a warming world, consumers considering a company's environmental record before purchasing products—are these all things that back companies into a corner? Or is it an instinct that arises from within companies as managers review their operations in light of higher raw material and energy costs for example, which makes them hatch resources to boost the bottom line and inspires them to find better ways of running their business?

The answer is simple; yes to all. In a globalized world facing resource scarcity and a carbon-constrained future, companies that manage their exposure to environmental risks, while at the same time seeking new opportunities for profit are the ones that generate competitive advantage over rivals (Figure 7.5).

### 7.4.1 A balanced approach to environmental innovation

Despite multiple causes explaining what make companies embrace sustainability, the academic theories stumble in capturing the complexity of it all. Case in point, the two main theories used in environmental management are institutional theory and resource-based view (RBV). For instance, while it addresses the influence of external pressures, institutional theory fails to address efficiency issues or the impact of strategies on performance, only explaining the implementation of practices without any obvious economic value. The theory explains that managers who only ever wait for unavoidable pressures before acting are less likely to spawn genuine innovation. Instead, they become mere copycats or wait until the long arm of the law gets hold of them and then pay the price.

Figure 7. 5  Pressures and a Firm's Responses

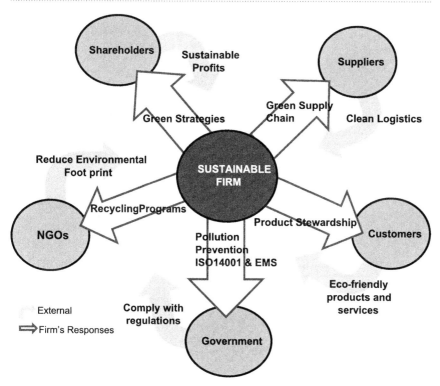

*Source:* Own.

The opposite of institutional theory is the RBV of the company. Under RBV, market success occurs when the firm creates, develops and combines resources and capabilities in such a way that rivals cannot imitate them. Here the main challenges arise from inside rather than outside the organization. When faced with this sort of pressure, managers have more flexibility to choose an appropriate strategy; they can tap into internal resources and capabilities with profit potential, such as their people, property and capital, along with intangible resources such as skills and know-how.

> **"** One has to look at the dilemma on one end regarding resource intensity, environmental footprint … and the business side on the other. It is the only way … to move forward. **"**
>
> *Xavier Houot*
> *SCHNEIDER-ELECTRIC*

The profit, therefore, arises from the uniqueness, scarcity and value of these innate resources and capabilities, which are difficult for rivals to obtain or duplicate. For this reason, companies are able to generate above-normal rates of return. To ensure that this competitive advantage remains sustainable rather than short term, these resources must be heterogeneous in nature and non-transferable, meaning they cannot be perfectly imitated or substituted without great effort. According to the RBV, companies must have the power within themselves to respond to environmental challenges in innovative ways. By doing so, they will build up a bank of resources that will give them an edge over rivals.

On the downside, RBV can be criticized for excessive emphasis on resource markets and economically rational choices without taking into account the social context within which companies' choices are embedded. Not to mention its tautological nature and circular reasoning under which competitive advantage is seen as a value-creating, resource-based strategy that is highly valuable.

In the end, true environmental innovation depends on a mix of institutional theory and RBV, because in real-life situations, such as the ones addressed above, a firm has to contemplate both the relevance of proper responsiveness to institutional forces and the importance of creating valuable resources. Combining the two is critical to identifying new business opportunities and establishing the grounds for innovation.

From a practical point of view, all evidence suggests that driving sustainability in a profitable way, depends first and foremost upon a company's culture and overall strategy. Without a sincere commitment from the top and bottom of the organization, sustainability become a "fake stance strategy" that will eventually backlash.

> **"** Why are we here? Who are we serving? These are some of the key questions firms must ask themselves to identify the organic role they play within society. [This will] allow them to respond and adapt to environmental challenges, which evidently leads to stakeholder engagement. **"**
>
> Luis Piacenza
> CROWE HORWATH

## 7.5 Six Steps to Remove the Wash From Your Green

The complaint that has repeated itself the most over time, is how CEOs struggle to make the business case for action. While they remain convinced of the transformational power of sustainability, they see a significant market failure that is hindering business efforts. Linking sustainability tangibly and quantifiably to value creation is the secret to unlocking key transformations, leaving incremental improvements behind in order to concentrate on ambitious and large-scale projects.

The first thing we must keep in mind is that every company is different and has its own reality, but there are certain themes that repeat themselves. Regardless of the industry, the behavior of those companies that are willing to act rather than react, can be broken down into six basic steps, a cheat sheet of sorts. **These steps are:**

1. **Define what sustainability means to YOU**

2. **Ensure company-wide commitment**

3. **Establish goals and monitor results**

4. **Align your corporate governance structure**

5. **Dialogue with customers and stakeholders**

6. **Collaborate with NGOs, policymakers, and industry peers**

### 1) Define what sustainability means to YOU

Acknowledging the scale of the global challenges we face is not enough. Companies must understand where they fit and how sustainability applies to their particular industry and individual activities. Many make the mistake of believing sustainability should only have one universal meaning, an assumption that has proven to be wrong. Of course, the main idea behind the word is applicable to all, but what each of us can interpret according to our particular situation is a whole different story.

What do a large multinational bank and an oil and gas corporation have in common? Nothing really. Besides operating in multiple countries, you wouldn't expect them to carry out their daily activities in a similar way. Why should they? Their entire supply and value chain is worlds apart. Well, the same can be said of their sustainability strategies. You wouldn't expect them to have similar goals or objectives as their impacts on society and the planet cannot be compared.

> **"** The terminology used may differ from case to case. For example, within our industry the terms 'responsible business' or 'responsible banking' make more sense than corporate sustainability. This little detail can make all the difference, as one has to use the term that fits and connects with what you do. Within a bank, if you want senior management to get on board and address these issues, not as a parallel or marginal strategy but as part of their day to day activities, the term responsible banking is more appropriate. It makes sense within our particular organization. In the past terms such as CSR or sustainability haven't managed to get the message across, failing to connect with the activities of our industry. However responsible banking is a concept that can be easily understood. **"**
>
> *Antoni Ballabriga Terreguitart*
> *BBVA*

While aspiring to become a sustainable bank may not make much sense within the financial sector, becoming a responsible bank does. A bank can invest in waste reduction schemes and recycling programs but at the end of the day, being transparent and responsible towards their customers is their biggest contribution to society. Presenting themselves as a positive driver of today's global economy and society, has had to become their highest priority considering the collapse in public trust after the recent global financial crisis.

> " It is impossible to adopt all the sustainability measures in the world, which is why organizations need to find their particular role in society. Only then will they be able to operate in a sustainable fashion, where performance won't be limited by their own organizational restrictions, [and they can] go beyond a mere declaration of intent. "
>
> *Luis Piacenza*
> *CROWE HORWATH*

On the other hand, corporations in typically polluting industries such as oil and gas are more concerned with reducing their impact on the environment as much as possible. This involves reducing environmental exposure to risks through proper safety, and risk management to prevent oil spills or other disasters such as those that occurred in the past (the most recent of which was suffered in 2010 at a BP offshore platform). Furthermore, the shift towards a low carbon economy is real and is happening, hence sustainable strategies should be directed towards facing these challenges and investing in alternative and renewable energies.

So figuring out what sustainability means to you, and how it makes sense to your business, is the first step. Also denominated "material sustainability," makes reference to the sustainability issues that are relevant to the company's ability to continue operations in the future. This is likely to differ depending on the industry and individual resources of each business. Again, for a food company such as Mondelez, sustainable sourcing is logical; it "greens" their products as much as it guarantees future access to resources that are critical to their manufacturing process and overall survival.

> " The sooner companies enjoy a shared vocabulary on $CO_2$ and a broader environmental foot printing, the better. Such clarity will help avoid some form of—sometimes unintended—greenwashing. "
>
> *Xavier Houot*
> *SCHNEIDER-ELECTRIC*

In the words of Paul Polman, CEO of Unilever, **"find a purpose or perish."** Thus, identifying how sustainability fits into your supply chain and value creation is the first step (and perhaps the only way) of developing a realistic and relatable sustainable strategy, which brings us to our next step; ensuring a company-wide commitment.

## 2) Ensure a company-wide commitment

Once the value and relevance of integrating sustainability has been identified, an appropriate strategy must be developed, for which commitment at all levels is imperative.

Take Norsk Hydro for example. When the Norwegian aluminum and petrochemical company came under pressure from the first wave of environmental protest movements in the 1960s and 1970s, it realized that something had to give. Its response was to modernize its plants, manufacture more environmentally friendly product mixes and reduce pollution through strict control measures.

Today, Hydro is barely recognizable from its former self. Having divested its oil, gas and agrochemical operations, the company now focuses on manufacturing aluminum and developing renewable energy. The company has produced a social responsibility directive, as well as a code of conduct to ensure that all people acting on behalf of Hydro perform activities in an ethical way. What is particularly striking about the Hydro case is that the company was operating in industries notorious for their damaging social and environmental impact, very much like BP, which comes to show how important commitment is.

> " There is usually an element of inadequate governance present in greenwashing companies, which has to be improved on in order to achieve appropriate corporate assurance. "
>
> *Antoni Ballabriga Terreguitart*
> *BBVA*

Moreover, the company embarked on the transformation in the face of stiff resistance from an internal corporate culture that had traditionally taken a hostile stance towards environmental issues. Essentially the key to their success was not being afraid to make radical changes to its governance structures in order to build a more sustainable business model.

This brings us to our second point; real change can only come from the inside out, not the other way around. It is amazing to see the impact that a genuine commitment from the top can have in the way organizations think and act. When commitment is sincere, the speeches and editorials CEOs make about the pressing need for climate action are inspirational and transformational. I myself have witnessed this from the CEOs of Unilever, The North Face and Patagonia.

> " How is greenwashing avoided? The same way any
> other important matters are avoided or promoted;
> with leadership from management and establishing a
> corporate culture accordingly. "
>
> *Ernesto Lluch Moreno*
> *G-ADVISORY*

I have also seen this heartfelt commitment to the environment in many family owned firms. In fact, my early academic research has revealed a tendency for family firms to outperform larger corporations when it comes to the environment. This can be easily explained, as family business owners are often willing to sacrifice short-term financial results in order to build a more sustainable business model that will stand the company in good stead for future generations. Much of it also has to do with the emotional attachments that lead family owners to do everything in their power, even when it is economically risky, not to fail their own company. They're highly motivated to safeguard their reputations as good corporate citizens in the local communities in which they operate. Ultimately sustainability is ingrained in the DNA of many family owners.

There is something that non-family firms can learn from their family counterparts. Perhaps the most crucial variable here is the time horizon. Above all, governance (ownership and management) would do well to adopt a "generational investment" strategy, which requires a long-term vision and uninterrupted commitment. After all, the beneficial effects of investing in social and environmental activities take a long time to feed through. The key, therefore, is to ensure a real long-term commitment from senior management that will lead efforts in the same direction throughout the organization.

Leadership has been found to be one of the main drivers of sustainable profitability, with successful businesses claiming sustainability has become a permanent fixture on their management agenda (MIT and BCG 2013; Walls and Berrone 2015). CEOs must focus and make sustainability a priority to prevent it from eventually falling off the radar and becoming empty promises.

Unfortunately, in order to guarantee sustainability maintains its position at the forefront of corporate efforts, certain internal structural changes are usually required which is where many firms seem to fail. The board of directors should play a key role in navigating the sustainability journey, working together with the owners and management.

## 3) Establish goals and monitor results

> " Adopting a clear strategy and objectives, with measurable indicators and traceable results are key to ensuring that the work done on sustainability is underpinned by real data. "
>
> – Carlos Salvador

To start with, a company must determine what their strategy is set to achieve; is your firm looking to take advantage of positive opportunities that may arise, or seeking to reduce its negative social and environmental impact, or both? This has to be considered taking into account other aspects such as who your networks are.

> " The feeling that there is a certain trade off—that [one must] renounce short term benefits in order to obtain higher returns in the long run (such as stakeholder engagement or employee satisfaction)—complicates things. "
>
> *Antoni Ballabriga Terreguitart*
> *BBVA*

Supply chain providers as well as other stakeholders such as governments, employees and NGOs have a direct or indirect influence in determining the type of environmental strategy you pursue.

Either way, one thing must be crystal clear: **it is necessary to accept trade-offs between economic and social results.**

The ultimate obstacle many a company fails to overcome is accepting the trade-offs between economic and social results. However, sometimes it feels as though firms willing to do so, are fighting a losing battle. The pressure to constantly deliver results makes it extremely difficult for managers to keep sight of the bigger picture and continue to bet on long-term commitments. But experience has shown that doing nothing is no longer an option as the reputational cost of adopting a reactive stance is ever increasing.

> " The key obstacle is identifying what is relevant and adds value to our customers, within the framework of a responsible practice, which in turn is relevant and profitable for the company's competitive edge and reputation. "
>
> *Antoni Ballabriga Terreguitart*
> *BBVA*

In this sense, Unilever has been a recognizable pioneer, having come to terms with the need to go beyond by prioritizing environmental and social issues on the corporate agenda regardless of the trade-offs. One of the company's boldest moves was eliminating quarterly profit reports for the sake of putting "the greater good ahead of self-interest." Funnily enough, this approach has actually rewarded shareholders, as Unilever has increased profits at a steady pace over the last few years. By reducing short-term pressures the company has attracted long-term investments, as well as successfully developing products with purpose and reducing their reputational risk. All of this has been translated into lower capital costs and higher shareholder returns.

The management guru Peter Drucker once said, "What gets measured gets managed." Thus, once a company has settled on the purpose behind its overall strategy, the next step is establishing clear and measurable objectives that will help you meet your goals. Clear measures will allow you to make a better assessment of the trade-offs involved in becoming more sustainable. Implementing strategic initiatives requires central coordination, integration and connections with others to source talent, ideas and technologies.

> **"** If your business is based on a particular set of products and/or services, the transition required to implement a sustainable strategy [is one] that addresses your core business activities [rather than] something on the side or parallel to the company's corporate strategy. **"**
>
> *Antonio Fuertes Zurita*
> *GAS NATURAL FENOSA*

Most importantly, conflicting departmental goals have proven to be a source of unintentional greenwashing in the past, which is why targets throughout the organization must be coherent and move in one direction. This can require revisiting existing functional, departmental and production processes to gear them towards environmental goals.

> **"** Many companies believe that publishing a series of sustainability indicators and numbers makes them sustainable. But these do not necessarily drive any major improvements: it is not just about the numbers. And while disclosing certain facts and figures may help track the progress made, at the end of the day what sticks is the [actual] progress made. Information must be complete and companies must be willing to provide easy access to further data and information. **"**
>
> *Gael Gonzalez*
> *SUSTAINABILITY EXPERT, LUXURY SECTOR*

Finally, once the objectives are clear, it is necessary to keep close track of the effects of your sustainability efforts. Companies that seek to shift from an incremental approach must not only measure and manage environmental performance such as tracking carbon emission and water usage footprints, but must also develop the ability to quantify the value of sustainable initiatives. If this is done successfully, the likelihood of moving towards more sustainable business models will undoubtedly increase.

In short, metrics must be clear and reporting should be thorough and transparent at all levels, because communicating your efforts and the pace at which you're evolving is important. Do not become a "green mute" out of fear. Measure progress and communicate, provide your stakeholders with all the necessary information to contrast your claims. This means becoming "brutally honest" (or "transparent" in its more polite form). By sharing your success, you're not only helping yourself but you can help fellow peers and regulators as well. Each individual contribution counts and helps push the sustainability agenda a bit further along.

### 4) Align your corporate governance structure

> " Internal alignment is critical. Commitment from senior management, and consistency throughout the company. "
>
> – Antoni Ballabriga Terreguitart

This is probably the most important step, as without the proper structures, commitment and goals will be unlikely to materialize. To avoid possible implementation gaps between ambitious sustainability strategies and what is actually achieved, businesses need to develop new skills, knowledge and mindsets, so that they have the capabilities to manage sustainable development properly. For any business to achieve this, there is one factor of overriding importance: its corporate governance model. By aligning the interests of owners and managers, depending on who exerts greater control over the firm, with board composition variables and managerial compensation policies, a company can achieve substantive improvements.

The following points address alignment and needs at an ownership level, board level, and managerial level, as well as an overall approach to executive compensation.

## ► Ownership level

At the ownership level, the main governance factors are shareholder activism, shareholder concentration, and investment horizon (the total length of time an investor expects to hold a security or portfolio).

> **"** Internal communication is necessary, recruiting people that understand sustainability as part of the company's culture and values from the very beginning and not as just a parallel strategy, but as part of its DNA. This implies far more than mere statements, and written values, and requires consistency and coherence amongst departments, commitment from the company's management, and overall cohesion of the corporate culture. **"**

*Gael Gonzalez*
*SUSTAINABILITY EXPERT, LUXURY SECTOR*

Arguably the most critical variable here is to attract investors with a long-term commitment, and whenever possible, to give more speculative investors a wide berth. This includes deeper engagement with the investor community to communicate the impact of the firm's sustainability activity on its core business metrics.

Obviously, this is much more difficult for publicly listed companies, which have less influence over which investors they attract. However, with the responsible investment movement definitely on the rise, and the ability to screen investment opportunities according to industry and company performance on issues related to sustainability, it is likely to become easier to attract like-minded investors. However, if a firm's diverse investors or shareholders are proving to be resistant to such thinking, then the task of driving through the necessary reforms must fall to the firm's board of directors and management team.

Figure 7. 6 Key Variables That Affect Performance

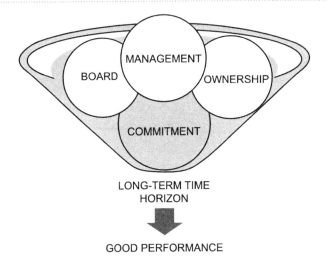

Source: Own

► **Board level**

My research on corporate sustainability has found significant associations between a firm's social and environmental performance and variables such as board independence, specialized committees, board diversity and board size (Walls, Berrone et al. 2012). Let's consider some of these issues in turn.

> 66 Some companies may have engaged in greenwashing in some
> form or the other over the last few years, however this may not
> be possible any longer. ... Green corporate governance is likely
> to evolve to make sure sustainability practices are adopted
> successfully. Green corporate governance is likely to improve. 99

*Xavier Houot*
*SCHNEIDER-ELECTRIC*

With regards to diversity, for an advisory board to take a proactive role in supporting or even driving a company's sustainability agenda, it must be diverse. That is to say, it must reflect a broad representation of stakeholder interests, including those of employees, suppliers, customers and shareholders; this model has long been used by German companies.

Another key aspect of board composition is that of female representation. As many studies have confirmed, the higher the concentration of women, the more likely it is to proactively address issues of sustainability and CSR. Women bring alternative perspectives, which can foster innovative responses to complex issues.

> 66 When sustainability is seen merely as a convenient
> opportunity, greenwashing is likely to come up as a solution.
> Therefore the better informed the board, with the ability to
> form their own views on environmental issues, the easier
> it is to understand and explain these arguments, and
> consequently drive the change within the organization. 99

*Luis Piacenza*
*CROWE HORWATH*

Finally, the last two relevant issues relate to the creation of specialized committees and the quality of board members. In recent years, many companies have opted to create CSR committees, so as to address sustainability issues better. Curiously, studies assessing their effectiveness have produced mixed results; no association exists between the use of environmental committees and environmental violations (McKendall, Sánchez et al. 1999) although some work suggests committees can encourage extra vigilance (Kassinis and Vafeas 2002). This is most likely because firms use them for one or two reasons; either to provide support to firms that are serious about cleaning up their acts, or to help heavily polluting firms provide "cover" for their poor environmental performance.

Nevertheless, if used for the right reasons, specialized committees actually play a decisive role because they require firms to draw upon expertise and resources through highly qualified board members as well as placing emphasis on environmental performance at the highest levels of the organization. To put it in another way, they ensure sustainability does not fall off the radar. This also leads us to our next point; the quality of board members.

While managers may be knowledgeable in their own particular fields, they may in fact, lack the knowledge necessary to address sustainability thoroughly. Therefore, it is essential to appoint experts, whether from within the organization or from without, who are familiar with the issues at stake. They can then provide counsel and monitor actions accordingly. Their position on the board needs to be notable, on equal footing with other directors and members of the senior management team.

The board plays a key role in intermediating between shareholders and managerial levels of a company when it comes to sustainability.

## ▶ Managerial level

At the managerial level, focus must be placed on three main issues: CEO duality, managerial control and CEO compensation.

At first glance, CEOs occupying a chair on the board seems like a bad idea, primarily because it may result in agency costs. However, CEO duality may be applied as a last resort, when a board's independent directors are opposed to addressing sustainability concerns, and only if the CEO is genuinely determined to pursue a strong sustainability agenda. In such a scenario, occupying the chair of the board will provide the CEO with much greater leeway to steer the company in an appropriate direction.

> **"** If we describe greenwashing as a major risk when communicating to specific stakeholder groups, employees and so forth, then roles and responsibilities should be clearly set, and qualified people should be entrusted to take charge of what is then communicated. **"**
>
> *Xavier Houot*
> SCHNEIDER-ELECTRIC

Secondly, when adopting strategies with uncertain benefits, "empowering" managers is important otherwise they will have little chance to innovate. Evidence suggests environmental performance is better when managerial control is high; in other words, they are able to act without having their hands tied. Autonomy, freedom, and control make it easier for managers to set the tone for the rest of the organization regarding sustainability issues.

Box 7. 1  A New Approach to Managing Risks

### Risk Management: The Three Lines of Defense

To ensure the effectiveness of an organization's risk management framework (in this case with regards to environmental and social impacts) many companies have begun to apply **"the three lines of defense"** model. This approach establishes a control system that ensures sustainability efforts within the organization are monitored at different levels, in order to avoid accidental greenwashing and potential disengagement.

While the board provides direction to senior management and establishes the overall strategy and identifying main risks, the CEO and senior management are delegated primary ownership and responsibility for operating risk management and control. In this regard, it is management's job to provide leadership and direction to the employees, and to control the organization's overall operational activities accordingly.

Nevertheless, the board and senior management need to be able to rely on adequate monitoring and compliance functions within the organization, which is why the "Three Lines of Defense" model comes in handy. It helps explain the relationship between these functions and guides how responsibilities should be divided:

1. **First line of defense:** functions to identify and manage risk (managers).

2. **Second line of defense:** functions to oversee risk management and compliance.

3. **Third line of defense:** functions to provide independent assurance (internal auditors).

*Source:* Adapted from The Three Lines of Defense. Copyright 2009 by KPMG.

### ► Contingent executive compensation

Finally, the issue of CEO and managerial compensation has received a great deal of attention. CEO salaries have been found to be higher amongst firms that have to deal with higher stakes on the environmental front. However, firms that paid higher salaries usually did less well in terms of their actual environmental performance, probably because CEOs still emphasize short-term financial performance, to the detriment of longer term goals. This effect was found to be more pronounced when boards were larger, hinting at the tensions that may arise between CEOs and board members when it comes to making environmental and financial trade-offs.

One way to encourage commitment to a more sustainable approach is to make at least part of CEO's and manager's pay contingent on the company's long-term performance. Some firms, such as ING in the Netherlands, have taken clear steps to include a range of social, ethical and environmental sustainability indicators in annual incentive objectives for executives and managements boards. To incentivize managers to focus on long-term performance, others are calling for executive bonuses to be linked to bonds or escrow, which are released only upon fulfillment of certain social, financial and environmental criteria after 10 or 20 years. Again, research indicates the importance of boards to ensure that sustainability performance forms a core component of compensation packages and incentive plans for all executives.

Furthermore, scorecards, key performance indicators and other metrics are all being used by company leaders in order to ensure efforts are paying off and meet the fulfillment of desired goals at each level. For instance, Kimberly-Clark has developed a bottom-up/ top-down approach and matrix to drive and monitor sustainability initiatives within the company. Once the company's CEO and senior management agree on five-year goals, the potential plans are communicated within the organization for vetting and input at each individual level. This enables each team, department and manager to own their goals and move in the same direction on one united front.

> **"** Companies have to be open to both external and internal opinions; even if a particular department has nothing to do with a certain matter, they must still be entitled to an opinion as a new perspective or point of view can be brought into the equation that hadn't been considered before. Promote interdepartmental cooperation and collaboration. Establish better relations and connections amongst employees to avoid compartmentalizing. **"**
>
> *Gael Gonzalez*
> *SUSTAINABILITY EXPERT, LUXURY SECTOR*

## 5) Dialogue with customers and stakeholders

Once managers are adequately incentivized to embrace their firm's sustainability agenda, who better to turn for advice and innovative ideas than the firm's own customers and other key stakeholders? Establishing a two-way dialogue with consumers, policymakers, investors and employees amongst others, has become somewhat of necessity. Businesses that fail to actively engage with their main stakeholders will also be at a loss when attempting to understand and negotiate the role they play within society (Accenture 2013).

Otherwise, companies run the risk of prioritizing the wrong issues and responding to external expectations incorrectly. Instead of wasting resources to no avail, by acting and then communicating industry leaders are striving to properly anticipate stakeholder's priorities through constructive relationships.

> 66 From a business perspective, the challenge we face is trying to satisfy the expectations regarding our company, our products and our services, expressed by different interest groups, and for that it is essential for our clients, employees, investors and society in general to have certain appreciations of the company. Managing the mismatch between expectations and perceptions is critical. Therefore finding the right balance between what is done and what is communicated is key. 🙰
>
> *Antoni Ballabriga Terreguitart*
> *BBVA*

Patagonia, is a good example of reaching out. The company has been able to identify the opportunities social media has to offer, not only to satisfy society's thirst for information, but most importantly, to connect with consumers that are eager to be heard. On the one hand, *The Footprint Chronicles* is an interactive site that enables users to track the environmental impact of products throughout the supply chain, from design to delivery, giving consumers the chance to verify the firm's environmental claims, and even set an example for others by sharing success stories (Patagonia 2014). On the other hand, *The Cleanest Line* is a blog that encourages employees, customers, or whoever else may be interested, to share stories, experiences or environmental concerns and talk openly about the company's products (Patagonia 2014). Hence, users are able to express their thoughts and offer feedback that can help the company improve their standards and functionality, while keeping track of consumer expectations and demands. In short, Patagonia has found a way of tapping into an invaluable source of information, innovation and opportunities simply by listening to their customers.

> 66 If a company claims that it has a policy of energy saving (for example), they should be required to say how much has been saved over the last three years and how much they expect to save over the next three. 99

*Ernesto Lluch Moreno*
*G-ADVISORY*

Ikea has established a social and environmental coordination group that engages with forestry organizations, transportation and distribution companies, as well as its own suppliers, to find ways to minimize the overall impact of its operations. Moreover, since Ikea enjoys enormous economies of scale and market power, the company is in a position that allows it to influence the behavior of all of its various supplier groups.

> 66 Doing things right but not communicating about it appropriately isn't good either (green mutes) because you miss the opportunity to properly value everything that is being done. In the end, communicating good efforts and successful measures is what contributes to generating the virtuous cycle that lead interest groups to value and recognize ethical corporate behavior. [This] incentivizes the company to continue investing as well as encourages others to do the same. This not only helps generate better practices, but can ultimately raise sector standards regarding sustainability issues. 99

*Antoni Ballabriga Terreguitart*
BBVA

As a matter of fact, promoting greater transparency through company supply chains had been a major development these past few years. In the past, many corporate scandals have actually taken place at some point or other of the supply chain, forcing companies to take a closer look at and monitor suppliers.

In other words, communicating is key. Companies should not be afraid to share their successes; they are entitled to take the credit and be rewarded for their efforts. Furthermore, sharing your success stories contributes to the sustainable movement in the sense that it may encourage fellow competitors, employees and consumers to jump on board too. The cascading effect is of vital importance. Paul Polman once said "If we achieve our sustainability targets and no one else follows, we will have failed."

Claims need to be coupled with evidence, and promises must be followed through. As long as companies remain truthful and humble about their efforts, missing the target is not as important as trying to hit in the first place.

> **"** (…) One has to stay well away from vague, or worse, inaccurate claims. Moreover it does not have to come across as bragging as there are many ways of communicating. When a company goes beyond regulation, when it goes the extra mile and invents 'planet-positive solutions,' it can be proud, and this need not be hidden. **"**
>
> *Xavier Houot*
> *SCHNEIDER-ELECTRIC*

## 6) Collaborate with NGOs, policymakers, and industry peers

Due to the complexity of global challenges, new approaches have started to emerge. Leading companies have also started to look beyond just stakeholder engagement, towards partnerships and collaborations with NGOs, governments or industry peers. Acknowledging the role each actor can play by bringing its own resources, skills and knowledge is helping to build a shared commitment following the realization that no one can do it alone. Hence, businesses that recognize the shortcomings in their ability to tackle sustainability issues, are more likely to collaborate with others to find for new answers and innovative responses.

This tendency was particularly highlighted by the UNGC, which noted that many CEOs are beginning to see the advantages and opportunities of long-term partnerships, not only with public entities, but with fellow industry peers as well. More than 50% of CEOs expressed a willingness to co-invest with other companies to move forward on environmental and social issues (UNGC 2013; MIT, BCG et al. 2015).

> " In the long-term, having a strong culture based on corporate responsibility helps build and maintain good relationships with suppliers as well as motivating employees. Ultimately, this adds value to the business. Instead of stressing suppliers/ economic partners with prices and budgets, when you create a collaborative environment the likelihood of reaching win-win situations increases dramatically. "
>
> *Gael Gonzalez*
> *SUSTAINABILITY EXPERT, LUXURY SECTOR*

For example, in 2010, the World's Economic Forum's "A New Vision for Agriculture" promoted an agreement with 18 global partners who have since collaborated to change agricultural practices. The numerous projects launched in recent years aim to improve food security, environmental sustainability, and economic opportunity across Africa, and have mobilized billions of dollars from leading organizations around the world (WEF 2015).

> Sustainability should of course be based on making money, increasing profitability and shareholder value, whilst building a future for all those involved with the company (customers, employees, institutions...). By considering the necessities and making use of the information available, the company will [in the long run] become prosperous [in addition to] serving society.
>
> *Antonio Fuertes Zurita*
> *GAS NATURAL FENOSA*

An example of an unusual collaboration and "strange" alliance was Walmart, the retailing behemoth, and Patagonia, the do-no-evil outdoor-apparel company. In 2010, Patagonia shared with Walmart (for free!) its knowledge about greening its supply chain. Another notable collaboration was the creation of the "The Sustainable Apparel Coalition," comprising bold-face names such as Adidas, Esprit, Gap, H&M, Levi Strauss, Nike, Marks & Spencer, Patagonia, Timberland, Target, and Walmart.

Transformational leaders are also using their position to publicly advocate for policy and market incentives that will both push and complement business contributions and efforts. This involves taking a proactive stance in helping policy makers address existing market failures (that have at times made greenwashing tempting) and shape future regulations.

Table 7. 1  Building Relevant Partnerships

| INDUSTRY PEERS | •Cooperate with industry peers to develop voluntary standards<br>•Co-invest in new solutions and diffuse knowledge |
| NGOs | •Partner with NGOs and other groups to maximize on-the-ground impact |
| CONSUMERS | •Collaborate with consumers to design new products and services |
| INVESTORS | •Work with investors to quantify and communicate the business value of sustainability |
| POLICYMAKERS | •Actively engage with governments and policy makers to shape future regulations and systems |

*Source:* Own adapted from "The UN Global Compact-Accenture CEO Study on Sustainability 2013." Copyright 2013 by Accenture.

## 7.6  Developing Six Strategic Capabilities

What all of this means is that environmental strategies must conform (proactively *not* reactively) to institutional demands. This is the only way to ensure social legitimacy and organizational success. Moreover, environmental innovation is a valuable policy for managers to follow, since a company's competitive advantage depends greatly on its ability to innovate in ways that allow it to create new scenarios that its rivals cannot easily imitate. Additionally, innovation does not have to be limited to R&D; it can also come in the form of new partnerships and collaborations.

> " Changes in processes, procedures, patents, human capital,
> are all necessary, so even though many sectors are subject
> to external pressures and opportunities certainly exist, the
> internal transformation needed to do so continues to be seen
> as an obstacle, a cost. "
>
> *Antonio Fuertes Zurita*
> *GAS NATURAL FENOSA*

To do this, management must be proactive. You must pay close attention to and draw inspiration from external influences in order to develop unique resources. Managers must constantly screen and survey the environmental landscape and take the lead on innovation. You must foresee institutional pressures and anticipate the consequences of penalties and sanctions. But above all, you must remain truthful and transparent.

> " No product or service can be 100% sustainable, which
> is why first and foremost companies need to be humble.
> Avoid making statements or claims that insinuate they
> are perfectly sustainable or better than the rest…this
> is both idealist and surreal. "
>
> *Gael Gonzalez*
> *SUSTAINABILITY EXPERT, LUXURY SECTOR*

Curiously, despite having numerous resources, some companies have preferred to greenwash, pay the piper if necessary, and move on. However, in light of growing environmental concern on behalf of all actors (civil society, governments and even businesses) this is no longer a viable alternative. This stance will damage company performance both in the short and long term. The aim for those who wish to become true leaders should be **innovate, not compensate.**

> " We've been trained to follow a linear logic where communication is one-directional. But if there is [one] thing that characterizes the sustainability movement as revolutionary, it is this idea that although managing boards are indeed responsible for deciding the course of the company, stakeholders now constitute an extremely powerful pressure group. And that is where the opportunities lie. "

*Luis Piacenza*
*CROWE HORWATH*

To do so, managers should aim to develop several of the following six capabilities identified as critical for creating value and establishing a competent, competitive and proactive environmental strategy.

Box 7. 2  Developing Six Strategic Capabilities

### 1. Historical Orientation

If your company has a history of addressing environmental concerns, so much the better. The more years you have implemented an environmental program, the more you will be able to incorporate such considerations into new strategies, products and processes, and spread these values throughout your supply chain.

### 2. Network Embeddedness

Who are your networks? Supply chain providers as well as other stakeholders such as governments, employees and NGOs have a direct influence in determining the type of environmental strategy you will pursue.

### 3. Top Skills

Are you on the executive team and reporting to the senior management team or the board? Implementing strategic initiatives requires central coordination, integration and connections with others to source for talent, ideas and technologies, and managers must be well-placed to do so.

### 4. Endowments

The amount of money you invest in R&D and supporting structures such as an EMS or ISO 14001 creates necessary slack. The greater the degree of discretionary slack within your control, the more likely you can address environmental issues and respond in a timelier manner to changes in environmental technologies.

### 5. Vision

Have you prioritized the environment on the corporate agenda? Do you champion and gear functional, departmental and production processes towards environmental goals? Do you emphasize a long-term, global commitment?

### 6. Human Resources

Do you evaluate managers according to environmental performance criteria? Do you provide a formal environmental training program? Is there environmental reporting in your firm?

*Source:* Own

Remember, simply having good intentions is not enough. Instead, materialize your ambitions. Make sure that all three elements of your corporate governance structure are fully aligned, so that sustainability principles pump through the heart of your organization.

# Conclusion: Optimism in the Face of Reality

> " You cannot escape the responsibility of tomorrow
> by evading it today. "
>
> – Abraham Lincoln

As the climate change agenda ramps up, executives should be preparing themselves for what is shaping up to be a major shift across the business world. It is happening now, and there is a great deal of value at stake. Soaring energy prices and the drive to reduce greenhouse gas emissions are already taking their toll in some sectors. But as the evidence indicates, this same set of conditions can also present a whole new world of opportunities.

By taking into account both the institutional forces at work in the wider world and the resources that you have in-house, your company can blaze a green trail and gain competitive advantage through environmental innovation. Green can mean gold.

## 8.1 Reality: The Six Reasons Companies Still Engage in Greenwashing

For years society has accepted companies' twofaced strategies regarding the impact that their products and activities have on the natural environment. Firms believed that making exaggerated or absurd claims, or even in some cases resorting to downright lies, would suffice to present themselves as environmentally friendly. And let us not forget that, even in the corporate world, greenwashing is not just a defensive mantra helping maintain business as usual. Some people are out there pushing the environmental agenda with sinister intent.

But as society has matured and eco-concerns have become more widespread, the reputational risks associated with greenwashing have also became more apparent. We have shown the deleterious effect these practices can have on firm's legitimacy, reputation, and economic outcomes.

Yet some firms still find themselves overstating their environmental credentials. As testified to by the volume of complaints to the regulatory agencies such as the ASA, the risk of being conned by slick corporate "greenwash" has never been greater. But why? Here's a quick recap of six of the reasons:

*1. Aggressive self-interest*

Sometimes greenwashing is done with outright bad intentions on behalf of the decision maker. There are people aggressively pushing an environmental agenda in order to serve their own interests, and hoping they will never get caught.

*2. Resistance to change*

Some companies are simply rigid. This book has shown that the path to sustainability is not easy. On the contrary, it is a long and winding road.

There are a number of obstacles that firms need to overcome in order to clean up their act in a sincere and meaningful way. These range from technical restrictions, to quality concerns, to lack of commitment present at the very top of firm management. Some companies use the fact that the path is both difficult and complex as an excuse not to walk it.

### 3. Narrow-minded corporate culture

In some cases the culture of the company is to blame. While some companies are risk averse by nature, other businesses have a compliance oriented culture, usually adopting a narrow-minded legal approach focused solely on compliance when addressing environmental concerns. Generally speaking, greenwashing is far more likely to occur in companies that do not value attention to detail, transparency and honesty. This kind of culture can lead to potentially misleading claims.

### 4. Myopic view and short-termism

Companies that lack a long-term orientation have also fallen for greenwashing on many an occasion. Spurious environmental claims made by companies are usually driven by short-termism; that is, seeking to reap off immediate benefits without taking into consideration the long-term consequences of their actions.

### 5. General ignorance

In some cases misleading claims are made due to something as simple as ignorance. Being unfamiliar with the applicable legislation, or not fully understanding what is expected of them can result in companies engaging in unintentional greenwashing. In the absence of proper stakeholder engagement, it is almost impossible for firms to discern whether an action will be considered a valuable improvement or will just be perceived as a green puff. A poor grasp of the environmental issues relevant to one's particular business operations can also be problematic, as without the proper expertise, the potential for error is high. Nevertheless, it should be noted that with increasing societal pressure, alleging to be ignorant about sustainability is going to become virtually impossible in the future. A lack of knowledge is no longer a credible excuse.

### 6. Good intentions but poor implementation

Having good intentions isn't everything. Companies may be taking sustainability seriously yet, in all their enthusiasm, make the mistake of talking faster than they can actually walk. Some firms blur the lines separating an aspiration from an action. Furthermore, impatience can also cause problems. When companies and managers publicly commit to an environmental agenda, they want to show results as soon as possible, sometimes at the cost of jumping the gun beforehand.

But, does the above mean that greenwashing will never stop? Not necessarily. We'd like to be optimistic about the future. And there are reasons to be so.

## 8.2  Optimism: The Promising Shift Towards Sustainability 4.0

Having reached this point, let us take a step back and consider where each of us stands today. While in the recent past, the predominant logic was related to profit maximization, leading companies have slowly changed the way they approach value creation. Examples such as the Mondelez salad container (mentioned in section 7.3.3.) show it is possible to balance both economic and social goals. It's possible to reduce the impact on the environment while increasing the company's profits, improve the customer interaction with an existing product in the process. Short-term goals must give way to long-term visions, and sustainability can no longer be considered a marginal, almost separate part of the company's strategy but be seamlessly integrated.

> 66 If the company proves it is on the right track and measures
> are being taken, the fact that they might not fulfill
> expected goals does not mean that the firm has engaged in
> greenwashing strategies. Moreover, precisely because they
> have gone public, is sure to make them even more motivated to
> take measures to show they are on the path of doing so. 99

*Gael Gonzalez*
SUSTAINABILITY EXPERT, LUXURY SECTOR

A change of mentality is certainly required, as CEOs recognize the need to actively manage social, environmental, and governance issues as part of their core business. Sustainability has become the new business imperative, a key to survival, yet a challenging way of approaching innovation, markets, and decisions.

> 66 In an environment of advanced (but solvable) climate
> change, growing world population and increasing economic
> development, taking care of the environment in the long-
> term is going to be an imperative need, in the same way we
> have moved into a digital era. [Acknowledging] this fact,
> knowing that the transformation of a company is a slow
> and progressive process, can position a company against
> competitors more focused on the short term. 99

*Ernesto Lluch Moreno*
*G-ADVISORY*

Sustainability equates to change. And change means trade-offs (like creating value for interest groups other than shareholders), difficult decisions (such as thinking long term while managing the present), risks (like migrating towards a relational organizational culture), paradoxes (like securing survival by limiting growth), and the development of new skills like adaptation, collaboration, and dialogue.

Thus, in order to become part of the solution to the environmental challenge, firms need the combination of skills, resources, motivation, and agility to implement changes on a large scale. This is the essence of Sustainability 4.0; the sustainability for the 21st century.

> **"** Rather than greenwashing regarding certain 'sustainability' achievements, the goal is to embed this concept, finding ways to concurrently add value to customers and the company, making ourselves as light on earth as possible and as a result decouple global GDP from $CO_2$ and resource intensities. **"**
>
> *Xavier Houot*
> *SCHNEIDER-ELECTRIC*

Table 8. 1  Towards the Company of the 21st Century

| KEY ISSUES | TRADITIONAL COMPANY | Where is your company today? | COMPANY OF THE FUTURE |
|---|---|---|---|
| Value Creation Logic | Shareholder value | | Shared value |
| Decision Time Horizon | Short term | | Long term |
| Organizational Culture | Transactional | | Relational |
| Leadership Culture | Self-enhancing | | Group-enhancing |
| Competitive Strategy | Boxing match | | Learning ecosystem |
| Growth Strategy | Growth maximization | | Sustainable growth |
| Sustainability Strategy | Functional | | Business model (integrated) |

*Source:* Own

Indeed, a company aligned with these principles is the model for the sustainable enterprise of the next industrial revolution. Those who fail to keep up will not only lose their competitive edge, but will most likely find themselves in a poor position to comply with increasing regulatory requirements and societal demands which include:

> " It is important to question yourself…not enough time is dedicated to revisiting past decisions, question what is being done. It's almost as if we were in a constant race forward… "

*Gael Gonzalez*
*SUSTAINABILITY EXPERT, LUXURY SECTOR*

### 1. More pressure

As societal eco-concerns mature and consumers become more eco-conscious, companies will go to ever greater lengths to present themselves as environmentally friendly.

Society in general, and green consumers in particular, are becoming increasingly skeptical about many firms' environmental claims. As more and more customers demand environmental responsibility from companies, few large corporations with any degree of public profile, will dare to enter the marketplace without a blizzard of sustainability audits and low-carbon-emissions targets. Presently, institutional and market pressures are steadily creating the necessary conditions to make greenwashing an inconvenient, unattractive, and dangerous strategy to follow.

### 2. More information

Technological advances combined with commitments from NGOs and activists have spurred a new era of transparency, making greenwashing practices difficult to hide. Nowadays, the speed at which news spreads, means knowledge about greenwashing practices travels so fast that significant damage can be done in a very short time. Moreover, the high level of information available can be used by consumers to research a company's environmental footprint and make well informed purchasing decisions. As it becomes easier for consumers in particular, and society in general, to spot the fake and identify the misguiding, companies should become less inclined to engage in greenwashing.

### 3. More regulation

For years, companies have believed that private green certification programs were the best method for consumers to evaluate and compare claims. But reality has shown us this is not enough to grant legitimacy and reward a firm with green credentials. In fact, it seems as though institutions have a larger role to play. There is a widespread belief that government regulation is imperative in order to force companies to remain true to their claims, and when not be held accountable, as many governments at different levels are moving towards this direction. Adequate regulation coupled with proper enforcement will ultimately curb the temptation to greenwash companies and their products.

### 4. More research

To this day, the academic world has agreed, almost unanimously, agreed that climate change is indeed a fact and is here to stay. As a result, the discussion currently shifting from whether climate change is or not happening, to understanding how fast it is evolving and the impact it will have on our lives. A growing number of scholars are now following the steps of economist Nicholas Stern, whose 700-page report released in 2006, estimated the disastrous economic impact climate change could have on the world economy. He predicted that if global temperature eventually rises by 2-3 degrees, it would cost the equivalent to losing at least 5% of GDP each year, without including a wider range of risks and impacts that could ultimately increase this figure to 20% of the GDP or more.

Having a deeper knowledge and better understanding of the true impact climate change can have on our daily lives is changing the way governments are addressing the issue which can be a far more productive approach than simply tackling the issue based on moral grounds. Similarly, research enlightening our understanding of the economic consequences of greenwashing will also provide companies with strong evidence that of the extent to which greenwashing is detrimental and far from profitable. In the hope of making a small contribution, this book should be regarded an open call to produce more rigorous and relevant research about the issues surrounding greenwashing.

Those that are not able to engage profoundly with the challenges that sustainability entails, will become obsolete and disappear.

## 8.3 A Final Note on the Right Steps to Take

Few things can sink you as fast as bogus green initiatives. Companies sincerely willing to transform a green agenda into an opportunity and gain a competitive advantage, will have to do it in the right way, with evidential substance, as discussed in chapter 7. However, here's a final tip for those who sincerely wish to engage in a sustainable agenda: *"Avoid the circle of guilt."*

> **"** Systematically educating society on the consequences related to greenwashing is necessary, in the same way that [education helps to] prevent corruption. **"**
>
> *Luis Piacenza*
> *CROWE HORWATH*

In my experience, when talking about sustainability with representatives of different parts of society, I get the feeling we enter into a dynamic that I like to call the "circle of guilt," where everybody blames everybody else for the negative consequences the industrialized world has brought on us and our planet. Governments blame firms for failing to invest in necessary measures to curb pollution. Companies blame consumers for not being willing to pay premium for greener products.

NGOs blame governments for their lack of commitment. Consumers blame both governments and companies for their lack of concrete actions. And around we go.

I believe the time has come for each and every party involved to sincerely reflect on and become aware about the level of responsibility we have as individuals and the role we can play to become a part of the solution, rather than remaining part of the problem.

I envision a world in which:

- ▶ our lifestyle changes dramatically to consume only what is needed,

- ▶ businesses are really serious about their environmental impact and have a strategy in place for changing the way they work as a whole,

- ▶ companies leverage technology to create products that are so green that it would be better to buy two rather than one,

- ▶ governments and NGOs cooperate to create reasonable legislation and secure objective scrutiny to make companies follow the rules without reservation,

- ▶ and collaboration replaces the "blame game," since it is unlikely that only one social actor will be able to resolve the issues on its own.

Ultimately, I picture a transparent and honest society where actions speak louder than words and where even the most cynical hack will be hard pushed by the strength of our behavior. I hope you share this vision with me, and that this book serves its purpose in helping firms take the first step towards a greener future, beginning with the avoidance and elimination of greenwashing.

# REFERENCES

(2015, 2015). "One For The Planet: Supporters." Retrieved 23rd October, 2015, from http://onepercentfortheplanet.org/supporters/.

AAM. (2015, 2015). "About the Alliance: Overview: Our Vision." Retrieved 16th June, 2015, from http://www.autoalliance.org/about-the-alliance.

Accenture (2010). A New Era of Sustainability: UN Global Compact-Accenture CEO Study 2010, UN Global Compact & Accenture: 1-57.

Accenture (2013). The UN Global Compact-Accenture CEO Study on Sustainability: Architects for a Better World UNGC

AccountAbility (2008). AA1000 Assurance Standard. U.K., AccountAbility.

Agle, B. R., R. K. Mitchell, et al. (1999). "Who matters to CEOs? An investigation of stakeholder attributes and salience, corporate performance, and CEO values." Academy of Management Journal 42(5): 507-525.

Al-Tuwaijri, S. A., T. E. Christensen, et al. (2004). "The relations among environmental disclosure, environmental performance, and economic performance: a simultaneous equations approach." Accounting, Organizations and Society 29: 447-471.

Aldrich, H. E. and C. M. Fiol (1994). "Fools rush in? The institutional context of industry creation." Academy of Management Review 19: 645-670.

Alger, C. F. (1998). The Future of the United Nations system: Potential for the twenty-first century. Tokyo, United Nations University Press.

Alvarez-Gil, M. A., P. Berrone, et al. (2007). "Reverse logistics, stakeholders' influence, organizational slack, and managers' posture." Journal of Business Research 60(5): 463-473.

Alves, I. M. (2009). "Green Spin Everywhere:How greenwashing reveals the limits of the CSR paradigm." Journal of Global Change & Governance II(1): 1-26.

Aragon-Correa, J. A. (1998). "Strategic proactivity and firm approach to the natural environment." Academy of Management Journal 41: 556-567.

Aragon-Correa, J. A. and S. Sharma (2003). "A contingent resource-based view of proactive corporate environmental strategy." Academy of Management Review **28**(1): 71-88.

Arthurs, J. D., L. W. Busenitz, et al. (2009). "Signaling and initial public offerings: The use and impact of the lockup period." Journal of Business Venturing **24**(4): 360-372.

ASA (2012). Ad Bank: Misleading Advertising, Advertising Standards Authority.

Bansal, P. and I. Clelland (2004). "Talking trash: Legitimacy, impression management, and unsystematic risk in the context of the natural environment." Academy of Management Journal **47**(1): 93-103.

Barney, J., M. Wright, et al. (2001). "The resource-based view of the firm: Ten years after 1991." Journal of Management **27**: 625-641.

Barrios, J. (2009). "Is bamboo really an eco friendly material?" Retrieved 7th June, 2015, from http://ecovillagegreen.com/641/is-bamboo-really-an-eco-friendly-material/.

Basdeo, D. K., K. G. Smith, et al. (2006). "The impact of market actions on firm reputation." Strategic Management Journal **27**(12): 1205-1219.

Baysinger, B. D., R. D. Kosnik, et al. (1991). "Effects of board and ownership structure on corporate R&D strategy." Academy of Management Journal **34**(1): 205-214.

Bennear, L. S. and S. M. Olmstead (2008). "The Impacts of the 'Right to Know': Information Disclosure and the Violation of Drinking Water Standards." Journal of Environmental Economics and Management **56**: 117-130.

Bennet, G. and F. Williams (2011). Mainstream Green: Moving sustainability from niche to normal. The Red Papers, Ogilvy & Mather.

Berrone, P., A. Fosfuri, et al. (2013). "Necessity as the mother of 'green' inventions: Institutional pressures and environmental innovation." Strategic Management Journal **34**(8): 891-909.

Berrone, P., L. Gelabert, et al. (2008). "Can institutional forces create competitive advantage? An empirical examination of environmental innovation." IESE Working paper series.

Berrone, P. and L. Gomez-Mejia (2009). "Environmental performance and executive compensation: An integrated agency-institutional perspective." Academy of Management Journal **52**(1): 103-126.

Berrone, P., J. Surroca, et al. (2007). "Corporate ethical identity as a determinant of firm performance: A test of the mediating role of stakeholder satisfaction." Journal of Business Ethics **76**(1): 35-53.

Bitektine, A. (2011). "Toward a theory of social judgments of organizations: The case of legitimacy, reputation, and status." Academy of Management Review **31**(1): 151-179.

Bloomberg. (2012). "Sustainability Report." From http://www.bloomberg.com/bcause/content/themes/sustainability/report/BloombergSustReport2012.pdf.

Bloomberg. (2014). "2014 Impact report." From http://www.bloomberg.com/bcause/content/uploads/sites/6/2015/06/15_0608-Impact-Report_Web.pdf.

Bonini, S. M. J. and J. M. Oppenheim (2008). "Helping 'green' products grow" The McKinsey Quarterly.

Borial, O. (2007). "Corporate greening through ISO 14001: A rational?" Organization Science **18**(1): 127-146.

Bromley, P. and W. W. Powell (2012). "From Smoke and Mirrors to Walking the Talk: Decoupling in the Contemporary World." The Academy of Management **6**(1): 483-530.

Busch, T. and V. H. Hoffman (2009). "Ecology-driven real options: An investment framework for incorporating uncertainties in the context of the natural environment." Journal of Business Ethics **90**(2): 295-310.

Butler, S. (2013) "Ethical shopping growing in popularity, survey suggests." The Guardian.

Certo, S. (2003). "Influencing initial public offering investors with prestige: Signaling with board structures." Academy of Management Review **28**(3): 432-446.

Clarkson, P. M., Y. Li, et al. (2008). "Revisiting the Relation Between Environmental Performance and Environmental Disclosure: An Empirical Analysis." Accounting, Organizations, and Society **33**: 303-327.

Clémençon, R. (2012). "From Rio 1992 to Rio 2012 and Beyond: Revisiting the Role of Trade Rules and Financial Transfers for Sustainable Development." Journal of Environment & Development(21): 9.

Colby, M. E. (1991). "Environmental management in development: the evolution of paradigms." Ecological Economics **3**: 30.

Commissioner, M. L. A. (1991). Options for Helping the Market Work on Behalf of the Environment. T. A. C. American Bar Association Section of Antitrust Law, National Symposium on the "Greening" of Trade Regulation. Washington D.C., Federal Trade Commission.

Connelly, B., S. Certo, et al. (2011). "Signaling Theory: A review and assessment." Journal of Management **37**(1): 39-67.

Conner, C. (2012). "It's A Dirty Business: The Green Entrepreneurs Who Create Treasure (And Profit) From Trash." Entrepreneurs. Retrieved 5th May, 2015, from http://www.forbes.com/sites/cherylsnappconner/2012/10/27/its-a-dirty-business-the-green-entrepreneurs-who-create-treasure-and-profit-from-trash/.

CorpWatch. (2001, 2015). "Greenwash Fact Sheet." Greenwash Awards. Retrieved 20th May, 2015, from http://www.corpwatch.org/article.php?id=242.

CRP. (2007, 2015). "Lobbying Industry: Automotive." Influence and Lobbying. Retrieved 17th June, 2015, from http://www.opensecrets.org/lobby/indusclient.php?id=M02&year=2007.

Cullen, J., P. Parboteeah, et al. (2003). "The Effects of Ethical Climates on Organizational Commitment: A Two-Study Analysis." Journal of Business Ethics **46**(2): 127-141.

Christmann, P. (2000). "Effects of 'best practices' of environmental management on cost advantage: The role of complementary assets." Academy of Management Journal **43**(4): 663-680.

Christmann, P. and G. Taylor (2006). "Firm self-regulation through international certifiable standards: determinants of symbolic versus substantive implementation." Journal of International Business Studies **37**(6): 863-878.

Christofi, A., P. Christofi, et al. (2012). "Corporate sustainability: historical development and reporting practices." Market Research Review **35**(2): 15.

David, P., M. Bloom, et al. (2007). "Investor activism, managerial responsiveness, and corporate social performance." Strategic Management Journal **28**: 91-100.

Deephouse, D. L. (1999). "To be different, or to be the same? It's a question (and theory) of strategic balance." Strategic Management Journal **20**: 147-166.

Deephouse, D. L. (2000). "Media reputation as a strategic resource: An integration of mass communication and resource-based theories." Journal of Management **26**(6): 1091-1112.

Deephouse, D. L. and S. M. Carter (2005). "An examination of differences between organizational legitimacy and organizational reputation." Journal of Management Studies **42**(2): 329-360.

Deléage, J. P. (2000). L'environment au vingtienne siecle. Dep. de Geographie. Orleans, Université d'Orleans. **DEA Environnement: temps, espaces, sociétés**.

Delmas, M. and M. Montes-Sancho (2010). "Voluntary agreements to improve environmental quality: Symbolic and substantive cooperation." Strategic Management Journal **31**(6): 575-601.

Delmas, M. and A. Terlaak (2001). "A framework for analyzing environmental voluntary agreements." California Management Review **43**(3): 44-63.

Delmas, M. A. and V. C. Burbano (2011). "The Drivers of Greenwashing." California Management Review: 38.

Delmas, M. A. and M. W. Toffel (2008). "Organizational Responses to Environmental Demands: Opening the Black Box." Strategic Management Journal(29): 1027-1055.

Demmerling, T. (2014). Corporate Social Responsibility Overload? Intention, Abuse, Misinterpretation of CSR from the Companies' and the Consumers' Point of View. Hamburg, Anchor Academic Publishing

DiMaggio, P. and W. Powell (1983). "The Iron Cage Revisited: Institutional Isomorphism and Collective Rationality in Organizational Fields." American Sociological Review **2**(48): 147-160.

DJSI. (2015). "Corporate Sustainability." Retrieved 12th April, 2015, from http://www.sustainability-indices.com/sustainability-assessment/corporate-sustainability.jsp.

Dowling, J. and J. Pfeffer (1975). "Organizational Legitimacy: Social values and organizational behavior." Pacific Sociological Review 18(1): 122-136.

Drexhage, J. and D. Murphy (2010). Sustainable Development: From Brundtland to Rio 2012. U. Nations. New York, International Institute for Sustainable Development: 26.

Dunn, C. (2007). Get a Green Job: GreenCareers by MonsterTRAK. Treehugger. 2015.

EC (2013). Environmental Claims: report from the Multi-Stakeholder Dialogue, European Union.

EC (2014). A Healthy and Sustainable Environment for Present and Future Generations. The European Union Explained. Luxembourg, Publications Office.

Eccles, R. G., I. Ioannou, et al. (2012). "The Impact of Corporate Sustainability on Organizational Processes and Performance." NBER Working Paper Series(17950).

EEA (2015). The European environment: state and outlook 2015: synthesis report. Copenhagen, European Environment Agency.

Ehrlich, P. R. (1968). The Population Bomb, Ballantine Books.

Ekins, P. (1993). "'Limits to growth' and 'sustainable development': grappling with ecological realities." Ecological Economics(8): 269-288.

Elkington, J. (1998). Cannibals with Forks: Triple Bottom Line of 21st Century Business. New Society Publishers.

EnviroMedia. (2015). "Greenwashing Index." from http://www.greenwashingindex.com/.

EuromonitorInternational. (2013). "Home Care in UK." Retrieved 17th July, 2015, from http://www.portal.euromonitor.com/portal/magazine/homemain.

Eurosif (2014). European SRI Study. Paris, European Sustainable Investment Forum.

Fell, D., P. Downing, et al. (2009). Assessment of Green Claims in Marketing: A report to the Department for Environment, Food and Rural affairs. London, Department for Environment, Food and Rural Affairs.

Feyer, A. M. and A. Williamson (1998). Occupational Injury: Risk, Prevention and Intervention. London, Taylor & Francis Ltd.

FOE. (2015). "Friends of the Earth: Background." from https://www.foe.co.uk/what_we_do/about_us/friends_earth_values_beliefs.

Fombrun, C. J. (1996). Reputation: Realizing value from the corporate image. Massachusetts, Harvard Business School Press.

Fombrun, C. J. and M. Shanley (1990). "What's in a name? Reputation building and corporate strategy." Academy of Management Journal 33(2): 233-258.

Freeman, E. R., Ed. (1984). Strategic Management: A Stakeholder Approach. New York, Cambridge University Press.

Freeman, E. R. and J. McVea (2001). A Stakeholder Approach to Strategic Management. Handbook of Strategic Management. M. Hitt, E. R. Freeman and J. Harrison. Oxford, Blackwell Publishing.

Friedman, M. (1970). The Social Responsibility of Business is to Increase its Profits. New York Times Magazine. New York, New York Times.

FTC. (2009, 2015). "FTC Charges Companies with 'Bamboo-zling' Consumers with False Product Claims." Press Releases. Retrieved 7th June, 2015, from https://www.ftc.gov/news-events/press-releases/2009/08/ftc-charges-companies-bamboo-zling-consumers-false-product-claims.

Futerra (2008). The Greenwash Guide. F. S. Communications.

Gallup (2014). Engagement at Work: Its Effect on Performance Continues in Tough Economic Times.

Gingerich, E. and G. Karaatli (2015). "'Eco-Friendly' Marketing: Beyond the Label." Journal of Applied Business and Economics 17(3): 45-62.

Gleim, M. R., J. S. Smith, et al. (2013). "Against the green: A multi-method examination of the barriers to green consumption." Journal of Retailing 89(1): 44-61.

Godfrey, P. C. (2005). "The relationship between corporate philanthropy and shareholder wealth: A risk management perspective." Academy of Management Review **30**(4): 777-798.

Gomez-Mejia, L., G. Martin, et al. (2015). "Principal conflict in publicly traded family firms: A minority shareholder perspective." IESE Working paper.

GPF. (2007, 2015). "NGOs Criticize 'Blue Washing' by the Global Compact." Retrieved 9th May, 2015, from https://www.globalpolicy.org/global-taxes/32267-ngos-criticize-qblue-washingq-by-the-global-compact.html.

Greenpeace. (2008, 2015). "GM's Attempt to Greenwash Its Image." Greenwash Ads. Retrieved 16th June, 2015, from http://stopgreenwash.org/casestudy_gm.

Greenpeace. (2015). "About Us." from http://www.greenpeace.org/international/en/.

GRI. (2015). "Global Reporting Initiative." Retrieved 14th April, 2015, from https://www.globalreporting.org/.

Gunther, M. (2011, 2015). "Patagonia's Conscientious Response to Black Friday Consumer Madness." Retrieved 23rd October, 2015, from http://www.greenbiz.com/blog/2011/11/28/patagonias-conscientious-response-black-friday-consumer-madness.

Gupta, S. and D. T. Ogden (2009). "To buy or not to buy? A social dilemma perspective on green buying." Journal of Consumer Marketing **26**(6): 376.

Hafber-Burton, E. M. and K. Tsutsui (2005). "Human Rights in a Globalizing World: The Paradox of Empty Promises." American Journal of Sociology 110(5): 1373-1411.

Hamilton, J. (1995). "Pollution as news: Media and stock market reactions to the TRI data." Journal of Environmental Economics and Management **28**(98-113).

Hart, S. L. (1995). "A natural resource-based view of the firm." Academy of Management Review **20**(4): 986-1014.

Harvey, F. (2015) "Everything you need to know about the Paris climate summit and UN talks." The Guardian.

Helper, L. and B. Grady. (2015). "How much do companies really care about COP21?" GreenBiz Retrieved 30th December, 2015, from http://www.greenbiz.com/article/how-much-do-companies-really-care-about-cop21.

Henriques, I. and P. Sadorsky (1996). "The determinants of an environmentally responsive firm: An empirical approach." Journal of Environmental Economics and Management 30(3): 381-395.

Henriques, I. and P. Sadorsky (1999). "The relationship between environmental commitment and managerial perceptions of stakeholder importance." Academy of Management Journal 42(1): 87-99.

Henson, R. (2011) "What is the Kyoto protocol and has it made any difference?" The Guardian.

Hillman, A. J. and G. D. Keim (2001). "Shareholder Value, Stakeholder Management, and Social Issues: What's the Bottom Line?" Strategic Management Journal 22(125-139).

Hoffman, A. J. (1999). "Institutional evolution and change: Environmentalism and the U.S. chemical industry." Academy of Management Journal 42(4): 351-371.

Hoffman, A. J. (2000). Competitive Environmental Strategy: a guide to the changing business landscape. Washington, Island Press.

Hoffman, A. J. (2001). From Hersey to Dogma: An Institutional History of Corporate Environmentalism. Stanford, Stanford University Press.

Hooghiemstra, R. (2000). "Corporate communication and impression management: New perspectives why companies engage in corporate social reporting." Journal of Business Ethics 27: 55-68.

Hoskisson, R. E., M. A. Hitt, et al. (1993). "Managerial incentives and investment in R&D in large multiproduct firms." Organization Science 4: 325-341.

ICC (1990). The Business Charter for Sustainable Development: Principles for Environmental Management. Paris, ICC.

ICC (2000). The Business Charter for Sustainable Development: Principles for Environmental Management. Paris, ICC.

Jensen, M. and A. Roy (2008). "Staging exchange partner choices: When do status and reputation matter?" Academy of Management Journal **51**(3): 495-516.

Johnstone, M.-L. and L. P. Tan (2014). "Exploring the Gap Between Consumers' Green Rhetoric and Purchasing Behaviour." Journal of Business Ethics **132**(2): 311-328.

Kannan, A. (2012). Global Environmental Governance and Desertification. New Delhi, Concept Publishing Company Pvt. Ltd.

Karliner, J. (1997). The Corporate Planet: Ecology and Politics in the Age of Globalization. San Francisco, Sierra Club Books.

Kassinis, G. and N. Vafeas (2002). "Corporate boards and outside stakeholders as determinants of environmental litigation." Strategic Management Journal **23**(5): 399-415.

Kim, E.-H. and T. P. Lyon (2011). "Strategic environmental disclosure: Evidence from the DOE's voluntary greenhouse gas registry." Journal of Environmental Economics and Management **61**: 311-326.

Kim, E.-H. and T. P. Lyon (2014). "Greenwash vs. Brownwash: Exaggeration and Undue Modesty in Corporate Sustainability Disclosure." Organization Science: 20.

Kimberly-Clark (2013). Employee Engagement: Crystal Tree Awards. Sustainability Report 2013, Kimberly-Clark Corporation.

King, A. A. and M. J. Lennox (2000). "Industry self-regulation without sanctions: The chemical industry's responsible care program." Academy of Management Journal **43**(4): 698-716.

Kirmani, A. and A. R. Rao (2000). "No pain, no gain: A critical review of the literature on signaling unobservable product quality." Journal of Marketing **64**(2): 66-79.

Klassen, R. D. and D. C. Whybark (1999). "The impact of environmental technologies on manufacturing performance." Academy of Management Journal **42**(6): 599-615.

Konar, S. and M. A. Cohen (1997). "Information as regulation: The effect of community right to know laws on toxic emissions." Journal of Environmental Economics and Management **32**: 109-124.

Korzeniewski, J. (2007). Automakers create radio and print ads in an attempt to stall fuel economy regulations. autoblog. **2015**.

Kovarik, P. W. (1996, 2012). "20th Century: Sixties 1960-1969" Environmental History Timeline. Retrieved 7th February, 2015, from http://66.147.244.135/~enviror4/20th-century/sixties-1960-1969/.

KPMG. (2011). "KPMG International Survey of Corporate Responsibility Reporting 2011." Retrieved 28th April, 2015, from http://www.kpmg.com/PT/pt/IssuesAndInsights/Documents/corporate-responsibility2011.pdf.

KPMG. (2013). "The KPMG Survey or Corporate Responsibility Reporting 2013." Retrieved 28th April, 2015, from http://www.kpmg.com/Global/en/IssuesAndInsights/ArticlesPublications/corporate-responsibility/Documents/kpmg-survey-of-corporate-responsibility-reporting-2013.pdf.

Lane, E. L. (2013). Greenwashing 2.0. Green Patent Blog. E. L. Lane. **2015**.

Leonidou, C. N., D. Palihawadana, et al. (2011). "Evaluating the green advertising practices of international firms: a trend analysis." International Marketing Review **28**(1): 6-33.

Lothe, S., I. Myrtveit, et al. (1999). "Compensation systems for improving environmental performance." Business Strategy and the Environment **8**(6): 313-321.

Love, E. G. and M. Kraatz (2009). "Character, conformity, or the bottom line? How and why downsizing affected corporate reputation." Academy of Management Journal **52**(2): 314-335.

Lovins, H. (2012). "Employee Engagement Is Key to Sustainable Success." Retrieved 9th May, 2015, from http://www.sustainablebrands.com/news_and_views/jul2012/employee-engagement-key-sustainable-success.

Lyon, T. P. and J. W. Maxwell (2011). "Greenwash: Corporate environmental disclosure under threat of audit." Journal of Economics & Management strategy **20**(1): 3-41.

Lyon, T. P. and J. W. Maxwell (2011). "Greenwash: Corporate Environmental Disclosure Under Threat of Audit." Journal of Economics & Management strategy **20**(1): 3-41.

Lyon, T. P. and A. W. Montgomery (2015). "The Means and End of Greenwash." Organization and Environment **28**(2): 223-249.

Macalister, T. (2011) "BP axes solar power business." The Guardian.

Macalister, T. (2015) "BP dropped green energy projects worth billions to focus on fossil fuels." The Guardian.

Makower, J. (2015). State of Green Business 2015. GreenBiz.com, GreenBiz Group Inc.

Mander, J. (1972). "Ecopornography: One Year and Nearly a Billion Dollars Later, Advertising Owns Ecology"." Communication and Arts Magazine **14**(2): 45-56.

Marquis, C. and M. W. Toffel (2011). The Globalization of Corporate Environmental Disclosure: Accountability or Greenwashing? Harvard Business School.

Marquis, C. and M. W. Toffel (2014). "Scrutiny, Norms, and Selective Disclosure: A Global Study of Greenwashing." Harvard Business School Working Paper: 11-115.

McCullough, D. G. (2014) "Putting your money where your mouth is: companies link green goals to pay." The Guardian.

McDonough, W. and M. Braungart (1998). "The NEXT Industrial Revolution." The Atlantic Monthly **282**(4): 10.

McKendall, M., C. Sánchez, et al. (1999). "Corporate governance and corporate illegality: the effects of board structure on environmental violations." International Journal of Organizational Analysis **7**(3): 201-223.

Meadows, D. L. (1974). The Limits to Growth, Signet.

Menon, A. and A. Menon (1997). "Environmental Marketing Strategy: The Emergence of Corporate Environmentalism as Market Strategy." Journal of Marketing **61**(1): 51-67.

Meyer, J. and B. Rowan (1977). "Institutional organizations: Formal structure as myth and ceremony." American Journal of Sociology **83**: 340-363.

Milgrom, P. (1981). "Good News and Bad News: representation theorems and applications." Bell Journal of Economics **12**: 191-380.

Milstein, M. B., S. L. Hart, et al. (2002). Coercion breeds variation: The differential impact of isomorphic pressures on environmental strategies. Organizations, policy, and the natural environment: Institutional and strategic perspectives. A. J. H. M. J. Ventresca. Stanford, Stanford University Press: 151-172.

Mishina, Y., E. S. Block, et al. (2012). "The path dependence of organizational reputation: How social judgment influences assessments of capability and character." Strategic Management Journal **33**(5): 459-477.

MIT and BCG. (2013). "The innovation Bottom Line." MIT Sloan Management Review, from http://sloanreview.mit.edu/reports/sustainability-innovation/.

MIT and BCG (2013). Sustainability's Next Frontier: Walking the talk on the sustainability issues that matter most. MIT Sloan Management Review.

MIT, BCG, et al. (2015). Joining Forces: Collaboration and Leadership for Sustainability. MIT Sloan Management Review: 36.

Motavalli, J. (2011) "A History of Greenwashing: How Dirty Towels Impacted the Green Movement." Daily Finance.

Müller-Rommel, F. (1998). "The new challengers: greens and right-wing populist parties in western Europe." European Review **6**(2): 191-202.

Mycoskie, B. (2008, 2015). "TOMS: Stories." Retrieved 6th May, 2015, from http://www.toms.com/stories/.

NCS (2012). Sustainability Pays: Studies That Prove the Business Case for Sustainability. Natural Capitalism Solutions.

Neslen, A. and E. Howard (2015) "Paris climate summit: Survey reveals 'greenwash' of corporate sponsors." The Guardian.

Nielsen. (2014). "Global consumers are willing to put their money where their heart is when it comes to goods and services from companies committed to social responsibility." Retrieved 29th December, 2015, from http://www.nielsen.com/us/en/press-room/2014/global-consumers-are-willing-to-put-their-money-where-their-heart-is.html.

Odell, A. M. (2007, 2015). "Working for the Earth: Green Companies and Green Jobs Attract Employess." Retrieved 7th May, 2015, from http://www.greenbiz.com/news/2007/10/16/working-earth-green-companies-and-green-jobs-attract-employees.

OGUK. (2015). "Oil & Gas UK, the voice of the offshore industry." Retrieved 20th April, 2015, from http://www.oilandgasuk.co.uk/aboutus/aboutus.cfm.

Oliver, C. (1991). "Strategic responses to institutional processes." Academy of Management Review **16**(1): 145-179.

Paddock, W. (1967). Famine 1975! America's Decision: Who Will Survive? Boston, Little, Brown.

Patagonia (2014). About. The Cleanest Line, Patagonia. Retrieved **2015**, from http://www.thecleanestline.com/about.html.

Patagonia. (2014, 2014). "Environmental and Social Responsibility: The Footprint Chronicles." Retrieved 26th October, 2015, from http://www. patagonia.com/eu/enGB/footprint.

Patagonia. (2015, 2015). "Worn Wear: Better Than New." Retrieved 26th October, 2015, from http://www.patagonia.com/eu/enGB/worn-wear?assetid=64443.

Patten, D. M. (1991). "Exposure, Legitimacy, and Social Disclosure." Journal of Accounting and Economics **10**: 297-308.

Patten, D. M. (1992). "Intra-industry environmental disclosure in response to the Alaskan oil spill: A note on legitimacy theory." Accounting, Organizations, and Society **17**(5): 471-475.

Pearce, F. (2008) "Greenwash: BP and the myth of a world 'Beyond Petroleum.'" The Guardian.

Pellus, C. (2014). "Regulations, Watchdogs, Eco-labels, oh my!: The Highly Fragmented and Uncoordinated State of Anti-Greenwashing Efforts." Law School Student Scholarship **619**.

Penhollow, S. (2015, 2015). "Patagonia and the Marketability of Antimaterialism." Blog Retrieved 26th October, 2015, from http://www.brittonmdg.com/the-britton-blog/case-study-patagonia-sustainable-marketing-corporate-social-responsibility.

Peteraf, M. A. (1993). "The cornerstones of competitive advantage: A resource-based view." Strategic Management Journal **14**(3): 179-191.

Pfeffer, J. and G. Salancik, Eds. (1978). The external control of organizations: A resource dependence perspective. New York, Harper and Row.

Piasecki, B. (1995). Corporate Environmental Strategy: The Avalanche of Change Since Bhopal. Canada, John Wiley &Sons.

Pickett-Baker, J. and R. Ozaki (2008). "Pro-environmental products: Marketing influence on consumer purchase decision." Journal of Consumer Marketing **25**(5): 281.

Podolny, J. M. (2010). Status signals: A sociological study of market competition. Princeton, Princeton University Press.

Polonsky, M. J. (1995). "A stakeholder theory approach to designing environmental marketing strategy." Journal of Business & Industrial Marketing **10**(3): 29-46.

Porter, M. E. (1980). Competitive strategy: Techniques for analyzing industries and competitors. New York, The Free Press.

Porter, M. E. and C. v. d. Linde (1995). "Toward a New Conception of the Environment-Competitiveness Relationship." The Journal of Economic Perspectives **9**(4): 21.

Portney, P. R. and R. N. Stavins (2000). Public Policies for Environmental Protection. Washington DC, Resources for the Future.

Prabhu, J. and D. W. Stewart (2001). "Signaling strategies in competitive interaction: Building reputations and hiding the truth." Journal of Marketing Research **38**(1): 62-72.

Prakash, A. (2000). Greening the Firm: The Politics of Corporate Environmentalism. Cambridge, Cambridge University Press.

PRI. (2015). "What is Responsible Investment?" Retrieved 3rd May, 2015, from http://2xjmlj8428u1a2k5o34l1m71.wpengine.netdna-cdn.com/wp-content/uploads/1.Whatisresponsibleinvestment.pdf.

Puybaraud, M. (2010). Generation Y and the Workplace 2010. Annual Report. Johnson Controls.

Ramus, C. A. and I. Montiel (2005). "When are corporate environmental policies a form of greenwashing?" Business & Society **44**(4): 377-414.

Redclift, M. (2005). "Sustainable Development (1987-2005): An Oxymoron Comes of Age." Sustainable Development(13): 15.

Rinuova, V. P., I. O. Williamson, et al. (2005). "Being good or being known: An empirical examination of the dimensions, antecedents, and consequences of organizational reputation." Academy of Management Journal **48**(6): 1033-1049.

Ring, K. (2013). The Bamboo Controversy. REDRESS. **2015**.

Roberts, P. W. and G. R. Dowling (2002). "Corporate reputation and sustained superior financial performance." Strategic Management Journal **23**(12): 1077-1093.

Rockness, H. and J. Rockness (2005). "Legislated Ethics: From Enron to Sarbanes-Oxley, the Impact on Corporate America." Journal of Business Ethics(57): 23.

Rogers, A. (1993). The Earth Summit; A Planetary Reckoning. Los Angeles, Global View Pr.

Rousseau, H., P. Berrone, et al. (2015). "Let's talk: Studying Dialogue between Firms and Outside Actors on Social and Environmental Issues." IESE Working paper.

Russo, M. V. and P. A. Fouts (1997). "A resource-based perspective on corporate environmental performance and profitability." Academy of Management Journal **40**(3): 534-559.

Russo, M. V. and N. S. Harrison (2005). "Organizational design and environmental performance: Clues from the electronic industry." Academy of Management Journal **48**(4): 582-593.

Sarkis, J. and J. J. Cordeiro (2001). "An empirical evaluation of environmental efficiencies and firm performance: Pollution prevention versus end-of-pipe practice." European Journal of Operational Research **135**: 102-113.

Scott, W. R., Ed. (1995). Institutions and organizations. Thousand Oak, Sage.

Schmidheiny, S. (1992). Changing Course: A Global Business Perspective on Development and the Environment. Cambridge, BCSD.

Schraum, B. (2015) "COP21: Businesses call for action on climate change as Paris environment talks begin." International Business Times.

Schuman, M. C. (1995). "Managing legitimacy: Strategic and institutional approaches." Academy of Management Review **20**(3): 571-610.

Shin, H. S. (2003). "Disclosures and Asset Returns." Econometrica **71**: 105-133.

Short, J. L. and M. W. Toffel (2010). "Making self-regulation more than merely symbolic: The critical role of the legal environment." Administrative Science Quarterly **55**(3): 361-396.

SIF. (2015). "COP21: About." Retrieved 25th December, 2015, from http://www. cop21paris.org/about/cop21.

Sinclair-Desgagne, B. and E. Gozlan (2003). "A Theory of Environmental Risk Disclosure." Journal of Environmental Economics and Management **45**: 377-393.

Skowronski, J. J. and D. E. Carlston (1989). "Negativity and extremity biases in impression formation: A review of explanations." Psychological Bulletin **105**(1): 131-142.

Sorescu, A., V. Shankar, et al. (2007). "New product preannouncements and shareholder value: Don't make promises you can't keep." Journal of Marketing Research **44**(3): 468-489.

SourceWatch. (2010). "Climate Action Partnership." Retrieved 16th June, 2015, from http://www.sourcewatch.org/index.php/Climate_Action_Partnership.

Spence, M. A. (1973). "Job market signaling." The Quarterly Journal of Economics **87**(3): 355-374.

Stevens, J. M., H. K. Steensma, et al. (2005). "Symbolic or Substantive Document? The Influence of Ethics Codes on Financial Executives' Decisions." Strategic Management Journal **26**: 181-195.

Sullivan, N. and R. Schiafo (2005) "Talking Green, Acting Dirty." The New York Times.

TerraChoice (2007). The "Six Sins of Greenwashing," TerraChoice Environmental Marketing Inc.

TerraChoice (2009). Environmental Claims in Consumer Markets. The Seven Sins of Greewashing, TerraChoice Group.

TerraChoice (2010). The Sins of Greenwashing: Home and Family Edition, UL Global Network.

Thogersen, J. (1999). "Psychological determinants of paying attention to eco-labels in purchase decisions: Model development and multinational validation." Journal of Consumer Policy **23**(3): 285-313.

Tolliver-Nigro, H. (2009) "Green Market to grow 267% by 2015." Green Marketing.

Turban, D. B. and D. W. Greening (1997). "Corporate social performance and organizational attractiveness to prospective employees." Academy of Management Journal **40**(3): 658-672.

UL (2014). The Sustainable Edge: Your Corporate Commitment—communicated effectively—brings bottom-line results.

UN (1969). General Assembly Resolution 2581. XXIV. G. Assembly. New York.

UN (1972). Declaration on the UN Conference on the Human Environment. UN Conference on Human Environment, Stockholm.

UN. (2012). "Secretary-General's statement at closing of Rio+20, UN Conference on Sustainable Development." 2015.

UN. (2015). "Global Issues: Environment." Retrieved 25th January, 2015, from http://www.un.org/en/globalissues/environment/.

UNEP. (2011). "Keeping Track of Our Changing Environment." from http://www.unep.org/geo/pdfs/keeping_track.pdf.

UNEP, GRI, et al. (2013). Sustainability Reporting Policies: Worldwide—today's Best Practices, Tomorrow's Trends. Carrots and Sticks.

UNFCCC. (2015). "Historic Paris Agreement on Climate Change." Retrieved 28th December, 2015, from http://newsroom.unfccc.int/unfccc-newsroom/finale-cop21/.

UNFCCC. (2015). "United Nations Conference on Climate Change: More about the agreement." COP21 Retrieved 28th December, 2015, from http://www.cop21.gouv.fr/en/more-details-about-the-agreement/.

UNGC (2013). Global Corporate Sustainability Report 2013. New York, United Nations Global Compact.

USSIFF (2014). US Sustainable, Responsible and Impact Investing Trends 2014, The Forum for Sustainable and Responsible Investment.

Vandermerwe, S. and M. D. Oliff (1990). "Customers drive corporations green." Long Range Planning **23**(6): 10-16.

Varadarajan, P. R. and A. Menon (1988). "Cause-Related Marketing: A Coalignment of Marketing Strategy and Corporate Philanthropy." Journal of Marketing **53**: 16.

Vogler, J. and A. Jordan (2003). Governance and Environment. Negotiating Environmental Change: New Perspectives from Social Science. F. Berkhout, M. Leach and I. Scoones. Cheltenham, Edward Elgar.

Waddock, S. (2008). "Building a New Infrastructure for Corporate Responsibility." Academy of Management Perspectives: 21.

Wade-Benzoni, K. A., A. J. Hoffman, et al. (2002). "Barriers to resolution in ideologically based negotiations: The role of values and institutions." Academy of Management Review **27**(1): 41-57.

Walker, H. (2010). Recapping on BP's long history of greenwashing. Greenpeace USA, Greenpeace. **2015**.

Walls, Berrone, et al. (2011). "Measuring environmental strategy: construct development, reliability and validity." Business & Society **50**(1): 71-115.

Walls, J., P. Berrone, et al. (2012). "Corporate Governance and Environmental Performance: Is there really a link?" Strategic Management Journal **33**: 885-913.

Walls, J. L. and P. Berrone (2015). "The Power of One to Make a Difference: How Informal and Formal CEO Power Affect Environmental Sustainability." Journal of Business Ethics: 1-16.

Washington, M. and E. J. Zajac (2005). "Status evolution and competition: Theory and evidence." Academy of Management Journal **48**(2): 282-296.

WCED (1987). Our Common Future. O. U. Press. New York/Oxford, World Commission on Environment & Development.

WCED (1987). Our Common Future, World Commission on Environment and Development: 300.

Weaver, G. R., L. K. Treviño, et al. (1999). "Integrated and decoupled corporate social performance: Management commitments, external pressures, and corporate ethics practices." Academy of Management Journal **42**(5): 539-552.

WEF. (2015). "World Economic Forum: New Vision for Agriculture." From http://www.weforum.org/projects/new-vision-agriculture.

Weigelt, K. and C. Camerer (1988). "Reputation and corporate strategy: A review of recent theory and applications." Strategic Management Journal 9(5): 443-454.

Welford, R. (1997). Hijacking Environmentalism: Corporate Responses to Sustainable Development. New York, Taylor & Francis.

Welford, R. (2002). "Globalization, Corporate Social Responsibility and Human Rights." Corporate Social Responsibility and Environmental Management(9): 7.

Whetten, D. A. and A. Mackey (2002). "A social actor conception of organizational identity and its implications for the study of organizational reputation." Business & Society 41(4): 393-414.

WMBC. (2015). "Take Action." Retrieved 31st December, 2015, from http://www.wemeanbusinesscoalition.org/take-action.

Wood, D. J. (1991). "Corporate Social Performance Revisited." Academy of Management Review 16(4): 691-718.

WRI (2010). Global Ecolabel Monitor. Washington DC, World Resources Institute.

Printed in Great Britain
by Amazon

59836097R00193